THE MIDSUMMER CUSHION

ACKNOWLEDGEMENTS

The Editors and Publishers wish to acknowledge their debt to Peterborough City Council for permission to work among Peterborough Museum's outstanding collection of Clare manuscripts. The unfailing help at all times of Mr Tony Cross, Curator of the Museum, is gratefully appreciated, as is the assistance by Mr G. L. Laidler with much tedious checking in the early editorial stages. The approval of Dr Eric Robinson is also acknowledged.

The publication has been grant-aided by the Arts Council of Great Britain and Northern Arts.

The original illustrations are by Birtley Aris.

JOHN CLARE

THE MIDSUMMER CUSHION

Edited by Anne Tibble
Associate Editor: R K R Thornton

MID NORTHUMBERLAND ARTS GROUP
in association with
CARCANET PRESS

Copyright © 1978 The introduction, Anne Tibble

SBN 85635 250 0

First published 1979 by
The Mid Northumberland Arts Group
Wansbeck Square, Ashington, Northumberland
in association with Carcanet Press Limited
330–332 Corn Exchange Buildings, Manchester M4 3BG

Printed by Billing & Sons Limited
Guildford, London and Worcester

CONTENTS

INTRODUCTION

THE MANUSCRIPT AND ITS HISTORY

In 1831, when he was thirty-eight, Clare realized that John Taylor, the London publisher who had given his previous volumes to the public, could not help him further. Tired of patrons' and of editorial tutelage, Clare determined to try to publish *The Midsummer Cushion* by subscription. Since before *The Shepherd's Calendar* of 1827, poems had been accumulating. Out of what he himself called the "disordered state" of his papers he began to fair-copy. The resulting manuscript, *The Midsummer Cushion*, shows him to have been perfectly capable of editing his work without undue interference. By any standards it is a fine manuscript.

Clare set about finding subscribers locally. How many he secured is not certain. As far as we know no list survives. Since the paper of the manuscript is watermarked 1831 we may conclude that he began copying some time in that year. He finished toward the end of 1832. In June of that year he, with wife and children, moved from their cottage at Helpstone, his birthplace, to a bigger cottage in the Fen village of Northborough, three miles distant.

Poems such as "Decay" and "The Flitting" indicate the date as well as the mental upheaval this caused him.

In August 1832 an account of Clare's project was, with some inaccuracies but with an encouraging editorial comment, printed in *The Athenaeum*, London:

> "Proposals for publishing in 1 volume, F.c. 8vo, The Midsummer Cushion, or Cottage Poems, by John Clare.
>
> 1st. The book will be printed on fine paper, and published as soon as a sufficient number of subscribers are procured to defray the expense of publishing.
>
> 2nd. It will consist of a number of fugitive trifles, some of which have appeared in different periodicals, and of others that have never been published.
>
> 3rd. No money is requested—until the volume shall be delivered, free of expense, to every subscriber.
>
> 4th. The price will not exceed seven shillings and sixpence, and it may not be so much, as the number of pages and the expense of the book will be regulated by the publisher."

Shortly afterward a local magazine, *The Bee* of Stamford, printed some ill-considered remarks calling in question the overall conduct of Clare's London publisher, John Taylor, and of his patrons, and stating that Clare had the Northborough cottage rent-free from Lord Milton. Angrily Clare wrote to the editor concerning "this officious misstatement": "I am no beggar for my income is £36 ...".

But already *The Athenaeum* had repeated the mischievous words. Taylor took offence, refusing to have anything to do with Clare's proposals for publication. When Clare received a request from the Peterborough publisher for a hundred pounds for steel engravings—and he had nothing like that amount of money—he returned to the idea of London help. He wrote to Taylor in apology, to other London friends. At last Taylor agreed to take a friendly interest in the book but no more. Mr and Mrs Emmerson, who were supplying a cow for the "two-acre piece" at the Northborough cottage, agreed to try to find a London publisher. The man they found was a relative of the Peterborough printer: J. How worked for the Almanack-printing firm of Whitaker.

Yet it was not the manuscript of *The Midsummer Cushion* that went to London for printing. Clare must have set to work and selected one hundred and thirty poems from that rich script. He had had a first attack of delusions in 1830. Ill again in 1832 he wrote distressed drafts of letters that he couldn't send or even finish. One letter to H. F. Cary in August 1832 runs:

> "... If you laugh at my ambitions I am ready to laugh with you at my own vanity for I sit sometimes & wonder over the little noise I have made in the world until I think I have written nothing as yet to deserve any praise at all so the spirit of fame of living a little after life like a name on a conspicuous place urges my blood upward into unconscious melodys & striding down my orchard & homestead I hum & sing inwardly those little madrigals & then go in and pen them down thinking them much better things than they are ..."

Nearly ten years ago he had seen "fames sun wither in its summer sky". By 1834 he sent a second carefully written manuscript to London. Eliza Emmerson selected forty-two poems and eighty-six sonnets, frequently verses already printed in the glossily engraved Annuals of the time. In 1835, with many of her emendations and lavish punctuation, *The Rural Muse* was published. Clare had sold the copyright outright in 1834 to How, who gave him £40 for it.

The Midsummer Cushion manuscript remained at Northborough during his "imprisonment" in two asylums and probably until his death in July 1864. What happened to it then is far from clear. Facts are further confused because there were two John Taylors, both publishers, the older man then about eighty-five and still in London, and a younger publisher also interested in Clare manuscripts who lived at Northampton. We have found no mention of *The Midsummer Cushion* until 1893 in the Clare Centenary Catalogue of the Peterborough Museum. Yet there may exist information still untapped about its whereabouts between Clare's death and its appearance among the Peterborough MSS.

What was called the "Whitaker collection" of 1893 was bought by local admirers of the poet from Joseph Whitaker who said he had bought them from the elder John Taylor and also from Clare's widow, Patty. What J. L. Cherry saw in 1873 for his *Life and Remains of John Clare* may have been all or some of the Whitaker MSS of which *The Midsummer Cushion* was part; but again, this is not provable. Arthur Symons, in his Introduction to his Selection, *Poems of John Clare, 1908*, speaks of "original manuscripts" seen by Cherry (who, we know, was in touch with Whitaker) which "I have tried in vain to find".

Thus, what happened to the manuscript of the following poems between 1864 and 1893, when it became the property of the Peterborough Museum, is still not known. It has lain in Peterborough since 1893, and is now published in entirety. About one third of the poems are published for the first time.

Clare's manuscript is number A54 in the Peterborough collection. The poems are neatly copied into a 12mo book, $9\frac{1}{2}'' \times 5\frac{1}{2}''$, bound on the short side, the paper watermarked "T Edmonds / 1831". It is bound in red quarter leather with marbled boards and endpapers, and all edges marbled. It looks like a ledger or cash book, though the paper is unlined. It is signed by Clare on the tape of the binding between the board and first endpaper.

We reproduce the title page, but scratched out is another still legible title: "The Midsummer Cushion / or Poems / Chiefly descriptive of / Cottage Life / & Rural Scenery by John Clare / (rule)".

The numbering of the MS is confusing, since it is paginated (by a later hand) in pencil only on those pages which are written on; it is best to stick to this convention in the following description of the MS: Title page; verso blank; 1 (Dedication); verso blank; 2 (Preface); verso blank; 3 ("To the Rural Muse"–19; 20 ("Tales") –54; 55 ("Poems")–272 (p. 65 is an inserted sheet with two stanzas of "Helpstone Statute" with nothing on verso—numbering begins again in book with 66 on next recto; p. 80 is an inserted sheet with one stanza of "Maying" with nothing on verso—numbering begins again with 81 on next recto; between 118 and 119 is a stub of a removed sheet on which are two lines of "On the Memory of the Honourable Lady—" but it is not numbered); 113 blank pages; numbering resumes on verso at 273 ("Ballads & Songs")–338 (between 317 and 318 a page is loosely inserted, unnumbered, with an extra stanza for "Love of the Fields", blank on verso); 47 blank pages; numbering resumes on recto at 339 ("Sonnets")–436; 12 blank pages.

"Natures Melodys" on p. 169 of the MS (180 of our text) may be meant as a general title for a section, but may apply only to a small number of poems.

CLARE'S LIFE

In the interim toward full recognition of any poet, biographical facts tend to be transformed as well as lost. A peasant's son, Clare is sometimes still "poor Clare", judged with a condescension however unconscious as "peasant poet" rather than just as poet. His tragic story still attracts as much attention as his poetry.

Born in 1793 in the village of Helpstone in Northamptonshire on the Fen verge, his father, a flail-thresher earning eight shillings a week, was also a ballad singer with over a hundred ballads in his memory—a repertoire unusual by then. Parker Clare was also a rustic wrestler at village feasts. Clare's mother was a neighbouring shepherd's daughter. He was small, the elder of twins, the only son, five feet two inches as Keats was—with immense endurance but without physical strength; he was fair-haired, blue-eyed.

Brought up in the Church of England, his village childhood was happy; he began at dame-school in Helpstone and then, until the age of about twelve, went to a school under a master in the church vestry of Glinton, two miles' walk away. There the master, a scholar, lent him books and rewarded him for his diligence and his astonishing memory.

At Glinton Church-vestry school Clare found Mary Joyce "the stillest and most good natured girl". She was four years his junior but they walked in the fields together. They parted finally when Mary was about seventeen. In "The Enthusiast", with its alternative title "A day dream in Summer", among *The Midsummer Cushion* poems, Clare gives his own version of his loss.

When he was twelve he walked five miles to Stamford to buy a copy of James Thomson's still popular *The Seasons*. For the next fifteen years he wrote and hoarded verses.

For about eighteen months, in 1812 and 1813, Clare was in the Northamptonshire Militia for the war against Napoleon. He was as unsatisfactory a recruit as was S. T. Coleridge. After the war, in days of agricultural unrest and unemployment through advance in farming methods, he joined "catchwork gangs" and was plough-boy, gardener, limeburner. Whilst limeburning at Casterton between 1817 and 1820, he met Martha Turner, got her with child, married her and took her back to the cottage at Helpstone to live with his father and mother.

In 1819 he showed his manuscript poems to a Stamford bookseller named Drury who showed them to his cousin John Taylor, who was the London publisher of Keats. The following year Taylor published Clare's first book, *Poems Descriptive of Rural Life and Scenery.* Four editions of this book within 1820 just caught the end of the fashion in rustic poetry begun by James Thomson in 1726–1730. Success took Clare on his first of four short visits to London where he met writers, artists and poets but missed Keats. Patrons provided a fund which gave him an income of £40 a year. He returned to Helpstone in 1820 to severe but preferred loneliness.

His second book—his own title "Ways in a Village" changed to a James Beattie echo, *The Village Minstrel*—came out in 1821. It sold poorly. A third which he wanted to call "Summer Walks" became, again through patron's or publisher's whim, the Spenser echo, *The Shepherd's Calendar,* of 1827. That, too, made little impact.

Next came the bitter frustration of his failure to get *The Midsummer Cushion* published by his own efforts. This was followed by the almost total failure of his fourth and last book, *The Rural Muse,* of 1835. After more than twenty years of incessant writing and of the poverty his obstinate independence of mind often led him to deny, he was driven over the brink into delusions. Determination, will-power (which he was thought to lack), or else a rigid defiance combined with an exhausting sensibility, did not, in Clare, deaden into middle-aged compromise, complacency, or disillusion. They resolved themselves into the strange swamp-barriers we call madness. *The Midsummer Cushion* poems show him writing intensely, taking long lonely walks, building an outlook of determined philosophic facing of life that he must have thought was an actual defence against insanity.

The poems speak of "my clouded mind" and my "sullen brow". "The Old Man's Song" reveals a slow estrangement from London acquaintances and from village friends. But Clare was not proof against delusions any more than he could stop writing.

In 1837 he was committed to High Beech Asylum in Epping Forest where he spent four years under the sympathetic and enlightened Dr. Matthew Allen. But in 1841 tired of "prison" Clare escaped and walked home to Northborough in about three days. Next morning he recorded his journey in one of the remarkable documents in literature. His wife Patty wished, according to a letter of Matthew Allen, to "try" him again at home. But after five months he was consigned, with John Taylor's help, to the new asylum of St Andrew's at Northampton. There he spent the remaining years of his life. As at High Beech, Clare was well treated and allowed to walk outside the grounds, to work and to write. But delusions—originating ideas may be found in many of the poems in the following pages—persisted. We are less contemptuous if not less afraid of madness today. Some psychologists even discern a kind of "sanity" in the delusions of the insane. Clare's idea of his having two wives, Mary and Martha, for instance, has obvious connotation. He claimed—when, one suspects, unwelcome, obtrusive visitors assailed him with questions— to be a well-known wrestler or boxer of his time, Tom Spring or Ben Caunt. His father had been a champion wrestler. Clare's own frame was slight, ineffectual—as if, treacherously, it let him down. That Byron's, Gray's, even Shakespeare's, poetic cloak had passed to him, holds a common poetic metaphor. I am not suggesting there was no delusion, no madness. But *The Midsummer Cushion* poems are importantly revealing in that they were written on either side of his first attack in 1830. At St Andrew's he was a quiet patient, still finding rapture in the green and watered land by the river Nene. He wrote, over those final twenty-three years, over a thousand poems. Many are traditional jingle. A few are on a level with poems by Blake, Coleridge, Wordsworth, Keats, Shelley, Burns.

THE POEMS

Editors have been selecting from *The Midsummer Cushion* only since Edmund Blunden in his *Poems Chiefly from Manuscript* (1920) brought Clare again to notice. The 361 poems are divided by Clare in his script into five sections. The first section, untitled by Clare, has only two poems. "To the Rural Muse" is Clare's goodbye to youthful ambitions. It is one of the key statements of his mature outlook. The second poem, "Pleasures of Spring", was first published by Professor Kenneth Richmond in *Poetry and the People* (1947).

A second, also shortish, section Clare has entitled "Tales". This contains "Valentine Eve" and "Going to the Fair", stories in rhyming couplets full of traditional local colour. Both, with their suspense and their country characters, show Clare following the advice of George Darley, Keats and other London friends to "people" his scenes, and achieving this aim with his own uncompromising honesty. His "clowns" are not only untaught ploughmen but farmers, soldiers. The other two poems of this section, "Adventures of a Grasshopper" and "The Birds & St Valentine", as well as "The Holiday Walk" of the third section, are poems for his children: all these some children of today might delight in.

That third, longest section, *Poems*, beginning with "Summer Images", and containing "Pastoral Poesy", "The Evening Star", "The Enthusiast", "A day dream in Summer", "The Progress of Ryhme" and "Autumn", all show Clare in his prime. Others of this third section, "The Yellow Wagtails Nest", "The Ravens Nest", "The Yellowhammers Nest", "The Landrail", "The Nightingales Nest" with its finely irregular rhymes, and "The Woods" with its half-rhymes, all indicate our most important naturalist-poet. The supremely accurate detail of these poems and of many more in the manuscript shows natural things many of us never see from beginning to end of our lives. The country round Helpstone and Northborough, dull to most people, is rich in its flora and fauna even today, and especially so seen through Clare's eyes. "Childhood", "St Martin's Eve", "The Cottager", "The Old Shepherd", and "The Village Doctress" show villagers young and old of the late eighteenth century and early nineteenth century with very different self-contained pastimes from the sophistications of villagers today.

"Love & Memory" and "Farewell to Love", also in this long third section, reveal the changing alchemy of Clare's early "visionary theme". They help to elucidate the origins and the continuity of his sense of loyalty, love, joy and innocence in a fusion of physical and spiritual meanings. Although "no words live to free the mind", these poems, and others among the sonnets—"Eternity of Time", "The Instinct of Hope", "The Truth of Time", "Vanity of Fame" and "Universal Goodness"—show his distrust of eighteenh-century "blind" reason. His searchingly unorthodox, yet archetypal, intuitive use of words such as "eternity", "eden" (or "edens"), "heaven" and "hell" support statements about earth's "natural" happiness, earthly eden, earthly heaven—among conventional poems such as "Thoughts in a Churchyard" and others of this section written to please patrons and publishers to whom he felt himself indebted.

The fourth section of this long manuscript Clare entitled "Ballads & Songs". This contains two humorous, long poems —"The Tankard" and "The Cellar Door—A Ballad", patriotic ballads like "Nelson & The Nile" and "Ocean Glories—tune Old

xiii

Benbow a beautiful melodie". These last two link with the coming disturbances of his mind. But this section also contains the rhythmically interesting "Remembrances" and the revealing "Decay—A Ballad".

A final, fifth section entitled "Sonnets" contains 219 sonnets, some of which are in groups of two or more poems. Some are conventional exercises in verse; others illustrate what he termed "natural" poetry.

This "natural" poetry of country life some see as his most important contribution, his "best" work. Others see a further importance in his later reflective lyrics written at St Andrew's—to which so many poems of *The Midsummer Cushion* point the way. The one genre surely completes the other. Arthur Symons wrote in 1908: "a gentle hallucination" comes into the later poems when "for the first time Clare's lyrical faculty gets free"; "Rhymically new" Edmund Blunden said around 1920; and in his selections of 1949 and 1950 Geoffrey Grigson emphasized the later poems of reflection. *The Midsummer Cushion* shows very clearly the links between Clare's country poetry and his 'spiritual' originality. It is the most important of all Clare's books.

NOTE ON THE TEXT

The manuscript of *The Midsummer Cushion* is careful, the essence of Clare's maturity. We have reproduced it as closely as possible, complete with Clare's spellings, dialect words, ampersands, and with his vestigial punctuation. This makes for some slight difficulties, but is essential. We have interfered with this exact transcription simply to correct the occasional errors of copying (this is a fair copy manuscript, not a working draft, where alterations and changes would represent aspects of the creative process): where Clare has written a word or words twice we have omitted one silently; where he has missed out a word which his rhythm demands and another manuscript supplies, we have added the missing piece in square brackets; where he has mistranscribed a related word, we have supplied the new part of the word (e.g. "that" for "the") in square brackets. The more significant of these changes are given in the appended list, so that the reader may feel he has the text as Clare wrote it. Our only other imposition is to insert a space in certain abbreviated forms which it would otherwise have been possible to confuse with other words, e.g. I ll, she ll, he ll, I d, she d, we ll, ye ll, he d, can t; sometimes Clare punctuated these forms himself.

Titles have been put in capitals and epigraphs in italic, although both are written in the manuscript in the same hand as the rest.

Clare's own spellings have been left; one soon becomes used to "hugh" for "huge", "breath" for "breathe", "enarmoured" for "enamoured", "ryhme" for "rhyme", "safty" for "safety", "carless" for "careless", "recieve" for "receive", "supprise" for "surprise", "sutty" for "sooty", "majic" for "magic" and so on. He does not spell by modern convention the words "where", "were", and "we're", but we have left what he wrote.

There are some elements in the manuscript about which one cannot be dogmatic. It is impossible to be certain when Clare writes "then" and when he writes "than"; it is not always clear when a final "s" is intended since some words end in an ambiguous flourish; it is often difficult to decide whether a word is one or two, like blackthorn or waistcoat, and it is not sufficient simply to divide when he has taken his pen from the paper since he does that in the middle of other words too; and capital letters in mid line are often ambiguous. We have simply tried to judge each case straight-forwardly.

Stanzas 18 and 19 of "Helpstone Statute" on p. 68 ("She soon broke up ..." etc.) are inserted from a separate slip in Clare's hand with the instruction "To follow after the 17th verse as the 18th and 19th", but the continuity of the story is a little disturbed. Similar insertions from similar instructions concern stanza 3 of "Maying", p. 85, and stanza 2 of "Love of the Fields", p. 356.

"The Wrynecks Nest" is printed twice (pp. 436 and 447) because Clare wrote it in his book twice, but its minor alterations show something of the attention which Clare was giving to his poems.

Some of the additions to correct Clare's slips of the pen are so minor and obvious as not to need separate listing, though it was possible to confirm all except one by reference to other manuscripts in the collection at Peterborough Museum. The slightly more substantial additions were as follows, giving the manuscript number and page reference as in Margaret Grainger's excellent and useful *A Descriptive Catalogue of the John Clare Collection in Peterborough Museum and Art Gallery* (Peterborough, 1973):

p. 3, "A. Hill" from A40-60; p. 103, "we" from A40-159; p. 110, the reading "we ll" from A40-102a; p. 128, "low" from A40-85a; p. 143, "cares" from A40-138; p. 172, "look" from A41-R82; p. 183, "with" from A45-15; p. 234, "that" from A40-81a; p. 237, "on" from A40-82; p. 238, "tender" from A40-82a; p. 250, superlative suffix of "coldest" from A37-34; p. 251, "&" from A37-35; p. 259, "see" from A57-R107; p. 272, "pleasantly" from A57-38; p. 273, "&" substituted for "at" from A57-41, which also supplies "hearth" for "heath"; p. 281, "meet" from B6-65; p. 289, "the" from B6-69; p. 317, the ending of "known" from A40-119; p. 370, "naked" for "naker", and "go" from B8-R118; p. 416, "on" from A50-R58; p. 425, "to" from A37-54; p. 425, the negative for "can t" from A37-23; p. 467, "surety" from A57-32, though the reading even there is difficult; p. 491, the ending of "asks" from B6-63.

On p. 10 we have put "in" for "is", but Clare may have meant "rose is" to represent "rose's". On p. 224 we have put "thy" for MS "my" since the sense requires it.

The text, then, is as near as one can get to the Clare of 1832.

THE MIDSUMMER CUSHION

CUSHION

OR COTTAGE POEMS

"How can such sweet & lovely hours
"Be reckoned but with herbs & flowers"
                                        Marvel

To the Right Honourable
Lord Viscount Milton

My Lord

    The alowing me to inscribe these Trifles to your Lordship confers many pleasures for I feel a deeper interest than self gratification in your Lordships early kindness to my lame Father long before I was personally known & this only confers another obligation to the many by alowing me to subscribe myself

My Lord

Your Lordships

grateful & obedient servant

John Clare

Although the fourth attempt may bring with it additional need of apology I am so confident of meeting success from the kindness of my readers if I deserve it as to render apology needless & so averse in apologizing for sympathy to aid successes that I may not be found to deserve that I shall so far deviate from the common place liscence of prefaces as to make none & merely occupy the space that a preface universally occupies to explain the title to these trifles.

It is a very old custom among villagers in summer time to stick a piece of greensward full of field flowers & place it as an ornament in their cottages which ornaments are called Midsummer Cushions   And as these trifles are field flowers of humble pretentions & of various hues I thought the above cottage custom gave me an oppertunity to select a title that was not inapplicable to the contents of the Volume—not that I wish the reader to imagine that by so doing I consider these Poems in the light of flowers that can even ornament a cottage by their presence—yet if the eye of beauty can feel even an hours entertainment in their perusal I shall take it as the proudest of praise & if the lover of simple images & rural scenery finds anything to commend my end & aim is gratified

TO THE RURAL MUSE

TO THE RURAL MUSE

"Smile on my verse & look the world to love" [*A. Hill*]

Muse of the fields oft have I said farewell
To thee my boon companion loved so long
& hung thy sweet harp in the bushy dell
For abler hands to wake an abler song
Much did I fear mine homage did thee wrong
Yet loath to leave as oft I turned again
& to its wires mine idle hands would cling
Torturing it into song—it may be vain
Yet still I try ere fancy droops her wing
& hopless silence comes to numb its every string

Muse of the pasture brooks on thy calm sea
Of poesy Ive saild & tho the will
To speed were greater than my prowess be
Ive ventured with much fear of usuage ill
Yet more of joy—tho timid be my skill
As not to dare the depths of mightier streams
Yet rocks abide in shallow ways & I
Have much of fear to mingle with my dreams
Yet lovely muse I still believe thee bye
& think I see thee smile & so forget I sigh

Muse of the cottage hearth oft did I tell
My hopes to thee nor feared to plead in vain
But felt around my heart thy witching spell
That bade me as thy worshiper remain
I did & worship on—O once again
Smile on my offerings & so keep them green
Bedeck my fancies like the clouds of heaven
Mingling all hues which thou from heaven dost glean
To me a portion of thy power be given
If theme so mean as mine may merit aught of heaven

For thee in youth I culled the simple flower
That on thy bosom gained a sweeter hue
& took thy hand along lifes sunny hour
Meeting the sweetest joys that ever grew
More friends were needless & my foes were few
Tho freedom then be deemed as rudeness now
& what once won thy praise now meet disdain

3

Yet the last wreath I braided for thy brow
Thy smiles did so commend it made me vain
To weave another one & hope for praise again

With thee the spirit of departed years
Wakes that sweet voice that time hath rendered dumb
& freshens like to spring—loves hopes & fears
That in my bosom found an early home
Wooing the heart to extacy—I come
To thee when sick of care of joy bereft
Seeking the pleasures that are found in bloom
& happy hopes that time hath only left
Around the haunts where thou didst erst sojourn
Then smile sweet cherubim & welcome my return

With thee the raptures of lifes early day
Appear & all that pleased me when a boy
Tho pains & cares have torn the best away
& winters crept between us to destroy
Do thou commend the reccompence is joy
The tempest of the heart shall soon be calm
Tho sterner truth against my dreams rebel
Hope feels success & all my spirits warm
To strike with happier mood my simple shell
& seize thy mantles hem O say not fare thee well

Still sweet enchantress youths stray feelings move
That from thy presence their existance took
The innocent idolatry & love
Paying thee worship in each secret nook
That fancied friends in tree & flower & brook
Shaped clouds to angels & beheld them smile
& heard commending tongues in every wind
Lifes grosser fancies did these dreams defile
Yet not entirely root them from the mind
I think I hear them still & often look behind

Aye I have heard thee in the summer wind
As if commending what I sung to thee
Aye I have seen thee on a cloud reclined
Kindling my fancies into poesy
I saw thee smile & took the praise to me
In beautys past all beautys thou wert drest
I thought the very clouds around thee knelt

4

I saw the sun to linger in the west
Paying thee worship & as eve did melt
In dews they seemd thy tears for sorrows I had felt

Sweeter than flowers on beautys bosom hung
Sweeter than dreams of happiness above
Sweeter than themes by lips of beauty sung
Are the young fancies of a poets love
When round his thoughts thy trancing visions move
In floating melody no notes may sound
The world is all forgot & past his care
While on thine harp thy fingers lightly bound
As winning him its melody to share
& heaven itself with him where is it then but there

Een now my heart leaps out from grief & all
The gloom thrown round by cares oershading wing
Een now those sunny visions to recall
Like to a bird I loose dull earth & sing
Lifes tempests swoons to calms on every string
& sweet enchantress if I do but dream
If earthly visions have been only mine
My weakness in thy service wooes esteem
& pleads my truth as almost worthy thine
Surely true worship makes the meanest theme divine

& still warm courage calming many a fear
Heartens my hand once more thine harp to try
To join the anthem of the minstrel year
For summers music in thy praise is high
The very winds about thy mantle sigh
Love melodies thy minstrel bards to be
Insects & birds exerting all their skill
Float in continued song for mastery
While in thy haunts loud leaps the little rill
To kiss thy mantles hem & how can I be still

There still I see thee fold thy mantle grey
To trace the dewy lawn at morn & night
& there I see thee in the sunny day
Withdraw thy veil & shine confest in light
Burning my fancies with a wild delight
To win a portion of thy blushing fame
Tho haughty fancies treat thy powers as small

& fashions thy simplicitys disclaim
Should but a portion of thy mantle fall
Oer him who wooes thy love tis reccompence for all

Not with the mighty to thy shrine I come
In anxious sighs or self applauding mirth
On mount parnassus as thine heir to roam
I dare not credit that immortal birth
But mingling with the lesser ones on earth
Like as the little lark from off its nest
Beside the mossy hill awakes in glee
To seek the mornings throne a merry guest
So do I seek thy shrine if that may be
To win by new attempts another smile from thee

If without thee neath clouds & storms & winds
Ive roamed the wood & field & meadow lea
& found no flowers but what the vulgar find
Nor met one breath of living poesy
Among such charms where inspirations be
The fault is mine & I must bear the lot
Of missing praise to merit thy disdain
To feel each idle plea tho urged forgot
I can but sigh—tho foolish to complain
Oer hopes so fair begun to find them end so vain

Then will it prove presumption thus to dare
To add fresh failings to each faulty song
Urging thy blessing on an idle prayer
To sanction silly themes it will be wrong
For one so lowly to be heard so long
Yet sweet enchantress yet a little while
Forgo impatience & from frowns refrain
The strong are not debarred thy cheering smile
Why should the weak who need them most complain
Alone in solitude soliciting in vain

But if my efforts on thine harp prove true
Which bashful youth at first so feared to try
If aught of nature be in sounds I drew
From hopes young dreams & doubts uncertainty
To these late offerings not without their sigh
Then on thine alter shall these themes be laid
& past the deeds of graven brass remain

6

Filling a space in time that shall not fade
& if it be not so—await disdain
Till dust shall feel no sting nor know it toiled in vain

PLEASURES OF SPRING

How beautiful the spring resumes its reign
Breathing her visions oer the earth again
The veriest clown that hath a pulse to move
Looks on her smiling face & falls in love
He plucks the wild flowers scattered from her hand
& feels warm rapture round his heart expand
Joys of the soul which nature prompts to seek
The all of poesy but its power to speak
Each bush & tree & sprouting weed is seen
Remembering spring & darkening into green
The hedgrow thorn unseals its tender shoots
& arum leaves sprout green about their roots
The ash tree swells its buds as black as jet
Whose pale green keys are not unfolded yet
The sallow glistens in its gay palm blooms
Studded with golden dust where earliest come
The solitary wild bees that survive
Their trance & keep their feeble songs alive
The rifted elm from cloathing spring recieves
Its hoplike pale forerunners of the leaves
& tasselled catkins on the hazels cling
The woodmans genial prophecys of spring
There is a calm divinity of joy
Breaths rapture round oer every ones employ
The Poet feels it neath some forward bush
The first in leaf to hide the singing thrush
Where cutting open with heart beating speed
Some book just purchased which he loves to read
Some brother poets new engaging song
Which warm anticipation sought so long
The Lover feels it in some secret place
Shut out from all but one endearing face
The idol of his heart that peerless maid
Who walks a goddess in the secret shade
Whose fairey form replete with every charm
Thrills to his heart while hanging on his arm
Listing with downward smiles some tender tale
Or sudden song of early nightingale
Bewitching woman what a boon of bliss
Hangs round thy lovliness in spots like this
When woman speaks mans heart delighted hears
Chaste conversations coupled with meek fears

Her innoscence from wrong her heart defends
Her smiles would change een savages to friends
In earthly charms she rivals heaven above
For what were angels without womans love
    The Hind too feels the happiness of spring
Chopping the wattling hedge while linnets sing
Around his labour all the live long day
& flowers spring up the chronicles of may
    The Boy too breaths it from the common air
While hurrying onward to the distant fair
In such glad haste as scarce can give him time
In neighbouring bush for peeping nest to climb
Or cowslip bunch that meets his eager view
About the meadows which he journeys through
& Shepherd Boy as soon as eer he finds
The brook untroubled with the winter winds
Trims up his pole & hunts in april storms
The cowdung hillocks on the moor for worms
Scarce giving patience leave his hooks to trim
Ere in he throws it from the weedy brim
Bent oer the leaning willow hour by hour
His chair for rest & house to shun a shower
    The Husbandman to see each freshening sight
Feels his heart warm & flutter with delight
& cheerful mid the lengthening days turmoils
Mingles full many a ballad with his toils
Those rude old themes his fathers sung with pride
Lost & half buried to the world beside
That wed a few fond hearts & linger on
Like sweet old poets when their fame is gone
Each feels the bliss on toil or leisure fall
Bestowed by spring who offers it to all
    Each flower again smiles th[r]o' its veil of dew
Like lovely abscent faces seen anew
Rich with the same perfumes & luscious smiles
They wake again our leisure to beguile
Like an old tale of pleasure told again
After long years of desolating pain
No fashions change them smell & hue the same
With memory old acquaintances proclaim
To manhoods withered root of faded joy
As when they met us while it bloomed a boy
Primroses among thorns now find their home
Like timid beautys shunning all that come

9

& lilys of the valley weeping dew
Live in their lonliness the season through
Save when a lovesick breeze with amourous sigh
Lifts their green veils to kiss them passing bye
The bark of trees puts gayer liveries on
& varied hues thro woodland thickets run
The black thorn deepens in a darker stain
& brighter freckles hazle shoots regain
The woodland rose [in] bright aray is seen
Whose bark recieves like leaves a vivid green
& foulroyce twigs as red as stockdoves claws
Shines in the woods to gain the bards applause
While the old oaks rude bulks in vigour warms
& mealy powder cloaths his rifted arms
  In spots like these the shepherd loves to fling
His careless limbs neath the young leaves of spring
To muse upon some wild brooks hasty streams
& idly revel over waking dreams
Or stretched in carless mood upon his back
To view the blue sky & its sweeping rack
Lifting his fancies to each passing cloud
& shaping every one that journeys proud
Oer its mysterious way to forms & things
That fancys visions to his memory brings
Some like to rocks gleam on his wondering eye
Mid shoreless seas & some go swifter bye
Like ships that onward other worlds pursue
Oer bounding billows of a different hue
Soft as the paper ships he used to make
& float in boyhood on each summer lake
Some white like pallaces of marble seem
The towers of heaven scaled in many a dream
& which to waking fancies grandly shine
The abodes of one whom instinct owns divine
Some like to mountains shadow high & some
Like the dear vales that nestle round his home
With cots & groves & fountains streaming bye
Spreading long edens to the musing eye
& thus he dreams away his idle hours
Stretched mid the totter grass & nodding flowers
& wishing often on his mossy bed
For the larks wings that whistles oer his head
To realize his glowing dreams & flye
To the soft bosom of that sunny sky

To trace the seeming vales & mountains there
Which hopeless height personifys so fair
For in the raptures of his warm delight
Mans reason keeps its wisdom out of sight
Leaving the sweets of fancy running wild
& half remains as he hath been a child
  By springs warm winds & gleaming smiles awoke
The noisey frogs in flaggy marshes croak
Of frost bound prisons fled & freedom won
& by each bauk that freshens in the sun
The snake curls up asleep or crooks along
Frighting the schoolboy from his sports & song
Who peeps for nests in the half feathered hedge
Or picks the pootys from the rustling sedge
  The prophets of the spring dart down the brook
& scarcely gives the shepherd time to look
In glad suspence he smiles & guesses on
If twas a swallow or his dream of one
Untill the bird as to convince the swain
Shortens his speed & circles round again
Oer fallow fields & moores of russet hue
Pewets again their restless flights renew
& swoop around with harsh & shrilly cry
Oer swains at plough & shepherds wandering bye
The schoolboy hears them with a mixed delight
Of hopes & pleasures & at morn & night
Spends many a leisure hour the meadows guest
In fruitless searches for their hidden nest
The gay woodpecker with its glossy wing
Green as the plumage of returning spring
Bores at decaying trees with wakening joys
& gives spring welcome with its jarring noise
Till startled by the noise of passing clowns
Then off it bounces in its ups and downs
  The Landrail now resumes its haunts again
Whom herdboys listen & pursue in vain
Its craiking noise how often when a child
Ive heard & followed with delusions wild
Wading knee deep the downy grass among
Startling grasshoppers from their idle song
How have I tracked the close & meadow ground
Listening & following the deluding sound
That onward still its craiking note renewed
Nor nearer seemed than when I first pursued

11

Hunt where I would or listen as I might
Twas here & there & ever out of sight
A very spirit to my wandering thought
Heard on but never to be seen or caught
So wearied with the chase I turned away
& sought new pleasure in my former play
Believing it some fairey left by night
To wander blinded by the sunny light
    The partridge mid the wheat that snugly shields
His russet plumage gladdens in the fields
& home bound hinds at sunsets dewy fall
Hears once again its well known evening call
    Tho these as simple trifles merely seem
To those whose souls are dead to every dream
That waking spring throws round them—there are some
Within whose bosom nature find a home
That deem them sweetest themes because they bring
The untutored music of returning spring
    Springs joys are universal & they fall
From an unsparing bounty blessing all
The meanest thing that lives to crawl or flye
Has equal claims in her impartial eye
Obscure & mean as they may seem to some
She always finds a pathway to their home
Een the coy hare blest with her cheering smile
Slinks from its buried solitudes awhile
From woodland lares all winters wants could find
Where brown sedge whistled to the res[t]less wind
To clover leas & there it squats to play
In timid raptures dewy hours away
Till dangers shadows haunt its nimble eye
& startling netherd boy goes whooping bye
Then off it scampers mid the shielding grain
Till all is still & out it skips again
& the wild rabbit less reserved & coy
Squats on the heaths thyme hills in nibbling joy
& crafty fox the blackthorn holts among
Plays round its den like kittens with her young
    March brought a little flower spring loves to wear
The brightest jewel in her shining hair
That like the daisey wears a lowly head
& scarcely peers above its grassy bed
& mingling in their blooms they shine afar
An earthly sky of gold & silver stars

Like them its open look smiles thro the day
& shuts at eve like pleasure tired of play
In botany it claims an humble shrine
& wears the name of "lesser celadine"
But by another name the shepherd swain
Marks it on young springs dewy paths again
With village boys he calls it buttercup
Yet not the one with which the faireys sup
That holds at night the nectar drops of dew
To cheer their mirth the feasting season thro
Which proudly leaves the grass to meet the sun
& waits till summer hath its reign begun
With head less haughty this is taught to shine
Of looks bewitching & of hues divine
It early comes & glads the shepherds eye
Like a bright star spring-tempted from the sky
Reflecting on its leaves the suns bright rays
That sets its pointed glories in a blaze
So bright that childerns fancies it decieves
Who think that sunshine settles in its leaves
& playful hold it neath each others chins
To see it stain with gold their lily skin
& he who seems to win the brightest spot
Feels future wealth & fortune as his lot
Ah happy childhood with that sunny brow
No wealth can match what nature gives thee now
& like these blossoms of the golden bloom
Thy spring *must* fade tho summers wealth *may* come
    From every village groups of merry boys
Throng field & meadow seeking after joys
& many a littered flower & broken bough
Wear the rude marks of their intrusions now
& moss & feathers scattered here & there
With birds left mourning oer their sad despair
Bespeak their young intrusions every day
& show the ravage of their tyrant play
With eager speed to woodland shades they rush
& peep around the pastures stumpy bush
Pushing the boughs aside with eager haste
& climbing bushes that consceal a nest
    Tho thorns full oft their little deeds chastise
& prick their fingers ere they gain the prize
The deepest wound costs but a tear or sigh
& new found nests soon warm such sorrows dry

Thus on they sport till liberty expires
& school again each runaway requires
To con his thumb soiled book with many a sigh
Oft turning to the door an anxious eye
Where sunbeams flicker thro' upon the walls
& sparrows chirp with freedoms welcome calls
Pictureing restraint more irksome to the mind
& heightening pleasures which they left behind
   Noisey marauders of the plashy green
Now spitefull geese with their young broods are seen
Nibbling the morning grass bejemmed with dew
As yellow as the flowers they wander through
Or rippling oer the pond in twittering glee
Chasing each waterflye or crossing bee
While their protectors watch with wary eye
Each fancied enemy that passes bye
Hissing & gabbling frightning far away
The meddling childern as they pass to play
Een dogs will loose their independant pride
& drop their tails & fearing turn aside
   Now walks the man of taste among the woods
& fields—& where small runnels rill their floods
Loud laughing on their errands watering flowers
& down the narrow lanes he walks for hours
All carpeted anew with young silk grass
So soft that birds hear not the feet that pass
Close by their nests—he peeps the leaves among
& marks with rapture how they brood their young
Then drops beneath the bushes to peruse
A pocket poet of some favoured muse
Then plucks a primrose from its leafey bed
To place between the pages which he read
Instead of doubling down to mark the place
& lye a relic in times withered space
Reminding him as seasons take to wing
What joys he felt on such a spot in spring
With such sweet essence of earths fading fruits
His soul is chronicled above the brutes
Such fine ideas that makes life sublime
& gains a look in heaven before its time
For heaven is happiness & he enjoys
That happy dream whoso his mind employs
He has his favourite bush & favourite tree
& nooks on commons where he loves to be

14

He makes his favourite bank a summer seat
& posts & stones he'll leave his path to greet
Where time with mossy prophecys presage
They are her favoured patriarchs for age
The stick he leans on was a favourite shoot
That ten years back was severed from the root
Of some prized relic or boy favoured tree
& keeps it still his daily friend to be
With such a waste of happiness he meets
As like a bee he strays collecting sweets
& gleans right covetous & never tires
But thro the dayspring saunters & admires
& when the night comes on his fancies wear
A wish to lodge with birds & still be there
    How beautiful the wind awakes & flings
Disordered graces oer the face of things
Stirring the shorter grass in twittering gleams
Like rippling shadows over shallow streams
& waving that which grows more rank & high
In deepening waves of darker majesty
A green & living sea in life arayed
Wave rolling over wave shade chasing shade
In every different grade of stirring hue
More swifter then the swallow can pursue
Who journeys low & rapid oer the lea
& seemly swims along the summer sea
The brushing billows rush oer passing feet
As waves are broken oer the rocks they meet
The woods too round the landscape roll a sea
Of varied hues & wild imensity
Heaving fantastic on the wandering eye
Hugh swelling billows to the smiling sky
Here oft the poet wanders & employs
His leisure midst this wilderness of joys
Seeking the spots his heart the most approves
& wild grown pastures which he dearly loves
The common furze clad heath all wild where sheep
Paddle their thousand tracks & rabbits leap
Playfully battering every little hill
Thrown up by moles that burrow at their will
Where tracks of waggons map the vagrant sward
That claims no fence or ownerships regard
Yet nature cloaths it oer with tastefull care
In garments which the may is proud to wear

Furze never out of blossom & the broom
That rivals sunshine with their golden bloom
Where mossy brooks their shallow floods distill
Forceing their way & wandering at their will
Here thoughts run wild by starts in various moods
Now eddying as the runnel thro the woods
Dallying with pleasant things as it with leaves
Then starts & wider space its glow recieves
Like cataracts led with hurried eager ire
As almost kindles water into fire
His thoughts rush out with joys unfelt before
& maddening raptures make his soul run oer
With its divine consceptions till they rise
Forgetting earth & mix with paradise
    Now long & green grows every laughing day
Till clouds seem weary with their length of way
& when the evening in her leisure comes
Night threats no terrors in its winter glooms
That prompted dismal tales round sooty hearth
& midnight murders left small room for mirth
Revealed by many a horrid screaming ghost
As heard by travellers upon wild heaths lost
Or seen in ancient rooms by folks abed
To draw the curtains with quick hand tho dead
& walk the stair case with unearthly tread
Makeing each listners very flesh to creep
& men & childern even dread to sleep
Night throws the mantle bye she wildly wore
& winter like a wizard reigns no more
Borrowing the voices of the bursting wind
To howl its dreads on the benighted hind
Who heard in tempests ringing oer his head
Ten thousand yells to stop him as he fled
These all have fled their sabbath glooms to keep
Till desolate winter startles them from sleep
In spellbound caves & charnel vaults they hide
Where bats are bred & dreadful dreams abide
Eve cometh now with her attendant moon
As pleasant as a cloudy day in June
& daylight ever stays the whole night long
To list the nightingales unsleeping song
& night grim tyrant in fears dread parade
Is now a bankrupt broken in his trade
The winds play harmless in the fledging bowers

Soft as the motion of the shaken flowers
Disturbing not the young moths easy flight
That steals to kiss the sleeping flowers at night
The clouds in beautious order thro the sky
Veil & not hide the moonlight passing bye
Mantled in beautious forms that seem to be
The travelling spirits of eternity
    The husbandman released from toiling day
Muses in pleasure on his homeward way
Oft gazing on the pale moons peaceful face
& pictures there a quiet resting place
Deeming it heaven or somthing near akin
To what all wishes are so warm to win
When dark hereafter takes him as her guest
He deems that place a sabbath land of rest
Thinking his soul shall gather wing & flye
To that pale eden on the soft blue sky
    The lingering milkmaid now tho far from town
Loiters along & sets her buckets down
Nor starts at sounds that meet her listening ear
For happy hope takes place of every fear
& paints her love in every object round
& fancy hears his voice in every sound
    The boy neer mends his pace but soodles on
Blessing the moonlight when the day is gone
& even dares to pause amid the shade
Of the old ruined castle undismayed
To mark the change—that some few weeks ago
Hid its blank walls in draperys of snow
Marking in joy on its once naked tower
Snub elders greening & full many a flower
Of Bloodwalls glowing with rich tawney streaks
Blushing in beauty from the gaping creeks
Swathy yet lovely by each zepher fanned
As the soft cheek of maidens summer tanned
Wreaths nature loves round ruins brows to bind
From seeds took thither by the birds & wind
He views those garlands & seems struck the while
That things so abject should be seen to smile
Oft turning to the moon a wondering eye
That seems to journey with him thro' the sky
Moves as he moves & stops as glad the while
To wait his leisure while he climbs a stile
He walks it walks & keeps his every pace

17

Runs when he runs & glories in the race
He trys his utmost speed to leave behind
His shining friend & thinks he beats the wind
For swiftness as he pants & hurries on
Inly exulting that the race is won
But spite of every vale & weary hill
He passed & clomb so swift it followed still
& while he hums oer each old tune he loves
Do as he will it moveth as he moves
Swift as his thoughts his speed is all in vain
He turns to look & there it is again
Plump opposite him gleaming pale & wan
As near as when his eager race began
He thinks on the long ways he left behind
& vain wild notions fill his puzzled mind
The gossip tales that winter did supply
Urge their faint shadows on his gazing eye
& the pale shades that cloud the moon so wan
His artless fancys fashions to a man
Oft has he heard at night when toil was done
Rude tales of jiants dwelling in the moon
& this as one of those his mind supplies
That takes his nightly journeys thro the skies
So here he stops nor urges speed again
Deeming a race with jiants doubly vain
      Now many an eve in simple moods of praise
The Hind right thankful for the lengthening days
Will oer his Bible in rich musings lean
Thats wrapt in baize to keep the covers clean
Noteing with joy as on he reads to see
The truth & power of sacred poesy
Those texts of spring he gets by heart to tell
His fellows which describe the time so well
As "now the time of singing birds is come"
& "lilys among thorns do make their home"
"The winters past the rain is oer & gone"
These are the texts that lead his raptures on
"The vine shoots forth & yields a goodly smell"
He finds no book that tells the time so well
& ere he goes to bed in humble ways
He breaths a prayer & fervently he prays
For blessings on his family around
That in the sooty corner sit profound
Begging alike to bear the worst when sent

All breathe amen & go to bed content
Prayers are the wings by which the soul doth flye
To gather blessings from the bountious sky
& they are blest whose days thus calmly wear
Each met in hope & finished in a prayer

TALES

VALENTINE EVE

Young girls grow eager as the day retires
& smile & whisper round their cottage fires
Listning for noises in the dusky street
For tinkling latches & for passing feet
The prophecys of coming joys to hark
Of wandering lovers stealing thro' the dark
Dropping their valentines at beautys door
With hearts & darts & love knots littered oer
"Aye" said a gossip by a neighbours hearth
While the young girls popt up in tittering mirth
To hear the door creek with heart jumping signs
& footsteps hastening bye & valentines
Drop rustling on the floor—"aye aye" she said
(As they kept back & smiled oer what they read)
Your fine love letters might be worth your smiles
If 'stead of coming from some creeping giles
Rich lovers sent them as it once befell
To one young maiden I remember well
Tho Madam Meers now lives at oakley hall
With coach & four & footmen at her call
Her father was none else than farmer Ling
& she plain Kate before she wore a ring
Tho I began about the valentine
The starting subject I ll awhile resign
But hear with patience & ye ll quickly learn
For I ll haste on & take it up in turn
    When the poor irish from their country rove
& like scotch cattle throng the road in droves
To seek the profits which the harvest brings
At that same season to old farmer Lings
A stranger came but not of foreign blood
He spoke plain english & his looks was good
& hired himself for toil the season thro
At any jobs the harvest had to do
& tho he seemed as merry as the clowns
He neer was noisey like such vulgar lowns
& when he heard them urge a vulgar joke
At passing maids he neither laughd nor spoke
But while he saw the blush their rudeness made
His manners seemed their freedom to upbraid
For he d turn round a moment from his toil
& say "good morning" & would kindly smile

23

Tho dressed like them in jacket russet brown
His ways betrayed him better than a clown
& many a guess from rumours whispers fell
& gossips daily had new tales to tell
Some said he once had been a wealthy man
& from a bankrupts painful ruin ran
Others with far worse causes marked his flight
& taxed him with a forgers name out right
& tho he heard such whispers passing bye
He d laugh but never stop to question why
Nor seemed offended think whatere he would
But always seemed to be in merry mood
Bad as folks thought him I was well aware
That he by one at least was welcome there
Who always mid their noisey idle prate
Would silent stand & that was rosey Kate
She seemed bewitched with his good mannered ways
& never spoke about him but to praise
She was the youngest daughter fair & gay
As flowers that open in the dews of May
Loves heart neer trembled at a sweeter face
When health & beauty courted its embrace
Nor lived a merrier girl beneath the sun
For romp & play when labours work was done
Wild as a Doe that overleapt the park
She'd laugh & play oer evenings games till dark
All noise & stir like an ill sitting hen
But shoy & timid in the sight of men
Her friends neer dreamed of what all else might see
His ways was plain as the "cross row" to me
When ere he caught her in her dissabille
Washing or aught—she ran as lovers will
Up stairs as quickly as she could from sight
To seek her glass & put her garments right
Anxious to meet him in her best attire
As he the more might love her & admire
& once at eve as we the cows did wait
He leaned beside her on the stackyard gate
& smiled & whispered as she stooped adown
To pull some burdocks from her sweeping gown
"Mary theres one whose thoughts when your away
"Always cling with you full as close as they
"Who hopes yet fears his growing love to name
"Lest you should throw it from you just the same"

24

She coloured like the fire & turned aside
But I saw quickly what her heart would hide
& up & told her when she milked at night
That be the harvest stranger who he might
A winning tongue neaths toils disguise was hid
That knew more manners then our farmers did
She laughd & said "aye so you love him then
But as for her she d no regard for men"
Tho such denials kept the secret worse
I took no heed but sanctioned her discourse
& when she dressed to walk on harvest eves
Spending an hour to glean among the sheaves
Things were to others eyes full often seen
That she'd more errands than the one to glean
She always follow'd in the strangers toil
Who oft would stop to wet his hook & smile
& loose when none percieved from out his hand
Some wheat ears now & then upon the land
& oft when running from a sudden shower
Or leaving off to take their beavering hour
He always from the rest would linger last
To leave a smile & greet her as he past
All that had any sense to use their eyes
Might easy guess beneath the thin disguise
Like to the burr about the moon at night
It seems to covert but still leaves it light
& sure enough he was a handsome swain
One any maiden had been proud to gain
Een I have often envied Kittys place
& felt the heartache at his smiling face
For when I passed him he would always smile
& often took my milk pail oer a stile
Jeering us both of sweethearts in our play
Tho nothing but in good behaviours way
He said to me—yet without shame I say't
I thought myself as fine a wench as Kate
    Dark as the strangers mystery were his ways
Here wandered round the field on sabbath days
& left to vulgar minds the noisey town
Nor made a partner of a fellow clown
Traceing the wood tracks overgrown with moss
Or with heath rabbits winding thro the goss
& oft neath black thorn shadows by the brook
Was seen by shepherds musing oer a book

25

& in his button holes was always seen
Wildflowers—that in his rambles he would glean
Folks often marvelled at each seeming whim
What we thought weeds seemd best of flowers with him
The ragged robbin by the runnel brinks
Seemed in his eye much finer flowers then pinks
& tall wild woad that lifts its spirey tops
By stone pits—nay een briony & hops
He would from hedges in a poesy bind
& leave the woodbine & the rose behind
All wondered at his ways & some believed
The man was crazed but rumour gets decieved
 When busy harvest to its end had come
& childern ran to hollow "harvest home"
Bawling half hidden neath each green ash bough
For cross plumb skittles out of fashion now
Kate was the queen upon that merry night
& rode upon the waggon drest in white
The stranger oft looked up to see her stand
& smiling called her "queen of fairey land"
That harvest supper we had morts of fun
& Farmer Sparks was there a neighbours son
He was her fathers choice who dreamed of gain
& talked of marriage as he would of grain
He vainly tryed young Kittys smiles to share
& next her without bidding took his chair
Full oft with gracious simperings looking up
To drink to Kitty oer the silver cup
While she but with a careless look replied
Or turned like one that would not heed aside
But if the stranger gazed above his horn
She smiled as lovely as a mayday morn
Soon as the racket & the fun began
Young Farmer Sparks up from the table ran
To act the crane & poked the room about
Breaking the pipes & putting candles out
While wenches squealed & old dames fainted pale
Quickly recovering with an horn of ale
The stranger seemed to shun the rude uproar
& Kate slove with him to the kitchen door
I sat on thorns the live long night about
For fear their ways would blab the secret out
& had aught met the fathers jealous sight
Farewell to fun & frolic for the night

But all went right & naught was seen or done
To spoil the acting or to damp the fun
The old man smoked his pipe & drank his ale
& laughed most hearty at each sport & tale
On the next day for Kate a gloomy day
The harvest labourers took their parting pay
& the young stranger with a downcast eye
Turned round to Kate & bade us both "good bye"
Soon as he went she ran with eager feet
Up stairs to see him vanish down the street
I heard the creeking casement open thrown
& knew full well what she neer cared to own
For her swelled eyes their secrets badly kept
When she came down they told me she had wept
Twas harmless sorrows did her bosom move
& theres no sin nor shame to weep for love
Sometimes she seemed as sad & sometimes gay
But never more appeared so fond of play
Lone pastimes now did leisure hours engage
Dull as a tamed bird wonted to the cage
She seemed to be while time unheeding went
Nor left a hope to ease her discontent
    At length the postman with his wind pluft cheek
That brought the news & letters once a week
Some mornings after valentine was bye
Came in & gan his parcel to untie
Her sisters bustled up & smiling thought
That he some lovers valentines had brought
But hopes with them was quickly out of date
Soon as they found the letter was for Kate
Poor wench her colour came & went away
Now red as crimson then as pale as may
The old man thought it farmer Sparkes's son
That sent the thing & felt his wishes won
Laying his pipe down he began to joke
& clapt her on the shoulder as he spoke
Have at him wench thats all I have to tell
& bonny Kate will sell her beauty well
For he's got money wench as well as love
To make your ring sit easy as a glove
But when he found the postmark & the seal
Did different notions to his own reveal
He let the mystery undisturbed remain
& turned his chair & took his pipe again

Her sisters bit their lips in silent spite
& could not keep their envye out of sight
To think that bonny Kate above them all
Who never in her life had seen a ball
Nor spent an hour to curl her parted hair
Nor of her beauty seemed to have one care
That romped about in play & joined in toil
While they would sit & not a finger soil
Should be thus noticed—but they urged a doubt
& muttered some low bred ingenious lout
Had sent the thing & said with louder voice
"Be who he will he wears a vulgar choice"
& tho they might clowns valentines condemn
Een they were welcome when they came to them
For Sawney Sparks & each young farmer guest
Was little better then a clown at best
Be who he might it made their bosoms ache
& worse when time unriddled their mistake
    Kate had no pride about her she was free
As any maiden in the world could be
& while her sisters dressed in muslin gowns
& scorned on holidays to talk with clowns
She seemed to wear no better dress then I
Yet won a look from every passer bye
& some that passed would mutter praises loud
"Theres a sweet face" which never made her proud
She made all equals—used een beggars well
& all of Kate had some kind things to tell
    When summer eves the first come swallows meet
As Kate & I were looking down the street
These little summer visitors to view
Marking how lowley & how swift they flew
We heard the bustle of a coach & four
Race the lane dust & hurry towards the door
The yard dog never barked nor made a fuss
But dropt his tail & stopt to gaze with us
Een the old geese were silent at the sight
& in amazement half forgot their spite
The noisey childern in the street at play
Picked up their tops & taws & sneaked away
& Kate half startled sneaked & hurried in
While wonder heaved her bosom to her chin
& well it might for twas the very same
Man that at harvest as a reaper came

28

The same that sent her at the valentine
The clever letter that was wrote so fine
Old women that had muttered round the town
& called the stranger by worse names than clown
Peeped out & dropped their courtseys to the coach
& mixed in groups to question its approach
Fine as he was soon as he came in view
I knew his face & so did Kitty too
Who overcame turned white as was the wall
& almost fainted but he stopt the fall
& kept her in his arms with fondling pain
Till the fresh rose came to her face again
Her father gaped & wondered at the throng
& bowed & chattered wether right or wrong
Guessing that love was what the stranger meant
The coach was plenty to buy his consent
& thinking Kate had made her fortune now
He bustled up & gan to scrape & bow
& bade Kate welcome in her noble guest
With wine & ale the oldest & the best
But he was not to be by flattery fed
He only smiled & never turned his head
I want no formal welcomes keep your place
Old man he said—but why that blushing face
My bonny Kate I left thee fond & true
& wish to find thee as I used to do
Smiling & free as on each harvest morn
When I as labourer reaped thy fathers corn
I travelled in disguise alone to find
The native undisguise of womans mind
They're easy coyed to take a golden bait
& love in mockery—but my bonny Kate
I found in thee a heart I wished to prove
Who ignorant of wealth was caught by love
Then shrink not if thy heart is still sincere
Nor blush nor startle with confounding fear
To see thy mother at this finery awed
& father bow & christen me "my lord"
No honours & no titled names are mine
But all I have plain love & wealth is thine
Tho I have grown above thy fathers toil
In reaping corn & ploughing up the soil
Yet that fond love my Kitty showed to me
Was neer a moment from my memory

29

Thy beauty would bewitch a world with love
& Ive returned thy worth & vows to prove
Ive came as promised for thee many a mile
Then bid me welcome with thy usual smile
Reach not sweet Kate the silver cup for me
But bring the horn toil often drank to thee
& thus he said but how can words of mine
Relate a speech that he told oer so fine
However there they sat the night about
& drank the old brown pitcher nearly out
Kate often smiled but yet was still & shoy
& the old man got down right drunk for joy
Who often reached across his elbow chair
To gain the whisper of his daughters ear
Muttering when ere the stranger turned his head
His urgent wishes in her looks to wed
Fingers in vain were shook to keep him still
He een got wilder in his headstrong will
"—A good receipt neer makes a bargain wrong
"So Kate says he burn nothing with your tongue"
& drank her health anew—the strangers eye
Looked smiling at him but made no reply
When morning came Kate gave her hearts consent
The coach was ordered & to church they went
Before the sun the old man bustled up
& gave his blessing oer the silver cup
At the glad closing of that happy day
The stranger drove his blooming bride away
She left her presents for the cake & tea
Leaving old gossips in the highest glee
While he with gifts the ringers did regale
Who rung his praises both with bells & ale
& tho she promised me a handsome gown
When eer she married be he gent or clown
No wonder that her memorys were away
I quite excused her breaking it that day
    He was no lord tho he was full as great
A country squire with a vast estate
In the most trifling things she had her ends
& ere she d gone a twelvemonth from her friends
She wished once more to see us all again
& as indulgence to her lonely pain
They in their coach & four came shining down
To rent a dwelling near her native town

& Oakley hall that tops old cromwells hill
He took to please & occupys it still
A fine old place with ivy round the porch
That long had stood as empty as a church
Folks say it is a Cromwells castle been
& in the walls still cannon holes are seen
There they in happiness & luxury live
& share the all lifes pleasure has to give
Sometimes they visit at their own estate
& yearly drive to London with the great
     Whenever I have errands from the town
To seek the hall she gives me many a crown
Making me welcome in plain friendly ways
& often laughs about our younger days
"Hark thats the clock well I must up & roam
My man no doubt sits waiting me at home
Wholl scold & say by sitting here till nine
That Im an old fool keeping Valentine
So good night all" & hastening from her seat
She sought her clogs & clocked adown the street
The girls were glad twas done— & in her place
The happy cat leapt up & cleaned her face
While crickets that had been unheard so long
Seemed as she stopt to start a merrier song

GOING TO THE FAIR

Gay rose the morn fulfilling many a prayer
Of anxious maids—the day was Topal Fair
The month was may the meadows they were green
& full of flowers tho paths were far from clean
Moistened by showers that frequent tho not long
Fell & were done ere linnets could their song
That now by crowds in every thicket sung
& from the mill dam up the Heron sprung
In every field larks twittered oer the grain
As happy twas the fair so thought the swain
Who hastened oer his labour to get free
By times the pleasures of the fair to see
The very air breathed joy & all the May
To such appeared in joyouance with the day
As if the fair had put their pleasures on
Thus merry minds shape raptures from their own
In ivy bowers woodpiegons sat to coo
& smooth voiced cuckoos muttered as they flew
Free smiled the daisey from dull nights embrace
Flushed with his dewy kisses on its face
The sun was peeping oer the spreading rows
Of dark green elms alive with busy crows
& round the Lodge that darkened neath their shade
Loud was the strife that pigs & poultry made
A farmhouse now tho once a moated hall
As loud too farmer Thriftys morning call
"Come up boys up" re-echoed thro the Lodge
Where last to bed & first to rise was Hodge
Who heard the unwelcome shout mid yawns & sighs
& spent some minutes to unclose his eyes
Yet up he must to fetch his horses now
They needed corn & waiting lay the plough
& morning toil must needs be finished soon
As all had leave to join the fair at noon
So up Hodge got & soodled down the lane
Hirpling like one whose joints was stiff with pain
Tho urged by many a call till out of sight
To mend his pace & not be out till night
& Simon foremost of the servant clan
Who next the master ruled as master man
Was more than anxious to perform his part
Who stript already stopt his song to start

As love & hope with mingling fear & glee
Burnt every thought with madness to be free
Mary a maid whose fame was in her face
Who lived his partner in his last years place
& now tho distant from him many a mile
Her former fondness cheered his present toil
For she had vowed last martinmass when they
For their new places parted wide away
That come what would—on the returning Fair
She'd come to see her friends & meet him there
So Simons hopes who painted her as come
Burnt till they grew all rebels to their home
Forcing his heart on fancys wings to wend
In thought already at its journeys end
His mind all night on thoughts with dull delay
Its parting waited wide awake for day
& now the day had come he waited on
To end his mornings labour & begone
While mingling hopes unsatisfied desires
With their warm gushes & blood boiling fires
Scarce gave him time—so anxious to pursue
Even to think of what he had to do

  By kindness he had bought in seasons past
The love of Mary which he hoped would last
Who young & blushing was & sweet to see
Yet not like gaudy roses on the tree
For beauty blazed not in her face yet there
A twilight splendour owned her more then fair
Illumned by many a mellancholly smile
That taste while gazing might believe the while
The pastoral muse did in her beauty shine
Such as might warm far better songs than mine
The voice of woods & streams was in her looks
& wise she seemed tho ignorant of books
Her hair was swarthy brown & soft of hue
As the sweet gloom that falls with evens dew
That on her fine white forhead did divide
In the triumphant negligence of pride
Her eyes were dark but they wore lights to shine
That love adores & poets call divine
& her cheeks summer blooms wore hues the while
Of loves soft innoscence without its guile
& on the pouting of her amorous lip
Where love delicious nectar longed to sip

Beauty sat throned in that bewitching spell
That love adores & language cannot tell
Where charms triumphant made each gazer pay
Heartaches for looking ere he turned away
& so did Simons but the smiles that cured
Paid more then double for the pain endured
For in loves views to win her kind regard
He milked—& every sunday swept the yard
That she might on her errands safely go
Nor soil the gloss jet of her sunday shoe
& from the stack a faggot every night
He threw his Marys morning fire to light
Nay did all toils her sundays had to do
When she had on a garment that was new
& feared with thorns to tear or dirt to soil
While love was all the payment for his toil
By all these deeds he strove his love to show
Nor was she backward what they meant to know
& tho she shrieked to shun a stolen kiss
A chance to meet his smile she d never miss
& oft for syllabubs for cream she crept
When mistress gossiped & the master slept
& slove the cellar key from off the nail
Above her masters chair to steal him ale
While in those favoured hours most like to speed
Simon had sued & Mary had agreed
Live where they might or fair or foul the weather
Theyd meet this morning at the fair together
Altho six lingering months since then had now
Spread in between warm love to cool that vow
Altho six lingering miles with dreary view
Stretched loves frail charm—still he believed her true
    At length came Hodge with trouble in his speed
For when with quicker pace he did proceed
Bad news was sure the herald of his tale
To say a portion of his job did fail
& now he stopt his song ere nigh to bawl
Of gaps new broke & horses vanished all
For he seemed joyed to find them all astray
Wishing no doubt theyd neer be found that day
A truce from plough to rest each weary limb
Was more then fairs or holidays to him
Simon in silence like a statue stood
Dire dissapointment curdled up his blood

34

His hopes & holiday all seemed as done
While farmer Thrifty bade them search till noon
Sending out heralds famed for swifter speed
Than Hodge grown needless in the time of need
When soon the horses all were found but one
& Dobbin oftenest to transgress was gone
Dobbin a horse well known for miles around
In every village & in every pound
Altho so tame at toil that boys might guide
& childern walk uninjured by his side
When loose from geers he roved as freedoms mate
Hed find all gaps & open every gate
& if aught sweet beyond his pasture grew
No fence so thick but he would blunder thro'
His youth from gipseys did these tricks recieve
With them he toiled & worked his wits to live
Bare roads he traced all day with nought to bite
Then stole with them to stacks to feed at night
Tho now a better life was Dobbins lot
Well fed & fat youths tricks he neer forgot
Still gaps were broke & Dobbin bore the blame
Still stacks were pulled & Dobbin felt no shame
If fifty partners in his pasture lay
Dobbin was safe to lead them all astray
& yet a better horse all did alow
Was never yoked to waggon or to plough
   Old farmer thrifty now with vengance ripe
Cursed & laid down half smoked his morning pipe
Vowing old Dobbins tricks would loose his crop
Of corn if thus whole days they forced to stop
The harrow— & then threw his hands behind him
"If hes above ground curse him we will find him"
& Simon as the safest to succeed
Was posted off & tho to urge his speed
A flaggon of the best ere he did start
Was drawn that burnt like brandy round his heart
But nothing cheered it for his hopes was crost
& chance of meeting Mary seemed as lost
Yet he brushed onward on his doubtful rout
With best leg foremost to find Dobbin out
Muttering his threats in angers blustering tones
How he would thrash the wanderers lazy bones
Whittling a monstrous cudgel while he spoke
Proving therebye he did not mean to joke

Alas for Dobbin sore will be his back
If Simon finds him & he marks his track
For faithless dews his blundering steps betrayed
Oer close & field in crooked marks displayed
But the kind sun that smiles on all below
Was Dobbins friend tho Simon was his foe
Drying the tell tale dew from off the grass
Leaving the ploughman to proceed by guess
Who asked of almost every one he met
Searched in each pound & neer the wiser yet
Measuring his shadow every now & then
To guess the hour then hurried on agen
While Marys smiles & promise & the fair
Rose oer all hopes & drove them to despair
Search where he might enquire of whom he would
Dobbin was missing as if lost for good
For he was reckoned cunning & at least
Had more of reason then a common beast
Seeking such secret spots from summer skys
As if he hid from toil as well as flies
This Simon knew & searched in every spot
Where he might hide but yet had hidden not
So on he searched & cursed & searched again
Muttering the while his threatning oaths in vain
Laying to Dobbins tramp in reckless strife
The loss of love & happiness for life
While short his shadow grew & shifted on
Untill it tokened half the day was gone
& what was worse the hour when at the gate
Mary for Simons coming was to wait
When he had told her last & vowed as how
That spot should sink ere he would break his vow
That vow was broke—at least the time expired
When Mary was to wait as love desired
& wait she did for half the morning there
Where two paths met the high road to the fair
She left her fathers cot before the time
To make her lover wait appeared a crime
"Decietful man" doubt burnt hopes taper dim
She sighed & muttered "I may wait for him"
"Here I may stand in doubt the morning long
"Altho he knows he never thinks it wrong
"Last night I came six weary miles in vain
"Cheered with the thoughts of seeing him again

"My mothers love could ill my absence spare
"But without Simon I was restless there"
So sighed the maid as oer the stile she bent
& sighed & onward to the fair she went
While every noise that floated in the wind
Would make her pause & turn a look behind
For Simons haloo she would list & look
Loitering & musing to be overtook
Altho still cheated—down each narrow lane
At every turn she'd stop & wait again
Till tired with hopes excuses for delay
The rosebud in her bosom dyed away
Which there was placed new graces to reveal
Or more for Simons tempted hands to steal
But Simon came not & the withered rose
Was the first omen sorrows to disclose
Stung with the void of abscence to the fair
Hopes curdled all to malice—& when there
To loose her thoughts she struggled to be gay
Passing in freakish whims the merry day
Mocking gay feelings that had small akin
To the perplexitys that lurked within
Changing her nature & in freedoms ways
Smiled as if courting amorous eyes to gaze
Taking with willing hand in merry cue
The glass to kiss from every youth she knew
Each proffered fairing too was freely taen
She cracked the nutts & threw the shells again
Resolved to change her old love for a new
& leave off Simon deemed no longer true
Yet half unconsious of the looks she raised
She blushed & seemed to wonder why they praised
While Footman Tim in his gilt gaudy suit
Tapping with pride his cane upon his boot
Grown bold with ale nipt up in smirking glee
& rudely made her welcome to his knee
Soon from his silken purse his cash was flung
& crown by crown upon the table rung
For every groat & een a penny paid
This purse & all this silver was displayed
The while he sat he'd chink his cash about
To let folk know his pockets wa'n't without
Tween thumb & finger oft he swung his cane
In haughty grace then sipt his glass again

37

Still leaving dregs at bottom to throw down
To show how fashion acted from a clown
& more in Marys presence to display
A careless waste as heeding not the pay
Full oft unbidden out his watch was taen
To show the hour but more to show the chain
& off his gloves were pulled his nails to bite
With vain excuse to show his hands were white
While open flew his waistcoat at the chin
Crimpt frills displaying & a golden pin
To raise his consequence in vulgar eyes
& win the girls to think a blank a prize
Mary seemed hurt yet suffered to be held
Bearing the seat with patience while compelled
& Simon now with weary feet & mind
Pursuing Dobbin whom he could not find
Gave up the hunt his master heard the tale
& swore yet paid him with a horn of ale
Saying as morn was bye he well could spare
Them all—so all made ready for the fair
His Ash plant Simon in his hand had got
Yet paused in doubt half willing & half not
Beside the door with kerchief smoothening down
The ruffled nap upon his beavers crown
Then starting off then still foreboding doubt
Dark fears strong impulse made him pause about
    Sweet was the day & sunny gleamed the weather
While sheep loud bleating called their lambs together
"Craik" went the Landrail in the wind waved grain
Whom idle schoolboys hearing chased in vain
In Simons mind the noise bespoke his fate
He thought it muttered he was all too "late"
"Chewsit" the Pewit screamed in swopping wews
"Chuse it" said Simon I know whom to chuse
Thus neer a bird could sing but Simons cares
Shaped it to somthing of his own affairs
& while he whiped the moisture from his brow
Fear chilled his spirit with his broken vow
& soon must love like lifes deciet decide
How nearly joys & sorrows are allied
The day was swiftly wasting with the wear
& some few girls were coming from the fair
Who left gay mirth & all his noisey crew
Not without sighs their evening jobs to do

& he when met got many a laughing look
Full loud their fears were urged to cross the brook
Knocking their pattens when no dirt was near
& finding danger where no danger were
Signals to urge the aid of Simons hand
But such he could or would not understand
He hurried by them all & would not stay
To ask a question or salute the day
Tho screams & shouts alternate rung behind
Raising their wanton ecchoes on the wind
He never once turned oer his arm to see
If they got oer or in the brook not he
His thoughts already at their journeys end
Left him no time on trifles to attend
With patten rings the path was thickly cut
Where fancy painted Marys nimble foot
In many a printing mark as on before
Which burnt his thoughts & hastened him the more
At length the noisey fair assailed his ear
Great grew his hope but greater grew his fear
& as he crushed among the crowds when there
His eyes dare scarcely wander oer the fair
Lest he—for fear was busy to alarm
Should see his Mary on anothers arm
& as his spirits worn in feeble guise
Needed the boldness barley stout supplies
He sought the ale house where by fear repelled
He scarce dare credit what his eyes beheld
When in a corner full of outward glee
He saw his Mary on anothers knee
He turned away nor would his looks repeat
She turned as white as death but kept her seat
For well she thought his carelessness foretold
He for a new love had forsook the old
While he with far more cause for dark distrust
Thought all was over & his actions just
& tho he could not stifle without pain
His love he thought it useless to explain
So sat in silence as if none the while
Was worth the notice of a word or smile
Yet as poor captives oft in hopeless plight
Look thro their bars on liberty & light
So did his eyes beneath his beavers brim
Steal looks on Mary half unknown to him

While lifting up when not athirst the quart
To drown the sigh fast swelling from his heart
& Mary smiling struggled to be gay
Tho dissapointment turned her cheek to clay
& eat like cankers every rose away
The deepest sorrow hath no tongue but steals
Signs from the heart betraying what it feels
Sighs come at deeper eloquence than speech
& tears touch chords that language cannot reach
—While footman Tim was busy with his tale
& toasting Mary oer each draught of ale
Simon as able to behold no more
Emptied his quart & hurried to the door
To seek amusement in the noise & rout
Within the fair & keep old memorys out
But all were blanks & every wish was vain
& search for peace still added more to pain
The showmans shouts which wonder yearly brings
The huge hung pictures of outlandish things
Where grinning tiger wavered in the wind
Raising more wonders than they hid behind
The merry fool that would his speeches make
Till at the sport old womens sides would ache
These without pleasure now he sauntered bye
& only turned a careless ear or eye
& weary with the frolic & the fun
He sauntered homeward ere the fair was done
While as in melancholly mood he went
In mutterings loud he gave his sorrows vent
'Is it for this' he said & turned behind
As if mistrustful of the listening wind
'Is it for this I watched till church was oer
Her hens & scoldings from the parson bore
Hunting the eggs all churchtime thro the day
That none should scold her cause they laid away
Is it for this my credit all at stake
& even life I ventured for her sake
When in the orchard while she milked her cows
I stole & clambered to the topmost boughs
To reach the reddest apple plumb or pear
For no more payment than a smile could spare
Smiles feed young love to madness & beguiles
So Ive rued sorely since I lived on smiles
In this same close which brings up happier hours

On sundays when we brushed these selfsame flowers
When glossy slippers did her feet bedeck
I took my kerchief even from my neck
To whipe off lingering drops of bygone showers
Or maybe tears from crushed & broken flowers
& dust that would their glossy hues oercast
Powdered from kingcups shaken as we past
But whats the use to bring up things gone bye
My best I did & the worst served am I'
Here Simon stopt for loud upon his ear
Stole merry voices fast approaching near
From many laughing home returning groups
Not sad like Simon under broken hopes
But wild with joy glad frolicked many a lass
On ploughmans arms light skipping thro the grass
Old men & women too with ale inspired
Felt young again & laughed till they were tired
While childern stooped & shouted by their sides
To see their shadows take such antique strides
As mocking the old dames who danced & sung
With aprons spread as nimble as the young
Simon right anxious for the nights disguise
Hurried along to hide from meddling eyes
While low the sun in evenings mellow light
Behind the meadow bridges sunk from sight
Yet as if loath to leave the merry crew
Peeped thro the arches in a last adieu
Simon tho filled with thoughts reflecting pain
Could not but turn to see it peep again
Remembering at the sight in happier days
How Mary stood that self same thing to praise
What sorrowful delights such dreams bequeath
What golden feelings clad in memorys wreath
Past reccolections in our bosoms move
That once were hopes attendants upon love
& Simon een in sorrow felt a joy
From memorys past that nothing could destroy
But such are reveries that will not last
They come like thoughts & ere we muse are past
Hopes change like summer clouds from shape to shape
Setting the restless fancies all agape
& painting joys as beautiful & fair
Till all disolves into the common air
So Simon proved it as he onward sped

Who soon as home went supperless to bed
& tho at toil next day he bawled & sung
Twas but to smother how his heart was wrung
His mind still laboured over past affairs
& strove in vain to get the start of cares
While hope proposed a medicine for pain
Making it up to see her once again
Resolving if next sunday should be fine
To look oer all & ere he would resign
Loves all hed go & clear himself from wrong
& tell what kept him from the fair so long
For he believed & did his follys scoff
That Mary fancied he had left her off
& at the fair in hurt loves jealous whim
To be revenged took up with Footman Tim
Thus Simon thought & often stopt his song
To curse lost Dobbin that had caused the wrong
   Soon Sunday came & to make worse the matter
Rain drops from off the eves did quickly patter
He heard it while abed for sorrow aches
Around the heart & haunts it while it wakes
Sad sad he listened to the pattering sound
While every plash left hope a deeper wound
Ere the gray cock nights watchman did supprise
Nights startled sleep & bid the sun to rise
& up he got & with an anxious eye
From out the window looked upon the sky
That darkly glowered as if it meant to last
Raining away so thickly & so fast
That every drop made bubbles as they fell
In the mossed duckpond & uncovered well
While brimming ruts did headlong journeys go
As if like springs they ever meant to flow
Vain hope what is it as its sun declines
A balm on which the sick heart feeds & pines
& many a heart from whence its rapture came
Is nothing now but memory & a name
Victims of love that cheated them too long
Sunk to the burthen of a mournful song
But Simon tho perplext felt not that smart
So deep that endeth in a broken heart
Of ruder mould was he & ruder form
That like the oak grows stubborn in a storm
Not like the weaker sort that bend & sigh

& at a frown cling to despair & die
The rain it ceased at noon the sky looked thro
The breaking clouds in many a patch of blue
As breaks the thick ice in a sudden thaw
Showing the bottom of the brook below
When Simon instantly from off the nail
His bran new beaver reached & without fail
Brushed oer the plashy fields & dripping stiles
Careless of shortening day & lengthening miles
For Marys smiles would be to him as light
& make een sunshine of the darkest night
& so they ought for ere he reached the place
The sun sunk low & bade good night apace
& while the spire peeped oer the woodland bough
He stopt to whipe the moisture from his brow
Asking a shepherd where the farm might be
About the town where Mary lived—& he
Scarce raised him on his elbow from his lare
& holding out his sheephook halooed "there"
When on his greedy ear her well known voice
Ecchoed amain & made his heart rejoice
As in a milking nook she called her cows
When on he sped & hid among the boughs
Of black thorn growing in disorder near
The sad revealings of her mind to hear
For grief in solitude will tell tho vain
Its sorrows to itself to ease the pain
That stifling silence round the heart inurned
Simon thus much by self experience learned
So down he dropt amid the thickets shade
To list unseen the unsuspecting maid
Staining his garments with the bruising grass
For he thought little of his sunday dress
Nor was his expectation long decieved
Her sighs soon told him how her heart was grieved
& while the brook in mingling mutterings ran
She milked & thus her sad complaint began
'Fye Simon fye to seem to love so true
'Your heedless follys know not what they do
'My hearts nigh broken with his broken vow
'I feel so sad I scarce can milk my cow
'Yet none will free me from my sunday toil
'So I must milk & sunday gowns must spoil
'& spoil they may—I feel in loves despair

'Few are the number I shall live to wear
'Simons unkindness made all pleasures vain
'& left me wounds that cannot heal again
'Ungrateful man to do as he hath done
'To take my pails that I the dirt might shun
'& lay fresh stones when eer the brook was high
'That I might cross in safety & be dry
'Then all at once to fling me from his mind
'Nor een on memory turn a look behind
'Around me as he did like Ivy cling
'& then to spurn me like a poison thing
'Dear what a terror of suspence Im in
'My heart een heaves my bosom to my chin
'& swelled with troubles that I could not see
'Unpins my kerchief as it would be free
'But sad to think of that can never be
'I felt no joy in fussy Footman Tim
'Twas downright malice made me notice him
'& vain I tryed to yield & he to win
'For love & malice claim but small akin
'False Simon first my foolish heart beguiled
'& to none else will it be reconsiled
'Would I could pluck his memory from my mind
'Just as a dewdrop trembles from the wind
'O dear I cannot for my heart must own
'The pain it feeleth to be left alone
'To weep unseen & all unheard to sigh
'Left all to silent loneliness am I
'Save that the Robin every time I come
'Peepeth & makes me welcome to his home
'Leaving in neighbouring bush its mossy nest
'To visit & invite me for its guest
'Perk nimble thing were I but half as free
'& half as happy I might sing with thee
'Thy love proves true but mine was false & bad
'& that which makes thee happy makes me sad
'—Well foolish griefs are follys many say
'& longs the night that never looks for day
'Well if the roads are bad & love unkind
'Ive got my pattens still so never mind
'Thank heaven Im neither blind or lame to need
'A arm to lean on or a guide to lead
'Yet will my heart be sad' so said her sighs
As she turned up her apron to her eyes

Simon heard all & from his hiding place
Rushed out & caught her in his hearts embrace
Cheered was his soul forgetting former toil
Glad as the hope that meets a lovers smile
Warmth did away the bashfulness of love
Leaving no pause to fear she might reprove
Alarm in her denials put to strife
& waked past pleasures into sudden life
Lost in his arms loves reverie beguiles
& kisses dry her sorrows into smiles
Till burning joy that speech to each denied
Did into reasons cooler light subside
Then Simon up & told her all & how
Misfortunes fell & made him break his vow
& laid it all to Dobbin who at large
Unfound remained as heedless of the charge
He told what kept him from the fair so long
She heard with joy yet grieved she judged so wrong
& from that night both pledged eternal love
Leaving the rest to him who rules above
& Simon when they parted in delight
Could not help singing tho twas sunday night
& sung so loud too on his homeward way
That birds awoke & thought it must be day
& day it was before he reached the farm
Where gaping wonder with enquirey warm
On tiptoe stood to question his delay
Where he had been & why he chose to stay
But silence whom no bribe can force to speak
Kept close her lips & left them still to seek
Time went on smooth & gaily with him now
& glad as larks that sung him to his plough
He toiled & sung & labour seemed as nought
While Marys smiles had share of every thought
Save now & then as oer his memory crost
The thought of Dobbin whom all reckoned lost
& many a week went bye & grew agen
To two whole months of mystery & then
With ribs nigh bare & shoulders gauled & sore
One morn they found him at the stable door
Waiting as not forgot the accustomed corn
Which he was wont to share of every morn
Hodge spied him first & with a joyous shout
Cried "heres old dobbin"—when from breakfast out

45

Came all & joy in every face did burn
Pleased as are mothers when their sons return
One clapped his sides one did his memory bless
While Dobbins looks bespoke his hearts distress
Low hung his lip nor in his former way
Did he give signs of frolic or of play
Yet when his name was called with freshened will
He prickt his ears as if he knew it still
The Farmer cursed the thieves he hoped to track
& clapped old Dobbin as right welcome back
& gave him extra corn & extra rest
Till he grew fat & frolic as the best
When he his former fame revived again
For breaking gaps & getting in the grain
& oft in after years with memorys mirth
Simon raised laughter round his cottage hearth
With tales of Dobbins strange eventful life
When happy Mary had become his wife
Who often laughed while in his elbow chair
He told the cause that kept him from the fair
& all the pains then felt now banished hence
Since Marys love had made them reccompence
Nay kisses now he claimed back debts to pay
& thus the winters evening wore away
Blessed each with each like birds in summer weather
Light was the chain that joined their hearts together

ADVENTURES OF A GRASSHOPPER

A grasshopper idle the whole summer long
Played about the tall grass with unthinking delight
& spent the whole day with his hopping & song
& sipp'd of the dew for his supper at night
Thus night brought him food & the red rising sun
Awoke him fresh fed to his singing agen
& thus he went on with his frolic & fun
Till winter winds whistled & where was he then

The plain wore no longer the hue of his wing
All withered & brown as a desert could be
In vain he looked round for the shelter of spring
While the longest green sprig scarcely reached to his knee
The rime feathered night fell as white as a sheet
& dewdrops were frozen before they could fall
The shy creeping sun too denied him his heat
Thus the poor silly soul was deserted of all

The ant had forewarned him of what he would be
When he laughed at his toil on the parched summer plain
He now saw the folly he then could not see
But advice taen too late is but labour in vain
If he wished to work now there was nothing to find
The winter told plain twas too late in the day
In vain he looked round in the snow & the wind
Unable to toil & too saddened for play

He looked back & sighed on his singing & racket
& employed the last hope he had left him to beg
So he sought in the woods withered leaves for a jacket
Of a rushe he made crutches & limped of a leg
The winds whistled round him while seeking for pity
Oer the white crimping snows he went limping along
Sighing sad at each cottage his sorrowful ditty
But a song out of season is povertys song

The first hut he came too belonged to a mouse
Beneath a warm bank at the foot of a tree
While dead rush & grass nodded over her house
& made it as snug as a dwelling could be
He told his sad tale & the mouse as in fear
Bade him work for a living & shrank from his sight

47

For she at that moment was nibbling an ear
Of barley she stole from a barn over night

He left her & journeyed half hopeless & chill
& met with a beetle that bustled away
To a crack called his home in a sun slanting hill
& he'd scarce stop to hear what the beggar would say
Though he held neath his arm a hugh crumble of bread
Which a shepherd boy dropped on his cold dinner seat
& well might he haste when from danger he fled
For his dog had nigh crushed him to death with his feet

At the hut of an ear wig he next made a call
Who crept from the cold in a down headed thistle
That nodded & minutely threatened to fall
While winnowing by it the tempest did whistle
The beggars loud rappings soon scared her from sleep
& her bosom for safety did terribly quake
For she thought it the treading down rustle of sheep
But slept undisturbed when she found the mistake

Hot summers sweet minstrel the large bumble bee
The one that wears clothing of tawney & brown
Who early in springs kindled suns we may see
Booming round peeping blossoms & bowing them down
Our beggar tho hopeless resolved to try all
& came to his hut in an old rotten oak
The bee thought it spring & was glad at the call
But frowned a denial as soon as he woke

He then sought a Ladycows cottage of moss
As old summer friends with as little success
& told his misfortunes to live by the loss
She pitied but pitys no food for distress
A chrysalis dwelt on the back of dead leaves
In a palace of silk & it gladdened his heart
But wealth rarely sleeps without dreaming of thieves
So she kept her door bolted & bade him depart

In a long hollow keck by the side of the road
As tall as in summer tho withered & old
A long legged shepherd had taen his abode
& made a good shift to keep out of the cold
Our beggar knocked hard at his door passing bye

48

& begged for a morsel & told his despair
The tennant looked out of his hole with a sigh
& pitied his fate—but had nothing to spare

He then shunned the road & went up by a hedge
Where some Gnats had collected to dance in the sun
& the day smiled so warm neath the bushes & sedge
That hopes had nigh whispered the summer begun
His heart even jumped at the sight of their play
But ere his sad steps to their revels had come
A cloud hid the sun that made night at noon day
& each gnat soon was missing away to his home

Over hill-spotted pasture & wild rushy lea
A poor houseless vagabond doomed for all weathers
He wandered where none was left wretched but he
While the white flakey snow flew about him like feathers
In vain he sought shelter & down in the vale
By the brook to an old hollow willow did roam
& there een a foot foundered slow creeping snail
Had crept in before him & made it her home

Her door was glued up from the frost & the snow
As a bee in its hive she was warm in her shell
& the storm it might drift & the wind it might blow
She was safe & could dream about spring in her cell
He knocked & begged hard een to creep in the porch
If she d no room for two in her parlour to spare
But as dead as a dormouse asleep in a church
All was silent & still as no tennnant was there

Thus pleading & praying & all to no good
Telling vainly a story of troubles & wants
He bethought of an old snubby oak by a wood
Where flourished in summer a city of ants
& though they reproved him for singing & play
& told him that winter would bring its reward
He knew they were rich & he hoped on his way
That pitys kind ear would his sorrows regard

From people so rich trifles could not be missed
So he thought ere his hopes to their finish had come
Though as to their giving he could not insist
Yet he might from such plenty be sure of a crumb

49

Thus he dreamed on his journey but guess his supprise
When come to the place where such bustle had been
A high wooden wall hid it all from his eyes
& an ant round about it was not to be seen

Their doors were shut up till the summer returned
Nor would one have come had he stood for a day
Again in despair with his wants he sojourned
& sighed lone & sad on his sorrowful way
He limped on his crutches in sorrow & pain
With neer a hope left to indulge his distress
While snows spread a carpet all over the plain
& hiding his path made him travel by guess

He roamed through the wood where he d fain made a stop
But hunger so painful still urged him away
For the oak tho it rocked like a cradle atop
Was as still at its root as a midsummer day
Where the leaves that the wind wirligigs to the ground
& feathers pruned off from the crows sooty wing
Lie mid the green moss that is blooming around
Undisturbed till the bird builds its nest in the spring

The night came apace & the clouds sailing bye
Wore the copper flushed tints of the cold setting sun
& crows to their rime feathered forests did flye
& owls round about had their whoopings begun
He hopped through rough hedges & rude creaking wickets
Till a shepherds lodgehouse in the fields met his eye
Where he heard with surprise the glad chirping of crickets
& hoped his companions & summer was nigh

He paused with delight oer the chitter & mirth
& tried to stare in thro a crack in the door
While a cat half asleep on the warm cottage hearth
Dreamed a mouse made the rustle & bounced on the floor
Our beggar half frighted to death at the sight
Hopped off & retreated as fast as he could
Better pleased to tramp on in the star studded night
Than hazard such danger for shelter & food

In passing a barn he a dwelling espied
Where silk hangings hung round the room like a hall
In a crack of the wall—once again he applied

& who but a spider should come at the call
The Grasshopper said he was weary & lost
& the spider gave welcome with cunning disguise
Altho a hugh jiant in size to his host
Our beggars heart trembled in terrors surprise

When he set down before him dried wings of a fly
& bade him with shy sort of welcome to eat
For hunger found nothing its wants to supply
& fear had him ready to sink thro his seat
Then to bed he went quaking & faith well he might
Where murdered things lay round the room in a heap
Too true did he dream oer his dangers that night
For the spider watched chances & killed him asleep

In the morning a cock robin hopped from his perch
& fluttered about by the side of the wall
Where the murdering spider peeped out on the lurch
& thought a new beggar was going to call
The Robin soon found what the spider was at
& killed him & bore the dead beggar away
But wether to bury or eat him or what
Is a secret he never would tell to this day

Thus idleness ever on sorrows attend
& often shakes hands with repentance too late
Till forced to take up with a foe as a friend
Then death & destruction is certain as fate
Had he taen the advice of the hardworking ant
He had shunned the sad snares of bad company then
& dwelt with his brothers & sisters from want
& lived to see summer & singing again

Now Anna my child to this story of truth
Pay attention & learn as thy reason comes on
To value that sweetest of seasons thy youth
Nor live to repent of its loss when its gone
Shun the idle that spend all their childhood in play
& pass them to school without care or regret
Where thy books they will show thee that this is the way
To shun the sad fate which the Grasshopper met

THE BIRDS & ST VALENTINE

Some two or three weeks before valentine day
At a time when Sir Winter grew kind & in play
Shook hands with Miss Flora he wooed her to spare
A few pretty snowdrops to stick in his hair
Intending for truth as he said to resign
His throne to Miss Spring & her priest Valentine
Which trifle he asked for before he set forth
To remind him of all when he got in the north
& this is the reason that snowdrops appear
Mid the cold of the winter so soon in the year
Flora gladly complied & the instant she heard
Flew away with the news to each bachelor bird
Who in raptures half moved on loves errands to start
Their songs muttered over to get them by heart
Nay the Mavis at once sung aloud in their glee
& looked for a spot where loves dwelling should be
& ever since then both in garden & grove
The Mavis tunes first a short ditty to love—
While all the young gentlemen birds that were near
Fell to trimming their jackets anew for the year
One & all they determined to seek for a mate
& thought it a folly for seasons to wait
So even agreed before valentine day
To join hearts in love but the ladies said nay
Yet each one consented at once to resign
Her heart unto Hymen on St Valentine
While winter who only pretended to go
Lapt himself out of sight in some hillocks of snow
That behind all the rest neath the wood hedges lay
So close that the sun could not drive them away
Yet the gentlemen birds on their love errands flew
Thinking all flora told them was nothing but true
Till out winter came & his frowns in a trice
Turned the lady birds hearts all as hardened as ice
In vain might the gentles in love sue & plead
They heard but not once did they notice or heed
From winter they crept who in tyranny proud
Yoked his horses of storms to his coach of a cloud
For on Valentines morn he was raving so high
Lady Spring for the life of her dare not come nigh
While Floras gay feet where so numbed with the snow
That she could not put on her best slippers to go

52

Then spring she fell ill & her health to regain
On a sunbeam rode back to her south once again
& as both were the bridemaids their teazing delay
Made the lady birds put off their weddings till may
Some sighed their excuses & feared to catch cold
& the redcap in mantle all bordered with gold
Sore feared that the weather would spoil her fine cloaths
& nought but complaints through the forrest arose
So St Valentine came on his journey alone
In the coach of the morn for he d none of his own
& put on his cassock & band & went in
To the temple of Hymen the rights to begin
Where the Mavis Thrush waited along with his bride
Nor in the whole place was a lady beside
The gentlemen they came alone to the saint
& instead of being married each made a complaint
Of Sir Winter whose folly had caused the delay
& forced love to put off the wedding till May
So the priest shook his head & undrest to be gone
As he had no day for his leisure but one
& when the May came with Miss Flora & Spring
They had nought but old cares & new sorrows to sing
For some of the lady birds ceased to be kind
To their old loves & changed for newcomers their mind
& some had resolved to keep single that year
Untill St Valentine with the next should appear
    Then the birds sung their sorrows the whole summer long
& the Robin first mixed up his ills with his song
He sung of his griefs—how in love hed been crost
& gave up his heart as eternally lost
Twas burnt to a coal as sly Cupid let fall
A spark that scorched through both the feathers & all
To cure it time tried but neer found out the way
So the mark on his bosom he wears to this day
& when birds are all silent & not a leaf seen
On the trees but the ivy & holly so green
In frost & in snow little Robin will sing
To put off the sorrow that ruffles his wing
& that is the cause in our gardens we hear
The Robins sweet note in the close of the year
    The Wagtail too mourned in his doubtlet of gray
As if powdered with rime on a dull winters day
He twittered of love—how he courted a fair
Who altered her mind & so made him despair

53

In a stone pit he chose her a place for a nest
But she like a wanton but made it a jest
Though he dabbled in brooks to convince her how kind
He would feed her with worms which he laboured to find
Till he een got the ague still nought could prevail
So ever since then he's been wagging his tail
In the white thorn the linnet bides lonely to sing
How his lady love shunned his embraces in spring
Though he found out a bush that the sun had half drest
With leaves quite sufficient to shelter their nest
& yet she forsook him no more to be seen
So that is the reason he dresses in green
Then aloud in his grief sings the gay speckled Thrush
That changes his music on every bush—
"My love she has left me to sorrow & mourn
"Yet I hope in my heart she'll repent & return"
So he tries at all notes her approval to meet
& that is the reason he singeth so sweet
& as sweet sang the Bulfinch although he confest
That the anguish he felt was more deep then the rest
& they all marvelled much how he'd spirits to sing
When to show them his anguish he held up his wing
From his throat to his tail not a feather was found
But what had been stained red as blood from the wound
   & sad chirped the Sparrow of joys fled & gone
Of his love being lost he so doated upon
So he vowed constant silence for that very thing
& this is the reason why Sparrows dont sing
   Then next came the Rook & the sorrowful crow
To tell birds the cause why in mourning they go
Ever since their old loves their embraces forsook
& all seemed to pity the Crow & the Rook
   The Jay he affected to hide his despair
& rather than mourn he had spirits to wear
A coat of all colours yet in it some blue
Denoted his passion though crossed was too true
So now in lone woods he will hide him all day
& aloud he scolds all that intrude in his way
   The Magpie declared it should never be said
That he mourned for a lover though fifty had fled
Yet his heart all the while was so burnt & distrest
That it turned all the feathers coal black on his breast
The birds they all marvelled but still he denied
& wore a black cap his deep blushes to hide

So that is the reason himself & his kin
Wear hoods with the lappets quite under the chin
   Then last came the Owl grieving loud as he flew
Saying how his false lover had bade him adieu
& though he knew not where to find her or follow
Yet round their old haunts he would still whoop & halloo
For no sleep could he get in his sorrowful plight
So that is the reason Owls halloo at night
   & here ends the song of each woe stricken bird
Now was a more pitiful story eer heard
The rest was all coupled & happy & they
Sung the old merry songs which they sung at this day
& good little boys when this tale they read oer
Will neer have the hearts to hurt birds any more
& add to the griefs they already have sung
By robbing their nests of their eggs & their young
But feel for their sufferings & pity tneir pain
Nor give them new cause of their lot to complain

POEMS

SUMMER IMAGES

Now swathy summer by rude health embrowned
Prescedence takes of rosey fingered spring
& laughing joy with wild flowers pranked & crowned
A wild & giddy thing
With health robust from every care unbound
Comes on the zephers wing
& cheers the toiling clown

Happy as holiday enjoying face
Loud tongued & "merry as a marriage bell"
Thy lightsome step sheds joy in every place
& where the troubled dwell
Thy witching charms weans them of half their cares
& from thy sunny spell
They greet joy unawares

Then with thy sultry locks all loose & rude
& mantle laced with gems of garish light
Come as of wont—for I would fain intrude
& in the worlds despight
Share the rude mirth that thine own heart beguiles
If haply so I might
Win pleasure from thy smiles

Me not the noise of brawling pleasures cheer
In nightly revels or in city streets
But joys which sooth & not distract mine ear
That one at leisure meets
In the green woods & meadows summer shorn
Or fields where beeflye greets
Ones ear with mellow horn

Where green swathed grasshopper on treble pipe
Singeth & danceth in mad hearted pranks
& bees go courting every flower thats ripe
On baulks & sunny banks
& droning dragon flye on rude bassoon
Striveth to give god thanks
In no discordant tune

Where speckled thrush by self delight embued
Singeth unto himself for joys amends

& drinks the honey dew of solitude
Where happiness attends
With inbred joy untill his heart oerflows
Of which the worlds rude friends
Naught heeding nothing knows

Where the gay river laughing as it goes
Plashes with easy wave its flaggy sides
& to the calm of heart in calmness shows
What pleasure there abides
To trace its sedgey banks from trouble free
Spots solitude provides
To muse & happy be

Or ruminating neath some pleasant bush
On sweet silk grasses stretch me at mine ease
Where I can pillow on the yielding rush
& acting as I please
Drop into pleasant dreams or musing lie
Mark the wind shaken trees
& cloud betravelled skye

There think me how some barter joy for care
& waste lifes summer health in riot rude
Of nature nor of natures sweets aware
Where passions vain intrude
These by calm musings softened are & still
& the hearts better mood
Feels sick of doing ill

Here I can live & at my leisure seek
Joys far from cold restraints—not fearing pride
Free as the winds that breath upon my cheek
Rude health so long denied
Where poor integrity can sit at ease
& list self satisfied
The song of honey bees

& green lane traverse heedless where it goes
Nought guessing till some sudden turn espies
Rude battered fingerpost that stooping shows
Where the snug mystery lies
& then a mossy spire with ivy crown
Clears up the short supprise

& shows a peeping town

& see the wild flowers in their summer morn
Of beauty feeding on joys luscious hours
The gay convolvulus wreathing round the thorn
Agape for honey showers
& slender kingcup burnished with the dew
Of mornings early hours
Like gold yminted new

& mark by rustic bridge oer shallow stream
Cow tending boy to toil unreconsiled
Absorbed as in some vagrant summer dream
& now in gestures wild
Starts dancing to his shadow on the wall
Feeling self gratified
Nor fearing human thrall

Then thread the sunny valley laced with streams
Or forrests rude & the oer shadowed brims
Of simple ponds where idle shepherd dreams
& streaks his listless limbs
Or trace hay scented meadows smooth & long
Where joys wild impulse swims
In one continued song

I love at early morn from new mown swath
To see the startled frog his rout pursue
& mark while leaping oer the dripping path
His bright sides scatter dew
& early lark that from its bustle flyes—
To hail his mattin new
& watch him to the skyes

& note on hedgerow baulks in moisture sprent
The jetty snail creep from the mossy thorn
With earnest heed & tremulous intent
Frail brother of the morn
That from the tiney bents & misted leaves
Withdraws his timid horn
& fearful vision weaves

& swallows heed on smoke tanned chimney top
As wont be first unsealing mornings eye

Ere yet the bee hath gleaned one wayward drop
Of honey on his thigh
& see him seek morns airy couch to sing
Untill the golden sky
Besprents his russet wing

& sawning boy by tanning corn espy
With clapping noise to startle birds away
& hear him brawl to every passer bye
To know the hour of day
& see the uncradeled breeze refreshed & strong
With waking blossoms play
& breath eolian song

I love the south west wind or low or loud
& not the less when sudden drops of rain
Moistens my palid cheek from ebon cloud
Threatening soft showers again
That over lands new ploughed & meadow grounds
Summers sweet breath unchains
& wakes harmonious sounds

Rich music breathes in summers every sound
& in her harmony of varied greens
Woods meadows hedgrows cornfields all around
Much beauty intervenes
Filling with harmony the ear & eye
While oer the mingling scenes
Far spreads the laughing sky

& wind enarmoured aspin mark the leaves
Turn up their silver lining to the sun
& list the brustling noise that oft decieves
& makes the sheepboy run
The sound so mimics fast approaching showers
He thinks the rain begun
& hastes to sheltering bowers

& mark the evening curdle dank & grey
Changing her watchet hue for sombre weed
& moping owl to close the lids of day
On drowsy wing proceed
While chickering crickets tremulous & long
Lights farewell inly heed

& gives it parting song

While pranking bat its flighty circlet makes
& gloworm burnisheth its lamp anew
Oer meadows dew besprent—& beetle wakes
Enquires ever new
Teazing each passing ear with murmurs vain
As wonting to pursue
His homeward path again

& catch the melody of distant bells
That on the wind with pleasing hum rebounds
By fitful starts—then musically swells
Oer the dim stilly grounds
While on the meadow bridge the pausing boy
Listens the mellow sounds
& hums in vacant joy

& now the homebound hedger bundles up
His evening faggot & with every stride
His leathern dublet leaves a rustling sound
Till silly sheep beside
His path start tremulous & once again
Look back dissatisfied
Then scour the dewy plain

& greet the soothing calm that smoothly stills
Oer the hearts every sense its opiate dews
In meek eyed moods & ever balmy trills
That softens & subdues
With gentle quiets bland & sober train
Which dreamy eve renews
In many a mellow strain

I love to walk the fields they are to me
A legacy no evil can destroy
They like a spell set every rapture free
That cheered me when a boy
Play pastime all times blotting pen consceals
Come like a new born joy
To greet me in the fields

For natures objects ever harmonize
With emelous taste that vulgar deed anoys

It loves in quiet moods to sympathise
& meet vibrating joys
Oer natures pleasing things—nor slighting deems
Pastime the muse employs
as vain obtrusive themes

HELPSTONE STATUTE OR THE RECRUITING PARTY

Unclouded rose the morning sun
Though autumns pleasant weather
In promise of some glorious fun
When all were got together
There wa'n't a road led to the town
But ye'd see clowns by dozens
For masters some & some for sport
& some to see their couzins

& skipping girls as sweet & fair
As smiles & dress could make 'em
With pattens in their sweethearts care
Who thought it pride to take 'em
They graceful lifted up their gowns
To show a taper ancle
Which made the hearts of following clowns
With beautys visions rankle

In gladdened speed awoke the morn
With holiday caresses
Young laughing clowns with beards new shorn
& girls in sunday dresses
& childern peeping in the street
For sisters & for brothers
& maids their coming swains to meet
& anxious watching mothers

Horses & gigs went whisking bye
With farming gent & lady
Although twas autumns cloudy sky
Joys blossomed as at may day
& soldiers gan their drums to rap
When near the town advancing
Which set like majic every chap
To capering & to dancing

Ah Helpstone thou art droning dull
Till statutes yearly find thee
& then thourt mad as any bull
& care is cast behind thee
Each house where lorn the year about

65

Signs creak to wind & weather
Relieved by thee & balmy stout
Draw scores of lads together

Thy fame with vigour yearly blooms
Round all the neighbouring towns
Renowned for cakes well stored with plums
& fun that pleases clowns
For civil Wills & winking jades
& E-O tables turning
Where gamesters oft are beggars made
& mirth is changed to mourning

There merry Punch displays his pranks
In squeaking jokes & blunders
& there the pale faced mountebanks
Spout loud their tale of wonders
Of balsams that will blooms secure
In fading belles & madams
& for the aged lives ensure
As long as father Adams

The place now thronged with young & old
For labour had its leisure
While every face its errand told
As seeking mirth & pleasure
Sweet beauty now displayed its blooms
Red cheeks & lily bosoms
Mirth buzzed like wild bees merry hum
Round fields of clover blossoms

With sweethearts hanging on their arms
In blushes softly blooming
Each maiden smiled in witching charms
Just blossoming to woman
& red coat gentry soon in style
For liquor 'gan a calling
& where their winks could meet a smile
Set maids in corners squalling

& loose laced sergant Macaroon
A hogshead sort of dandy
With visage like a harvest moon
& nose as burnt as brandy

He strutted round the room with ale
& drank to tittering wenches
Making clowns stare at valours tale
Of storming towers & trenches

He jested oer the battles strife
As play when theyd been school to't
& swore that to a soldiers life
King Williams were a fool to't
He bragged about their mints of cash
& swaggered & insisted
Till boys that scarcely reached his sash
Bawled teazing to be listed

Some listened & believed it true
& some disposed to quarrel
Swore he of valour never knew
A gunshot from the barrel
But he bragged on & spent his crowns
& tossed off foaming glasses
A very heroe with the clowns
& cupid with the lasses

The alehouse soon was in a rout
& all was helter skelter
& Molly Meek came puffing out
She said twas fit to melt her
The truth on't was that Coporal Sly
Had won her with his feather
& secret whispered by & by
To trample out together

A sweetheart she to Booby Briggs
Who soons he cleared the trick up
Cursed all the redcoats rougish rigs
& rumptions 'gan kick up
They cocked their consequential caps
& sneering filled their glasses
Saying theyd make lords of straw yard chaps
& ladies of the lasses

But Boobys heart was bad for fight
He could but rave & rattle
& when he d broke the peace his spite

Most cooly shunned the battle
The row got high boards gan to fall
Where stood the pipes & cans on
& alewife swore revenge on all
She eer could lay her hands on

& in she bounced with face as red
As if twas daubed with riddle
& first gan thump the fiddlers head
O fun protect the fiddle
The scrapers fist was soon for blows
Ales courage rarely failed him
& wo'd been to her brandy nose
If lasses hadnt quailed him

He loved the wenches monstrous well
& never wished to teaze 'em
But gloried in his fiddling skill
That had the power to pleaze 'em
& when hed found his trampled hat
Mid broken pipes & glasses
With vengance half appeased he sat
& struck up "Bonny Lasses"

She soon broke up the fighting rout
By soldier lads assisted
& sharply played the sticks about
The rebels that resisted
She boldly shoved & showed the door
In spite of oaths & cavil
Some cursed—& staggered while they swore
& wished her to the devil

But broken pots & broken pipes
All that were slain in battle
Made her for vengance fury-ripe
& loud her tongue did rattle
Till brawlings loud for quarts of ale
& sound of money chinking
Did bye & bye her vengance quail
& peace was signed by drinking

The Statute now was all in mobs
Each maiden interposes

68

Swooning with heartbursting sobs
Oer sweethearts bloody noses
Een boys bethought em men that day
As highs ones knee & hardly
& stript & bruised amid the fray
& acted most blackguardly

At length with bruising softened down
Those not so full of mettle
Got weary trying for renown
& battle gan to settle
& soon the aid of pipe & pot
Made up for hits & misses
In corners some with sweethearts got
To cure black eyes with kisses

& Coporal Sly had played his rigs
& Moll had proved his jesting
Who sneaked agen to Booby Briggs
Her innoscence protesting
No maid could simper more demure
& keep such meek parade up
Poor Booby thought it true besure
& matters soon were made up

To put a Soldiers heart in thrall
He thought her mighty clever
& then prize Booby after all
He loved her more then ever
& while his purse had sixpence int
With kindnesses he paid
& gifts almost without a stint
Of nuts & cakes he made her

The Soldiers now began to drum
& gaping stood the ninneys
To see the sergant neath his thumb
Hold out the tempting guineas
& rustics tempted at the sight
Their parents tears were scorning
& ranting oer their quarts till night
left sorrow for the morning

Some ere the daylight wore away
Went home with lovers happy
& others still inclined to stay
Sat ranting oer their nappy
Some drunk & weary sunk to rest
On leaning chairs reposing
& others lay more hap'ly blest
On sweethearts bosoms dozing

Soul stirring ale thy laurelled brow
Blooms an immortal fairly
Or long as England yokes a plough
& summers ripen barley
& curse the wretch who craving chink
Thy fame with drugs defaces
I wish him hell denied of drink
Who thus thy worth debases

Thus passed the day & weary night
Found some with empty purses
& some that scaped with hasty flight
From battles blows & curses
& some with headaches shoots severe
Felt the last tankards drainings
While maidens wept with secret fear
Incurable complainings

OUR OWN FIRESIDE

Our firesides easy chair
Is there any place beside
Can such pleasant cheer prepare
As our own fireside
Tho humble be the fare
That wants daily toils provide
Daintys pomp can neer compare
With the joy want meeteth there
By his own fireside

He may wish a better lot
With his own dissatisfied
Yet he ll never find a spot
Like his own fireside
With his little ones at play
& their mother by his side
Tho he toiled so hard the day
O what rest doth peace convey
To his own fireside

He can share his childerns mirth
He can in his friends confide
For the truest friends on earth
Grace his own fireside
They who share his care & hope
They who with his wants abide
Who from sorrows neer elope
Are the little honest group
By his own fireside

They who love him till he dies
Who through troubles have been tried
They who weep deaths closing eyes
When all are cold beside
Can such honest hearts abound
In this worlds deciet & pride
O its all enjoyed & found
In that little circle round
Our own fireside

The wanderer may have friends
That for present needs provide

Yet they make but small amends
For his own fireside
They whove been the longest kind
They who first his wants supplied
They who bare him most in mind
Are the friends he left behind
Round his own fireside

He may after fortune stray
& with providence his guide
Meet with comforts as he may
By a strange fireside
The kindest favours shown
Are by stranger tongues applied
Home lives not in the tone
& he feels himself alone
From his own fireside

He may ride a horse to death
He may speed with time & tide
He shall find no spot on earth
Like his own fireside
Tho a cold stone were his seat
Yet to kindred closely tied
Where his wife & childern meet
O theres neer a spot so sweet
As his own fireside

Man tho honest may be poor
& may feel an honest pride
While he counts his troubles oer
By his own fireside
Wealth may very easy fall
From his fortune & his pride
Yet he's not the worst of all
While he owns a place to call
His own fireside

Though the soldier in the war
Courteth honour as a bride
Doth he never turn from far
To his own fireside
Yes he often feels the pain
Though he strives the sigh to hide

While he wishes when in vain
For the rest & peace again
Of his own fireside

The sailor tossed in storms
Tho all fears he doth deride
Loves that snug spot free from harms
By his own fireside
& imprisoned on the sea
By every peril tried
O he d give his all to be
In that port at anchor free
By his own fireside

I have oft been plentys guest
Where forms welcome did abide
& my heart was ill at rest
From my own fireside
Tho but poor my homely fare
Yet I felt I d all beside
& the welcome I should share
From the little circle there
Round my own fireside

In this chimneys sooty nook
I with pleasure can abide
Tho the walls are dyed in smoke
Tis my own fireside
Wealth may boast its splendid hall
Carpet floor & painted wall
There is nothing in them all
Like our own fireside

NATURES HYMN TO THE DEITY

All nature owns with one accord
The great & universal Lord
The sun proclaims him through the day
The moon when daylight drops away
The very darkness smiles to wear
The stars that show us God is there
On moonlight seas soft gleams the sky
& God is with us waves reply

Winds breath from Gods abode we come
Storms louder call God is our home
& thunders yet with louder call
Sound him as mightiest over all
Till earth right loath the proof to miss
Echoes triumphantly he is
& earth & ocean make reply
God reigns on earth in air & sky

All nature owns with one accord
The great & universal Lord
Insect & bird & tree & flower
The witnesses of every hour
Are pregnant with his prophecy
& God is with us all reply
The first link in the mighty plan
Is still & all upbreaideth man

IMPULSES OF SPRING

Day burnishes the distant hills
& clouds blush far away
Lifes heart with natures rapture thrills
To hail this glorious day
The morning falls in dizzy light
On mountain tops & towers
But speeds with soft & gentle flight
Among these valley flowers

Theres music in the waking woods
Theres glory in the air
Birds in their merry summer moods
Now rant & revel there
Joy wakes & wantons all around
Love laughs in every call
Music in many hearts abounds
& poesy breaths in all

The merry newcome Nightingale
Woos nights dull hours along
Till daylight at the sound turns pale
& hastes to share the song
A waste of sunny flowers is seen
& insence fills the air
No sunless place is found too mean
Springs blushing gems to wear

The horse blob by the water mill
Blooms in the foaming dam
& pilewort blazes round the hill
Beside the sleeping lamb
Spring is the happy breathing time
For young loves stolen joys
Spring is the poets luscious prime
He revels in the noise

Of waking insects humming round
Of birds upon the wing
& all the gushing soul of sound
That echoes of the spring
For in their joys his own are met
Tho tears stand in his eye

In their gay mirth he half forgets
He eer knew how to sigh

He feeds on springs precarious boon
A being of her race
Where light & shade & shower & sun
Are ever changing place
To day he buds & glows to meet
To morrows promised shower
When crushed by cares intruding feet
He fades a broken flower

His hopes they change like summer clouds
& fairy phantasies
His pleasures wrapt in gayer shrouds
Are sorrows in disguise
The sweetest smiles his heart can find
Possess their tears as well
& highest pleasures leave behind
Their heartache & farewell

His are the fading "joys of grief"
Care grows his favoured guest
& sorrow gives his heart relief
Because it knows him best
The sweetest flower on pleasures path
Will bloom on sorrows grave
& earthly love & earthly mirth
Their share of grief shall have

& poesy owns a haunted mind
A thirst enduring flame
Burning the soul to leave behind
The memory of a name
Though life he deemed as sweetly sold
For toil so ill repaid
The marble epitaph how cold
Although with gold inlaid

While the rude clown of thoughtless clay
In feelings unrefined
Lives out lifes cloudless holiday
With nothing on his mind
Then sound as ever king hath slept

On earths green lap he lies
While beautys tear so sweetly wept
& friendships warmest sighs

Are left upon his lowly grave
& live his only fame
While frowning envy never gave
One insult to his name
Yet who would from their cares be free
For such unconsious bliss
A living blank in life to be
Pains sympathy to miss

To meet enthusiastic May
As but dull winters hours
& primrose pale & daisy gay
As white & yellow flowers
& not as friends in our esteem
To cheer dull lifes sojourn
Let me throughout its cheating dream
Much rather feel & mourn

The bliss or grief tho past controul
That with extremes inflame
Blood rushing feelings through the soul
Not uttered in a name
Where no words live to free the mind
Of hidden hopes or fears
The only utterance they can find
Are gushing smiles & tears

Yet woo I not that burning flame
Enkindling ecstasy
Blazing in dreams to win a name
From fames eternity
Fames yearning breath breeds not my sigh
Nor eats my heart away
Burning lifes every channel dry
To triumph oer decay

Yet with the minstrelsy on earth
I too would love the lyre
For heaven neer gave the meanest birth
To quench that holy fire

It owns the muses sweetest smiles
& scatters life around
Grief sick with hopes heart broken toils
Glows happy at the sound

The lyre is pleasures blest abode
& round it angels throng
The lyre it is the voice of God
The prophets spoke in song
& as the sun this day brings forth
Creations every hour
Cares wreath warms at the muses mirth
& blushes into flower

ON SEEING A SKULL ON COWPER GREEN

One morn I wandered forth neath spirits high
Those moods that mornings peering breath instills
& like my shade my mind in ecstasy
Stretched like a jiant oer the pasture hills
I mused on reasoning mans exalted sway
Oer the brute world—pride made my feelings brave
Creations lord to me he seemed that day
I felt as if all nature was his slave
But times glass soon did mock my visioned might
I saw & shrunk an insect at the sight

For as I wandered by a quarrys side
Where an old hoary weatherbeaten swain
Was delving sand—in lifes rude troubles tried
An humble pittance natures boon to gain
He stopt his toil & with a feeble hand
Pointed to where a human skull lay bare
& mingled with the refuse of the land
Fallen from life & pride to moulder there
I looked upon the relic with deep awe
While silence seemed to question what I saw

What wert thou upon earth perhaps a king
For such the relics of earths best renown
Thou pompous shadow thou proud trifling thing
Bare is the brow that triumphed neath a crown
By rank forsaken stript of prides attire
Deaths sad reality fate only claims
All else like shadows bidden to expire
Time keeps the wreck to mock at earthly fames
To show vain glory in its golden birth
Of what poor value it is held by death

Wert thou a tyrant that disdained though clay
The laws of God & man & with vain power
For earths vain glories threw the heavens away
How art thou fallen at this lonely hour
Thy vengance that did like the thunder sear
Ordaining hosts of murders at a breath
Hath vanished & the slave forgot his fear
Beneath the banner of that tyrant death
Even the little ant now undismayed

Creeps oer thy skull & feeleth not afraid

A warrior thou who sped in victorys ways
As overbearing as a mighty wind
Ah little thought thy pride that victorys praise
So soon would leave her heroes fame behind
From war & all its havoc long deterred
Thy courage withering in its mad career
Bowed before death tame as a broken sword
& ah how silent doth it harbour here
Its fame all sunk to nothingness away
As showers by night was[h] out the steps of day

Wert thou a lover ah what else so warm
As lovers thoughts that lead the heart to bliss
How sad the change in deaths oertaken storm
Cold wrecked & stranded in a place like this
Love that will nestle neath the eagles wing
& find a dwelling in the lions den
Hath long forsaken thee thou lonely thing
Of mystery & knows thee not agen
Warm hopes gay thoughts rapt joys & fond desires
Have lost their home death put out all their fires

Wert thou a poet who in fancys dream
Saw immortality throw by her veil
& all thy labours in fames temple gleam
In the proud glory of an aftertale
If so how cheated thy ambition died
How vain the hopes the muses visions gave
Death with eternity scarce took one stride
Ere thou wert left forgotten in the grave
Chilled all thy powers with thoughts oerflowing full
& nought left extant but this empty skull

Wert thou of poor descent & like to me
A toiling worm to earn lifes daily bread
If so death made thee rich as well as free
& left thee equal with the noblest dead
Emperors & kings no more by flattery fed
Poor as thou art their condescension spares
Even to thee a portion of their bed
& thines as soft a pillow now as theirs
& who could grudge the mightys guest to be

Where kings grow kind & share their pomp with thee

In vain I question nought will answer me
Of what thou wert yet know I that thou art
A faithful portrait of what life shall be
Thus much thy mystic vision doth impart
King Tyrant Warrior Lover Bard & all
Shall into nothing every name resign
& fames proud scroll at last shall be the pall
To hide them as oblivion hideth thine
While virtues deeds shall longest live & be
A wreath to girdle vast eternity

PURSUITS AFTER HAPPINESS

Some climb ambitions hill with many toils
& follow hope at length to hopeless be
Some seek for quiet in contentions broils
& suffer shipwreck that go not to sea
Some seeming warned a new consciet betrays
To worship phantoms who reward in pain
Vain follys fancys running divers ways
Seeking for somthing which they neer attain

Where truth meets foes & honesty no friends
Where good intents are ever ill repaid
Where highest merit earneth worst amends
& closest friendships soonest are betrayed
Where bribes & lies to honours place aspires
The props wereby ambition stays its fall
If to shun aught of these thy heart desires
Shun vain ambitions & so shun them all

Pride thus aye seeketh & so findeth not
Wearing vain flatterys phrases all threadbare
While the poor shepherd swain in lowley cot
Finds without seeking & has joys to spare
The ploughman blythe that whistles toil away
& oer the russet land aye speeds his plough
On pleasures lap fares sumptious every day
With laughing Maud who milks the brinded cow

To seek where pleasaunce in her mirth carouses
As from ambition to flee far away
& join where buxsome health wild mirth espouses
& all rejoiceth at the holiday
To laugh with shepherd Ralph & milking Molly
Who on the haycocks fare so merrily
Who in gray russet taunt at melancholly
& always laughing find no room to sigh

Where trees & hedges & astonished bushes
Are filled with music as if music grew
From happy blackbirds & delighted thrushes
Who daub their nests & love in happy cue
Where little blackcaps in their early song
Do calm the march winds with their merry throats

& cuckoo singeth blythe ere it be long
A full toned anthem with two simple notes

There trim a little garden at ones leisure
To watch the flowers to bud & so to bloom
To reap from present labour added pleasure
& have an hour for talk when friends do come
Hoeing up weeds that bed & path deforms
& smoothing grassplots with a roll & scythe
While tiney Robin poppeth down for worms
Then strokes his little bill & singeth blythe

Spending an hour with quiet now & then
By flood washed river & sedge flounced pool
Musing like hermit from the haunts of men
Indulging idless like a child from school
To find on leaning tree an easy chair
Where one can sit & bid the minutes pass
& mark the dodging float sink speedy there
Then land the large bream bouncing on the grass

Or seek out spots where nature doth disport
In curious phantasy her whims to please
Where the minds eye may shape a princely court
Without its cares from intertwining trees
Or muse in grottos by rock hidden spring
Where fairey folk from summers noon retires
There feel the place a throne oneself a king
With nought to govern but ones own desires

Safe are such antidotes such means supply
For what decayed ambition aye endures
& hearts grown sick of show may meet therebye
Coy pleasures long pursued & speedy cures
Tis but vain fashions tinsel gauds to shun
& speed where health & happiness employs
The simple swain to labour in the sun
Tending his toils therebye to share his joys

So would I live like such so pass away
When winter comes like any other flye
Sinking to sleep forgetting it were day
In pleasant nook with natures kind to lye
Who for their monuments plant flowers not stones

Whose epitaphs the little birds doth sing
Whose graves are not dull heaps of charnel bones
But shrines where seasons memorys offerings bring

MAYING OR LOVE & FLOWERS

Upon a day a merry day
When summer in her best
Like Sunday belles prepares for play
& joins each merry guest
A maid as wild as is the bird
That never knew a cage
Went out her parents kine to herd
& Jockey as her page

Would need go join her merry toils
A silly shepherd he
& little thought the aching broils
That in his heart would be
For he as yet knew nought of love
& nought of love knew she
Yet without learning love can move
The wildest to agree

He gathered flowers a pleasing task
To crown her queen of may
But dare not give nor would she ask
So threw them all away
Then from her path she turned aside
& took a double pain
To gather others far & wide
& so he sighed again

The wind enarmoured of the maid
Around her drapery swims
& moulds in luscious masquerade
Her lovely shape & limbs
Smiths "Venus stealing Cupids bow"
In marble hides as fine
But hers was life & soul—whose glow
Makes meaner things divine

In sooth she was a lovely toy
A worship moving thing
As ever brought the season joy
Or beautified the spring
So sweet a thing no heart might hurt
Gay as a butterflye

Though Cupid chased twas half in sport
He meant not to destroy

When speaking—words with breathing grace
Her sweet lips seemly wooed
Pausing to leave so sweet a place
Ere they could part for good
Those lips that pouted from her face
As a rosey bursts the bud
Which June so eager to embrace
Tempts from beneath its hood

Her eyes like suns did seem to light
The beautys of her face
Streaming up her forhead white
& cheeks of rosey grace
Her bosom swelled to pillows large
Till her so taper waist
Scarce able seemed to bear the charge
Of each lawn bursting breast

A very flower how did she shine
Her beautys all displaying
In sooth this modern Proserpine
Might set the angels maying
As like a fairy mid the flowers
She flew to this—now that—
& some she braided in her hair
Some wreathed within her hat

Then off she skipt in bowers to hide
By Cupid led I ween
Putting her bosoms lawn aside
To place some thyme atween
The shepherd saw her skin so white
Two twin suns newly risen
Though love had chained him there till night
Who would have shunned the prison

Then off again she skipt & flew
With foot so light & little
That Cinderellas fairy shoe
Had fit her to a tittle
The shepherds heart like blazing coal

Beat as 'twould leave the socket
He sighed but thought it silly fool
The watch within his pocket

& then he tried a song to sing
But sighs arose & dropt it
He thought the winds poor silly thing
Blew in his face & stopt it
& then he tried to sing again
But sighs again did flutter
Around his heart—& 'what a pain'
Was all that he could utter

'Fair flower' said he 'Whose that' quoth she
& tied her flowers together
Then sought for more 'ah woe is me'
He said or sighed it rather
Then grasped her arm that soft & white
Like to a pillow dinted
& blushing red as at a bite
His fingers there were printed
& ah he sighed to mark the sight
That unmeant rudeness hinted

And Daphne like she blushed & flew
Tho but to vex his pain
And soon to see if he d pursue
She turned to smile again
And like a bird with injured wing
That flutters but not flies
She waited for the sheepish thing
To catch her by surprise

But bold in love grow silly sheep
& so right bold grew he
He ran she fled & at bo-peep
She met him round a tree
A thorn enarmoured like the swain
Caught at her lily arm
& then good faith to ease her pain
Love had a double charm

She sighed he wished it well I wis
The place was sadly swollen

And then he took a willing kiss
And made believe twas stolen
Then made another make believe
Till thefts grew past concealing
For when love once begins to thieve
Their grows no end to stealing

They played & toyed till down the skies
The sun had taken flight
And still a sun was in her eyes
To keep away the night
And there he talked of love so well
Or else he talked so ill
That soon the priest was sought to tell
The story better still

THOUGHTS IN A CHURCHYARD

Ah happy spot how still it seems
Where crowds of buried memorys sleep
How quiet nature oer them dreams
Tis but our troubled thoughts that weep
Lifes book shuts here its page is lost
With them & all its busy claims
The poor are from its memory crost
The rich have nothing but their names

There rest the weary from their toil
There lye the troubled free from care
Who through the strife of lifes turmoil
Sought rest & only found it there
With none to fear his scornful brow
There sleep the master & the slave
& heedless of all titles now
Repose the honoured & the brave

There rest the miser & the heir
Both careless who their wealth shall reap
Een love found cures for heartaches there
& none enjoys a sounder sleep
The fair one far from follys freaks
As quiet as her neighbour seems
Unconsious now of rosey cheeks
& neer a rival in her dreams

Strangers alike to joy & strife
Heedless of all its past affairs
Theyre blotted from the list of life
And absent from its teasing cares
Grief joy hope fear & all their crew
That haunt the memorys living mind
Ceased where they could no more pursue
& left a painless blank behind

Lifes ignis fatus light is gone
No more to lead their hopes astray
Cares poisoned cup is drained & done
& all its follys far away
The bills made out the reckoning paid
The book is crossed the business done

On them the last demand is made
& deaths long happy sleep is won

THE VANITYS OF LIFE

"Vanitys of vanitys all is vanity" Solomon

What are lifes joys & gains
What pleasures crowd its ways
That man should take such pains
To seek them all his days
Sift this untoward strife
On which thy mind is bent
See if this chaff of life
Is worth the trouble spent

Is pride thy hearts desire
Is power thy climbing aim
Is love thy follys fire
Is wealth thy restless game
Pride power love wealth & all
Times touchstone shall destroy
& like base coin prove all
Vain substitutes for joy

Dost think that pride exalts
Thyself in others eyes
& hides thy follys faults
Which reason will despise
Dost strut & turn & stride
Like walking weathercocks
The shadow by thy side
Becomes thy ape & mocks

Dost think that powers disguise
Can make thee mighty seem
It may in follys eyes
But not in worths esteem
When all that thou canst ask
& all that she can give
Is but a paltry mask
Which tyrants wear & live

Go let thy fancys range
& ramble where they may
View power in every change
& what is its display

91

—The country magistrate
The meanest shade in power
To rulers of the state
The meteors of an hour—

View all & mark the end
Of every proud extreme
Where flattery turns a friend
& counterfiets esteem
Where worth is aped in show
That doth her name purloin
Like toys of golden glow
Thats sold for copper coin

Ambitions haughty nod
With fancys may decieve
Nay tell thee thourt a God
& wilt thou such believe
—Go bid the seas be dry
Go hold earth like a ball
Or throw thy fancys bye
For God can do it all

Dost thou possess the dower
Of laws to spare or kill
Call it not heavenly power
When but a tyrants will
Know what a God will do
& know thyself a fool
Nor tyrant like pursue
Where he alone should rule

O put away thy pride
Or be ashamed of power
That cannot turn aside
The breeze that waves a flower
Or bid the clouds be still
Though shadows they can brave
Thy poor power mocking will
Then make not man a slave

Dost think when wealth is won
Thy heart has its desire
Hold ice up to the sun

& wax before the fire
Nor triumph oer the reign
Which they so soon resign
In this worlds ways they gain
Insurance safe as thine

Dost think lifes peace secure
In houses & in land
Go read the fairey lure
To twist a chord of sand
Lodge stones upon the sky
Hold water in a sieve
Nor give such tales the lie
& still thine own believe

Whoso with riches deals
& thinks peace bought & sold
Will find them slippery eels
That slide the firmest [h]old
Though sweet as sleep with health
Thy lulling luck may be
Pride may oerstride thy wealth
& check prosperity

Dost think that beautys power
Lifes sweetest pleasure gives
Go pluck the summer flower
& see how long it lives
Behold the rays glide on
Along the summer plain
Ere thou canst say "theyre gone"
& measure beautys reign

Look on the brightest eye
Nor teach it to be proud
But view the clearest sky
& thou shalt find a cloud
Nor call each face ye meet
An angels cause its fair
But look beneath your feet
& think of what they are

Who thinks that love doth live
In beautys tempting show

Shall find his hopes ungive
& melt in reasons thaw
Who thinks that pleasure lies
In every fairey bower
Shall oft to his suprise
Find poison in the flower

Dost lawless pleasures grasp
Judge not thou dealst in joy
Its flowers but hide the asp
Thy revels to destroy
Who trusts an harlots smiles
& by her wiles are led
Plays with a sword the while
Hung dropping oer his head

Dost doubt my warning song
Then doubt the sun gives light
Doubt truth to teach thee wrong
& wrong alone as right
& live as lives the knave
Intrigues decieving guest
Be tyrant or be slave
As suits thy ends the best

Or pause amid thy toils
For visions won & lost
& count the fancied spoils
If ere they quit the cost
& if they still possess
Thy mind as worthy things
Plat straws with bedlam Bess
& call them diamond rings

Thy follys past advice
Thy hearts already won
Thy falls above all price
So go & be undone
For all who thus prefer
The seeming great for small
Shall make wine vinegar
& sweetest honey gall

Wouldst heed the truths I sing
To profit wherewithall
Clip follys wanton wing
& keep her within call
Ive little else to give
What thou canst easy try
The lesson how to live
Is but to learn to die

CHILDHOOD

The past it is a majic word
Too beautiful to last
It looks back like a lovely face
Who can forget the past
Theres music in its childhood
Thats known in every tongue
Like the music of the wildwood
All chorus to the song

The happy dream the joyous play
The life without a sigh
The beauty thoughts can neer pourtray
In those four letters lye
The painters beauty breathing arts
The poets speaking pens
Can neer call back a thousand part
Of what that word contains

& fancy at its sweetest hour
What eer may come to pass
Shall find that majic thrill no more
Time broke it like his glass
The sweetest joy the fairest face
The treasure most preferred
Have left the honours of their place
Locked in that silent word

When we look back on what we were
& feel what we are now
A fading leaf is not so drear
Upon a broken bough
A winter seat without a fire
A cold world without friends
Doth not such chilly glooms impart
As that one word portends

Like withered wreaths in banquet halls
When all the rout is past
Like sunshine that on ruins falls
Our pleasures are at last
The joy is fled the love is cold
& beautys splendour too

Our first believings all are old
& faith itself untrue

When beauty met loves budding spring
In artless witcherys
It were not then an earthly thing
But an angel in disguise
Where are they now of youths esteems
All shadows past away
Flowers blooming but in summer dreams
& thoughts of yesterday

Our childhood soon a trifle gets
Yet like a broken toy
Grown out of date it reccolects
Our memorys into joy
The simple catalogue of things
That reason would despise
Starts in the heart a thousand springs
Of half forgotten joys

When we review that place of prime
That childhoods joys endow
That seemed more green in winter time
Than summer grass does now
Where oft the task of skill was put
For other boys to match
To run along the churchyard wall
Or balls to cuck & catch

How oft we clomb the porch to cut
Our names upon the leads
Though fame nor anything akin
Was never in our heads
Where hands & feet were rudely drawn
& names we could not spell
& thought no artist in the world
Could ever do as well

We twirled our tops that spun so well
They scarce could tumble down
& thought they twirled as well again
When riddled on the crown
& bee-spell marbles bound to win

97

As by a potent charm
Was often wetted in the mouth
To show the dotted swarm

We pelted at the weathercock
& he who pelted oer
Was reckoned as a mighty man
& even somthing more
We leapt accross "cat gallows sticks"
& mighty proud was he
Who overshot the famous nicks
That reached above his knee

& then each others tasks we did
& great ambition grew
We ran so swift so strong we leaped
We almost thought we flew
We ran across the broken brig
Whose wooden rail was lost
& loud the victors feat was hailed
Who dared the danger most

& hopskotch too a spur to joy
We thought the task divine
To hop & kick the stone right out
& never touch a line
& then we walked on mighty stilts
Scarce seven inches high
Yet on we stalked & thought ourselves
Already at the sky

Our pride to reason would not shrink
In these exalted hours
A jiants was a pigmy link
To statures such as ours
We even fancied we could flye
& fancy then was true
So with the clouds upon the sky
In dreams at night we flew

We shot our arrows from our bows
Like any archers proud
& thought when lost they went so high
To lodge upon a cloud

98

& these seemed feats that none before
Ourselves could eer attain
& Wellington with all his feats
Felt never half so vain

& oft we urged the barking dog
For mischief was our glee
To chace the cat up weed green walls
& mossy apple tree
When her tail stood like a bottle brush
With fear—we laughed again
Like tyrants we could purchase mirth
& neer alow for pain

& then our playpots sought & won
For uses & for show
That Wedgewoods self with all his skill
Might guess in vain to know
& pallaces of stone & stick
In which we could not creep
Which Nash himself neer made so quick
& never half so cheap

Our fancys made us great & rich
No bounds our wealth could fix
A stool drawn round the room was soon
A splendid coach & six
The majic of our minds was great
& even pebbles they
Soon as we chose to call them gold
Grew guineas in our play

& carriages of oyster shells
Though filled with nought but stones
Grew instant ministers of state
While clay kings filled their thrones
Like Cinderellas fairey queen
Joy would our wants bewitch
If wealth was sought the dust & stones
Turned wealth & made us rich

The mallow seed became a cheese
The henbanes loaves of bread
A burdock leaf our table cloth

On a table stone was spread
The bindweed flower that climbs the hedge
Made us a drinking glass
& there we spread our merry feast
Upon the summer grass

A henbane root could scarcely grow
A mallow shake its seeds
The insects that might feed thereon
Found famine in the weeds
But like the pomp of princely taste
That humbler life anoys
We thought not of our neighbours wants
While we were wasting joys

We often tried to force the snail
To leave his harvest horn
By singing that the beggarman
Was coming for his corn
We thought we forced the lady cow
To tell the time of day
Twas one oclock & two oclock
& then she flew away

We bawled to beetles as they ran
That their childern were all gone
Their houses down & door key hid
Beneath the golden stone
They seemed to haste as fast again
While we shouted as they past
With mirth half mad to think our tale
Had urged their speed so fast

The stonecrop that on ruins comes
& hangs like golden balls
How oft to reach its shining blooms
We scaled the mossy walls
& weeds—we gathered weeds as well
Of all that bore a flower
& tied our little poseys up
Beneath the eldern bower

Our little gardens there we made
Of blossoms all arow

& though they had no roots at all
We hoped to see them grow
& in the cart rutt after showers
Of sudden summer rain
We filled our tiney waterpots
& cherished them in vain

We pulled the moss from apple trees
& gathered bits of straws
When weary twirling of our tops
& shooting of our taws
We made birds nests & thought that birds
Would like them ready made
& went full twenty times a day
To see if eggs were laid

The long & swaily willow row
Where we for whips would climb
How sweet their shadows used to grow
In merry harvest time
We pulled boughs down & made a swee
Snug hid from toil & sun
& up we tossed right merrily
Till weary with the fun

On summer eves with wild delight
We bawled the bat to spy
Who in the "I spy" dusky light
Shrieked loud & flickered bye
& up we tossed our shuttlecocks
& tried to hit the moon
& wondered bats should flye so long
& they come down so soon

We sought for nutts in secret nook
We thought none else could find
& listened to the laughing brook
& mocked the singing wind
We gathered acorns ripe & brown
That hung too high to pull
Which friendly winds would shake adown
Till all had pockets full

Then loading home at days decline
Each sought his corner stool
Then went to bed till morning came
& crept again to school
Yet there by pleasure unforsook
In natures happy moods
The cuts in Fennings Spelling book
Made up for fields & woods

Each noise that breathed around us then
Was majic all & song
Where ever pastime found us then
Joy never led us wrong
The wild bees in the blossom hung
The coy birds startled call
To find its home in danger—there
Was music in them all

& oer the first Bumbarrels nest
We wondered at the spell
That birds who served no prenticeship
Could build their nests so well
& finding linnets moss was green
& finches chusing grey
& every finches nest alike
Our wits was all away

Then blackbirds lining theirs with grass
& thrushes theirs with dung
So for our lives we could not tell
From whence the wisdom sprung
We marvelled much how little birds
Should ever be so wise
& so we guessed some angel came
To teach them from the skys

In winter too we traced the fields
& still felt summer joys
We sought our hips & felt no cold
Cold never came to boys
The sloes appeared as choice as plumbs
When bitten by the frost
& crabs grew honey in the mouth
When apple time was past

We rolled in sunshine lumps of snow
& called them mighty men
& tired of pelting Bouneparte
We ran to slide agen
& ponds for glibbest ice we sought
With shouting & delight
& tasks of spelling all were left
To get by heart at night

& when it came—& round the fire
We sat—what joy was there
The kitten dancing round the cork
That dangled from a chair
While we our scraps of paper burnt
To watch the flitting sparks
& Collect books were often torn
For parsons & for clerks

Nought seemed too hard for us to do
But the sums upon our slates
Nought seemed too hard for us to win
But the masters chair of state
The "Town of Troy" we tried & made
When our sums we could not try
While we envied een the sparrows wings
From our prison house to flye

When twelve oclock was counted out
The joy & strife began
The shut of books the hearty shout
As out of doors we ran
Sunshine & showers who could withstand
Our food & rapture they
We took our dinners in our hands
To loose no time in play

The morn when first [we] went to school
Who can forget the morn
When the birchwhip lay upon the clock
& our hornbook it was torn
We tore the little pictures out
Less fond of books than play
& only took one letter home
& that the letter "A"

I love in childhoods little book
To read its lessons through
& oer each pictured page to look
Because they read so true
& there my heart creates anew
Love for each trifling thing
—Who can disdain the meanest weed
That shows its face at spring

The daisey looks up in my face
As long ago it smiled
It knows no change but keeps its place
& takes me for a child
The Chaffinch in the hedge row thorn
Cries "pink pink pink" to hear
My footsteps in the early morn
As though a boy was near

I seek no more the finches nest
Nor stoop for daisey flowers
I grow a stranger to myself
In these delightful hours
Yet when I hear the voice of spring
I can but call to mind
The pleasures which they used to bring
The joys I used to find

The firetail on the orchard wall
Keeps at its startled cry
Of "tweet tut tut" nor sees the morn
Of boyhoods mischief bye
It knows no change of changing time
By sickness never stung
It feeds on hopes eternal prime
Around its brooded young

Ponds where we played at "Duck & Drake"
Where the ash with ivy grew
Where we robbed the Owl of all her eggs
& mocked her as she flew
The broad tree in the spinney hedge
Neath which the gipseys lay
Where we our fine oak apples got
On the twenty ninth of may

These all remain as then they were
& are not changed a day
& the Ivys crowns as near to green
As mine is to the grey
It shades the pond oer hangs the stile
& the oak is in the glen
But the paths of joy are so worn out
I cant find one agen

The merry wind still sings the song
As if no change had been
The birds build nests the summer long
The trees look full as green
As eer they did in childhoods joy
Though that hath long been bye
When I a happy roving boy
In the fields had used to lye

To tend the restless roving sheep
Or lead the quiet cow
Toils that seemed more than slavery then
How more then freedom now
Could we but feel as then we did
When joy too fond to flye
Would flutter round as soon as bid
& drive all troubles bye

But rainbows on an april cloud
& blossoms pluckt in may
& painted eves that summer brings
Fade not so fast away
Tho grass is green though flowers are gay
& every where they be
What are the leaves on branches hung
Unto the withered tree

Lifes happiest gifts & what are they
Pearls by the morning strung
Which ere the noon are swept away—
Short as a cuckoos song
A nightingales the summer is
Can pleasure make us proud
To think when swallows fly away
They leave her in her shroud

Youth revels at his rising hour
With more than summer joys
& rapture holds the fairey flower
Which reason soon destroys
O sweet the bliss which fancy feigns
To hide the eyes of truth
& beautious still the charm remains
Of faces loved in youth

& spring returns the blooming year
Just as it used to be
& joys in youthful smiles appear
To mock the change in me
Each sight leaves memory ill at ease
& stirs an aching bosom
To think that seasons sweet as these
With me are out of blossom

The fairest summer sinks in shade
The sweetest blossom dies
& age finds every beauty fade
That youth esteemed a prize
The play breaks up the blossom fades
& childhood dissapears
For higher dooms ambitions aims
& care grows into years

But time we often blame him wrong
That rude destroying time
& follow him with sorrows song
When he hath done no crime
Our joys in youth are often sold
In follys thoughtless fray
& many feel their hearts grow old
Before their heads are grey

The past—there lyes in that one word
Joys more than wealth can crown
Nor could a million call them back
Though muses wrote them down
The sweetest joys imagined yet
The beautys that surpast
All life or fancy ever met
Are there among the past

TO A POET

Poet of mighty power I fain
Would court the muse that honoured thee
& like Elishas spirit gain
A part of thy intensity
& share the mantle which she flung
Around thee when thy lyre was strung

Though factions scorn at first did shun
With coldness thy inspired song
Though clouds of malice passed thy sun
They could not hide it long
Its brightness soon exaled away
Dank night & gained eternal day

The critics wrath did darkly frown
Upon thy muses mighty lay
But blasts that break the blossom down
Do only stir the bay
& thine shall flourish green & long
With the eternity of song

Thy genius saw in quiet mood
Gilt fashions follys pass thee bye
& like the monarch of the wood
Towered oer it to the sky
Where thou couldst sing of other spheres
& feel the fame of future years

Though bitter sneers & stinging scorns
Did throng the muses dangerous way
Thy powers were past such little thorns
They gave thee no dismay
The scoffers insult passed thee bye
Thou smiled & made him no reply

Envy will gnaw its heart away
To see thy genius gather root
& as its flowers their sweets display
Scorns malice shall be mute
Hornets that summer warmed to flye
Shall at the death of summer die

Though friendly praise hath but its hour
& little praise with thee hath been
The bay may loose its summer flower
But still its leaves are green
& thine whose buds are on the shoot
Shall only fade to change to fruit

Fame lives not in the breath of words
In public praises hue & cry
The music of those summer birds
Are silent in a winter sky
When thine shall live & flourish on
Oer wrecks where crowds of fames are gone

The ivy shuns the city wall
Where busy clamorous crowds intrude
& climbs the desolated hall
In silent solitude
The time worn arch the fallen dome
Are roots for its eternal home

The bard his glory neer recieves
Where summers common flowers are seen
But winter finds it when she leaves
The laurel only green
& time from that eternal tree
Shall weave a wreath to honour thee

A sunny wreath for poets meet
From helicons immortal soil
Where sacred time with pilgrim feet
Walks forth to worship not to spoil
A wreath which fame creates & bears
& deathless genius only heirs

Nought but thy ashes shall expire
Thy genius at thy obsequies
Shall kindle up its living fire
& light the muses skies
Aye it shall rise & shine & be
A sun in songs posterity

AUTUMN

Siren of sullen moods & fading hues
Yet haply not incapable of joy
Sweet autumn I thee hail
With welcome all unfeignd
& oft as morning from her lattice peeps
To beckon up the sun I seek with thee
To drink the dewy breath
Of fields left fragrant then

To solitudes where no frequented paths
But what thine own feet makes betray thy home
Stealing obtrusive there
To meditate thine end
By overshadowed ponds in woody nooks
With ramping sallows lined & crowding sedge
Who woo the winds to play
& with them dance for joy

& meadow pools torn wide by lawless floods
Where water lilies spread their oily leaves
On which as wont the flye
Oft battons in the sun
Where leans the mossy willow half way oer
On which the shepherd crawls astride to throw
His angle clear of weeds
That crowd the waters brim

Or crispy hills & hollows scant of sward
Where step by step the patient lonely boy
Hath cut rude flights of stairs
To climb their steepy sides
Then tracking at their feet grown hoarse with noise
The crawling brook that ekes its weary speed
& struggles through the weeds
With faint & sullen brawls

These haunts long favoured but the more as now
With thee thus wandering moralizing on
Stealing glad thoughts from grief
& happy though I sigh
Sweet vision with the wild dishevelled hair
& raiments shadowy of each winds embrace

Fain would I win thine harp
To one accordant theme

Now not inaptly craved communing thus
Beneath the curdled arms of this stunt oak
We ll pillow on the grass
& fondly ruminate
Oer the disordered scenes of woods & fields
Ploughed lands thin travelled with half hungry sheep
Pastures tracked deep with cows
Where small birds seek for seeds

Marking the cow boy that so merry trills
His frequent unpremeditated song
Wooing the winds to pause
Till echo brawls again
As on with plashy step & clouted shoon
He roves half indolent & self employed
To rob the little birds
Of hips & pendant awes

& sloes dim covered as with dewey veils
& rambling bramble berries pulp & sweet
Arching their prickly trails
Half oer the narrow lane
& mark the hedger front with stubborn face
The dank blea wind that whistles thinly bye
His leathern garb thorn proof
& cheeks red hot with toil

Wild sorceress me thy restless mood delights
More than the stir of summers crowded scenes
Where jostled in the din
Joy pauled mine ear with song
Heart sickening for the silence that is thine
Not broken inharmoniously as now
That lone & vagrant bee
Booms faint with weary chime

& filtering winds thin winnowing through the woods
In tremelous noise that bids at every breath
Some sickly cankered leaf
Let go its hold & die
& now the bickering storm with sudden start

110

In flirting fits of anger carpeth loud
Thee urging to thine end
Sore wept by troubled skyes

& yet sublime in grief thy thoughts delight
To show me visions of most gorgeous dyes
Haply forgetting now
They but prepare thy shroud
Thy pencil dashing its excess of shades
Improvident of waste till every bough
Burns with thy mellow touch
Disorderly divine

Soon must I view thee as a pleasant dream
Droop faintly & so sicken for thine end
As sad the winds sink low
In dirges for their queen
While in the moment of their weary pause
To cheer thy bankrupt pomp the willing lark
Starts from his shielding clod
Snatching sweet scraps of song

Thy life is waning now & silence tries
To mourn but meets no sympathy in sounds
As stooping low she bends
Forming with leaves thy grave
To sleep inglorious there mid tangled woods
Till parch lipped summer pines in draught away
Then from thine ivied trance
Awake to glories new

ST MARTINS EVE

Now that the year grows wearisome with age
& days grow short & nights excessive long
No outdoor sports the village hinds engage
Still is the meadow romp & harvest song
That wont to echo from each merry throng
At dinner hours beneath hugh spreading tree
Rude winds hath done the landscape mickle wrong
That nature in her mirth did ill foresee
Who clingeth now to hope like shipwrecked folks at sea

The woods are desolate of song—the sky
Is all forsaken of its joyous crowd
Martin & swallow there no longer flye
—Hugh seeming rocks & deserts now enshroud
The sky for aye with shadow shaping cloud
None there of all those busy tribes remain
No song is heard save one that wails aloud
From the all lone & melancholly crane
Who like a traveller lost the right road seeks in vain

The childern hastening in from threatening rain
No longer round the fields for wild fruit run
But at their homes from morn till night remain
& wish in vain to see the welcome sun
Winters imprisonment is all begun
Yet when the wind grows troubleous & high
Pining for freedom like a lovesick nun
Around the gardens little bounds they flye
Beneath the roaring trees fallen apples to espye

But spite of all the melancholly moods
That out of doors poor pleasures heart alarms
Flood bellowing rivers & wind roaring woods
The fireside evening owns increasing charms
What with the tale & eldern wine that warms
In purple bubbles by the blazing fire
Of simple cots & rude old fashioned farms
They feel as blest as joys can well desire
& midnight often joins before the guests retire

& such a group on good St Martins eve
Was met together upon pleasure bent

112

Where tales & fun did cares so well decieve
That the old cottage rung with merriment
& even the very rafters groaned & bent
Not so much it would seem from tempests din
That roared without in roaring discontent
As from the merry noise & laugh within
That seemed as summers sports had never absent bin

Beside the fire large apples lay to roast
& in a hugh brown pitcher creaming ale
Was warming seasoned with a nutmeg toast
The merry group of gossips to regale
Around her feet the glad cat curled her tail
Listening the crickets song with half shut eyes
While in the chimney top loud roared the gale
Its blustering howl of outdoor symphonies
That round the cottage hearth bade happier moods arise

& circling round the fire the merry folks
Brought up all sports their memory could devise
Playing upon each other merry jokes
& now one shuts his hands & archly cries
Come open wide your mouth & shut your eyes
& see what gifts are sent you—foolish thing
He doth as he is bid & quickly rise
The peals of laughter when they up & fling
The ashes in while he goes spitting from the ring

& the old dame tho not in laughing luck
For that same night at one fell sweeping stroke
Mischieving cat that at a mouse had struck
Upon the shelf her best blue china broke
Yet spite of fate so funny was the joke
She laughed untill her very sides did shake
& some so tittled were they could not smoke
Laying down their pipes lest they their pipe should break
& laughed & laughed again untill their ribs did ache

Then deftly one with cunning in his eyes
With out stretched hand walks backward in the dark
Encouraged to the feet with proffered prize
If so he right can touch pretended mark
Made on the wall—& happy as a lark
He chuckles oer success by hopes prepared

113

While one with open mouth like greedy shark
Slives in the place & bites his finger hard
He bawls for freedom loud & shames his whole reward

Then came more games of wonderment & fun
Which set poor Hodges wisdom all aghast
Who sought three knives to hide them one by one
While one no conjuror to reveal the past
Blindfold would tell him where he hid the last
Hodge hiding two did for the third enquire
All tittered round & bade him hold it fast
But ah he shook it from his hands in ire
For while he hid the two they warmed it in the fire

Then to appease him with his burning hand
They bade him hide himself & they would tell
The very way in which he chose to stand
Hodge thought the matter most impossible
& on his knees behind the mash tub fell
& muttering said I ll beat em now or never
Crying out "how stand I" just to prove the spell
They answered "like a fool" & thing so clever
Raised laughter against Hodge more long & loud than ever

Nor can the aged in such boisterous glee
Escape the tricks for laugh & jest designed
The old dame takes the bellows on her knee
& puffs in vain to tricks of rougery blind
Nor heeds the urgin who lets out the wind
With crafty finger & with cunning skill
That for her life the cause she cannot find
Untill the group unable to be still
Laughs out & dame though tricked smiles too against her will

Yet mid this strife of joy—on corner stool
One sits all silent doomed to worst of fate
Who made one slip in love & played the fool
& since condemned to live without a mate
No youth again courts once beguiled Kate
Tho hopes of sweethearts yet perplex her head
& charms to try by gipseys told of late
Beneath her pillow lays an onion red
To dream on this same night with whom she is to wed

& hopes that like to sunshine warming falls
Being all the solace to her withering mind
When they for dancing rise old young & all
She in her corner musing sits behind
Her palid cheek upon her hand reclined
Nursing rude melancholly like a child
Who sighs its silence to the sobbing wind
That in the chimney roars with fury wild
While every other heart to joy is reconsiled

One thumps the warming pan with merry glee
That bright as is a mirror decks the cot
Another droning as an humble bee
Plays on the muffled comb till piping hot
With over strained exertion—yet the lot
Is such an happy one that still he plays
Fatigue & all its countless ills forgot
All that he wants he wins—for rapture pays
To his unwearied skill right earnest words of praise

Ah happy hearts how happy cant be told
To fancy music in such clamorous noise
Like those converting all they touched to gold
These all they hearken to convert to joys
Thrice happy hearts—old men as wild as boys
Feel nought of age creep oer their extacys
—Old women whom no cares of life destroys
Dance with the girls—true did the bard surmise
"Where ignorance is bliss tis folly to be wise["]

When weary of the dance one reads a tale
Tho puzzled oft to spell a lengthy word
Storys though often read yet never stale
But gaining interest every time theyre heard
With morts of wonderment that neer occurred
Yet simple souls their faith it knows no stint
Things least to be believed are most preferred
All counterfiets as from truths sacred mint
Are readily believed if once put down in print

Bluebeard & all his murders dread parade
Are listened to & mourned for & the tear
Drops from the blue eye of the listening maid
Warm as it fell upon her lovers bier

115

None in the circle doubt of what they hear
It were a sin to doubt oer tales so true
So say the old whose wisdom all revere
& unto whom such reverence may be due
For honest good intents praise that belongs to few

& Tib a Tinkers Daughter is the tale
That doth by wonder their rude hearts engage
Oer young & old its witchcraft scenes prevail
In the rude legend of her pilgrimage
How she in servitude did erst engage
To live with an old hag of dreadful fame
Who often fell in freaks of wonderous rage
& played with Tib full many a bitter game
Till een the childern round cried out for very shame

They read how once to thrash her into chaff
The fearful witch tied Tibby in a sack
& hied her to the wood to seek a staff
That might be strong enough her bones to whack
But lucky Tib escaped ere she came back
& tied up dog & cat her doom to share
& pots & pans—& loud the howl & crack
That rose when the old witch with inky hair
Began the sack to thrash with no intent to spare

& when she found her unrevenged mistake
Her rage more fearful grew but all in vain
For fear no more caused Tibbys heart to ache
She far away from the old hags domain
Ran hartsomely a better place to gain
& here the younkers tongues grew wonder glib
With gladness & the reader stopt again
Declaring all too true to be a fib
& urged full glasses round to drink success to Tib

& when her sorrows & her pilgrimage
The plot of most new novels & old tales
Grew to a close her beauty did presage
Luck in the wind—& fortune spread her sails
In favouring bounty to Tibs summer gales
All praised her beauty & the lucky day
At length its rosey smiling face unveils
When Tib of course became a lady gay

116

& loud the listeners laugh while childern turned to play

Anon the clock counts twelve & mid their joys
The startled blackbird smooths its feathers down
That in its cage grew weary of their noise
—The merry maiden & the noisey clown
Prepare for home & down the straggling town
To seek their cottages they tittering go
Heartened with sports & stout ale berry brown
Beside their dames like chanticleer they crow
While every lanthorn flings long gleams along the snow

117

TO ——
ON MAY MORNING

Lady tis thy desire to move
Far from the worlds ungentle throng
Lady tis thy delight to love
The muses & the suns of song
Nor taste alone is thine to praise
For thou canst touch the minstrel wire
& while thourt praising others lays
Wake notes that any may admire
Forgive if I in friendships way
Do offer thee a wreath of May

I greet thee with no gaudy flowers
For thou art not to fashions prone
But rather lovest the woodland bowers
Where natures beautys charm alone
The Passion flower & Ceres fine
By wealth & pride are reared alone
Yet flowers more sweet nor less divine
Springs humbler fields & forests own
To every hand & bosom given
And nourished by the dews of heaven

The little violets bloom I weave
In wreaths Im fain that thou shouldst prize
Although it comes at winters eve
& often in the tempest dies
The Primrose too a doubtful dream
Of what precarious spring would be
Yet would I not the type should seem
Aught fancy feigns resembling thee
& thus belie thy gentle heart
Where worldly coldness hath no part

Here too are boughs of opening May
And Lillies of the valley fair
Yet not with idle praise to say
Theyre types of what are sweet & fair
I cropt one from the pasture hedge
The others from the forrest dell
& thou hast given the muses pledge
Such scenes delight thy bosom well

Tis not thy person wakes my lays
Thy heart alone I mean to praise

Forgive me though I flatter not
Youths beauties it were thine to wear
Hath been by riper years forgot
Though thou hast had a happy share
& I might praise full many a grace
That lives & lingers yet behind
But they like flowers shall change their place
Not so the beauties of the mind
So I have Ivy placed between
To prove that worth is ever green

The little blue Forget me not
Comes too on friendships gentle plea
Springs messenger in every spot
Smiling on all remember me
But gaudy Tulips find no place
In garlands friendship would bestow
Yet here the cowslip shows its face
Prized for its sweetness more than show
Emblems to pride & pomp inclined
Would but offend a modest mind

I would not on Mays garland fling
The Laurel to the muse & thee
For fashions praise—a common thing
Hath made of that once sacred tree
& trust me many laurels wear
That never grew on parnass hill
Yet dare & speed tis thine to heir
The muses laurels if ye will
Let flattery think her wreaths divine
Merit by its own worth will shine

O when I view the glorious host
Of poets to my country born
Though sorrow was the lot of most
& many shared the sneers of scorn
That now by time & talent tried
Give life to fames eternal sun
O when I mark the glorious pride
That England from her bards hath won

Een I the meanest of the throng
Warm into extacy & song

The highest gifts each kingdom claims
Are minstrels on the muses throne
& bards whove won the richest fames
Tis Englands noblest pride to own
Shakspears & Miltons they that heir
The fames immortal oer decay
& Scotts & Byrons born to wear
The honours of a later day
That joins to present past renown
& sings eternity to crown

These from proud laurels never won
Their fames & honours more divine
They like the grand eternal sun
Confer their glories where they shine
The Laurel were a common bough
Had it not decked the poets crown
& even weeds so common now
Placed there would augur like renown
Bloom satellites in glorys way
Proud as the Laurel & the Bay

Lady & thou hast chosen well
To give the muses thy regard
There taste from pleasure bears the bell
There feeling finds its own reward
Tho genius often while it makes
Lifes millions happy with her songs
For sorrows cup her portion takes
& struggles under bitterest wrongs
To cares of life & song unknown
The poets fame be thine alone

ON A CHILD KILLED BY LIGHTNING

As fearless as a cherubs rest
Now safe above the cloud
A babe lay on its mothers breast
When thunders roared aloud
It started not to hear the crash
But held its little hand
Up at the lightnings fearful flash
To catch the burning brand

The tender mother held her breath
In more than grief awhile
To think the thing that brought its death
Should cause her babe to smile
Ay it did smile a heavenly smile
To see the lightning play
Well might she shriek when it turned pale
& yet it smiled in clay

O woman the dread storm was given
To be to each a friend
It took thy infant pure to heaven
Left thee impure to mend
Thus providence will oft appear
From Gods own mouth to preach
Ah would we were as prone to hear
As mercy is to teach

THE AUTUMN ROBIN

Sweet little bird in russet coat
The livery of the closing year
I love thy lonely plaintive note
& tiney whispering song to hear
While on the stile or garden seat
I sit to watch the falling leaves
The songs thy little joys repeat
My lonliness relieves

& many are the lonely minds
That hear & welcome thee anew
Not taste alone but humble hinds
Delight to praise & love thee too
The veriest clown biside his cart
Turns from his song with many a smile
To see thee from the hedgerow start
To sing upon the stile

The shepherd on the fallen tree
Drops down to listen to thy lay
& chides his dog beside his knee
Who barks & frightens thee away
The hedger pauses ere he knocks
The stake down in the meadow gap
—The boy who every songster mocks
Forbears the gate to clap

When in the hedge that hides the post
Thy ruddy bosom he surveys
Pleased with thy song in pleasure lost
He pausing mutters scraps of praise
The maiden marks at days decline
Thee in the yard on broken plough
& stops her song to listen thine
While milking brinded cow

Thy simple faith in mans esteem
From every heart hath favours won
Dangers to thee no dangers seem
Thou seemest to court them more than shun
The clown in winter takes his gun
The barn door flocking birds to slay

Yet shouldst thou in the danger run
He turns the tube away

The gipsey boy who seeks in glee
Blackberrys for a dainty meal
Laughs loud on first beholding thee
When called so near his presence steal
He surely thinks thou knew the call
& though his hunger ill can spare
The fruit he will not pluck them all
But leaves some to thy share

Upon the ditchers spade thoult hop
For grubs & wreathing worms to search
Where woodmen in the forrests chop
Thoult fearless on their faggots perch
Nay by the gipseys camp I stop
& mark thee perch a moment there
To prune thy wing awhile then drop
The littered crumbs to share

Domestic bird thy pleasant face
Doth well thy common suit commend
To meet thee in a stranger place
Is meeting with an ancient friend
I track the thickets glooms around
& there as loath to leave agen
Thou comest as if thou knew the sound
& loved the sight of men

The lonliest woods that man can trace
To thee a pleasant dwelling gives
In every town & crowded place
The sweet domestic Robin lives
Go where we will in every spot
Thy little welcome mates appear
& like the daiseys common lot
Thourt met with every where

The swallow in the chimney tier
The tittering martin in the eaves
With half of love & half of fear
Their mortared dwelling shyly weaves
The sparrows in the thatch will shield

Yet they as well as eer they can
Contrive with doubtful faith to build
Beyond the reach of man

But thourt less timid than the wren
Domestic & confiding bird
& spots the nearest haunts of men
Are oftenest for thy home preferred
In garden walls thoult build so low
Close where the bunch of fennel stands
That een a child just learned to go
May reach with tiney hands

Sweet favoured bird thy under notes
In summers music grows unknown
The consert from a thousand throats
Leaves thee as if to pipe alone
No listening ear the shepheard lends
The simple ploughman marks thee not
& then by all thy autumn friends
Thourt missing & forgot

The far famed nightingale that heirs
Cold public praise from every tongue
The popular voice of music heirs
& injures much thy under song
Yet then my walks thy theme salutes
& finds their autumn favoured guest
Gay piping on the hazel roots
Above thy mossy nest

Tis wrong that thou shouldst be despised
When these gay fickle birds appear
They sing when summers flowers are prized
Thou at the dull & dying year
Well let the heedless & the gay
Bepraise the voice of louder lays
The joy thou stealest from sorrows day
Is more to thee than praise

& could my notes win aught from thine
My words but imitate thy lay
Time would not then his charge resign
Nor throw the meanest verse away

124

But ever at this mellow time
He should thy autumn praise prolong
So would they share the happy prime
Of thy eternal song

ON THE MEMORY
OF THE HONOURABLE LADY ——

Lifes current journeyed smooth with thee
& travelled to eternity
Calm & untroubled as it ran
When thy unruffled course began
Wealth lulled thee on her golden breast
But power neer stained thy princely rest
Titles were thine & not the pride
That is with shadows dignified
Thou knew how vain such things to trust
& felt earths honours were but dust
While vain ambition joined the crowd
While folly still pursued the proud
& pride blazed oer a titled name
Thy meekness sought a better fame
Unpleased with pomp unused to shine
These own no claims to trumpet thine
Patron to one—to all a friend
Beloved & honoured to thy end
Not in the mockery flattery vents
The marble tales of monuments
Nor in the verse that only tells
How much thy worth the theme excells
But in the hearts of those that knew
The blameless course thou didst pursue
In prayers that want to heaven would send
For even want could call thee friend
Though fortune wrapt thy heart from care
Yet pity found a dwelling there
That thought oer troubles not its own
& felt for sorrows never known
These are the farewells following thee
To worths well won eternity
& thus thy memory lingers on
Like sun beams when the day is gone
They praised thee once with truths free will
& love to turn & bless thee still
Let pride to tinsel follys throng
& shine in flatterys birthday song
Both are at best in their display
The insects of a summers day
While thine in many a heart shall live

Till memory hath a thought to give
Truth speaks thy fame & while it mourns
Thy end its gratitude returns
Then rest while foes if foes can be
Turn from thy cherished memory
Envying when they cannot blame
The blessing of an honest fame
& folly sighs at lifes decline
For half the love that dwells with thine

THE QUIET MIND

Though [low] my lot my wish is won
My hopes are few & staid
All I thought life would do is done
The last request is made
If I have foes no foes I fear
To fate I live resigned
I have a friend I value here
& thats a quiet mind

I wish not it was mine to wear
Flushed honours sunny crown
I wish not I were fortunes heir
She frowns & let her frown
I have no taste for pomp & strife
Which others love to find
I only wish the bliss of life
A poor & quiet mind

The trumpets taunt in battle field
The great mans pedigree
What peace can all their honours yield
& what are they to me
Though praise & pomp to eke the strife
Rave like a mighty wind
What are they to the calm of life
A still & quiet mind

I mourn not that my lot is low
I wish no higher state
I sigh not that fate made me so
Nor teaze her to be great
I am content for well I see
What all at last shall find
That lifes worst lot the best shall be
& thats a quiet mind

I see the great pass heedless bye
& pride above me tower
It costs me not a single sigh
For either wealth or power
They are but men & I'm a man
Of quite as great a kind

Proud too that life gives all she can
A calm & quiet mind

I never mocked at beautys shrine
To stain her lips with lyes
No knighthoods fame or luck was mine
To win loves richest prize
& yet I found in russet weed
What all will wish to find
True love & comforts prize indeed
A glad & quiet mind

& come what will of cares or woe
As some must come to all
I ll wish not that they were not so
Nor mourn that they befall
If tears for sorrows start at will
Theyre comforts in their kind
& I am blest if with me still
Remains a quiet mind

When friends depart as part they must
& loves true joys decay
That leave us like the summers dust
The wirlwind puffs away
While lifes allotted time I brave
Though left the last behind
A prop & friend I still shall have
If Ive a quiet mind

SHADOWS OF TASTE

Taste with as many hues doth hearts engage
As leaves & flowers do upon natures page
Not mind alone the instinctive mood declares
But birds & flowers & insects are its heirs
Taste is their joyous heritage & they
All choose for joy in a peculiar way
Birds own it in the various spots they chuse
Some live content in low grass gemmed with dews
The yellowhammer like a tasteful guest
Neath picturesque green molehills makes a nest
Where oft the shepherd with unlearned ken
Finds strange eggs scribbled as with ink & pen
He looks with wonder on the learned marks
& calls them in his memory writing larks
Birds bolder winged on bushes love to be
While some choose cradles on the highest tree
There rocked by winds they feel no moods of fear
But joy their birthright lives for ever near
& the bold eagle which mans fear enshrouds
Would could he lodge it house upon the clouds
While little wrens mistrusting none that come
In each low hovel meet a sheltered home
Flowers in the wisdom of creative choice
Seem blest with feeling & a silent voice
Some on the barren roads delight to bloom
& others haunt the melancholly tomb
Where death the blight of all finds summers hours
Too kind to miss him with her host of flowers
Some flourish in the sun & some the shade
Who almost in his morning smiles would fade
These in leaf darkened woods right timid stray
& in its green night smile their lives away
Others in water live & scarcely seem
To peep their little flowers above the stream
While water lilies in their glories come
& spread green isles of beauty round their home
All share the summers glory & its good
& taste of joy in each peculiar mood
Insects of varied taste in rapture share
The heyday luxuries which she comes to heir
In wild disorder various routs they run
In water earth still shade & busy sun

& in the crowd of green earths busy claims
They een grow nameless mid their many names
& man that noble insect restless man
Whose thoughts scale heaven in its mighty span
Pours forth his living soul in many a shade
& taste runs riot in her every grade
While the low herd mere savages subdued
With nought of feeling or of taste imbued
Pass over sweetest scenes a carless eye
As blank as midnight in its deepest dye
From these & different far in rich degrees
Minds spring as various as the leaves of trees
To follow taste & all her sweets explore
& Edens make where deserts spread before
In poesys spells some all their raptures find
& revel in the melodies of mind
There nature oer the soul her beauty flings
In all the sweets & essences of things
A face of beauty in a city crowd
Met—passed—& vanished like a summer cloud
In poesys vision more refined & fair
Taste reads oerjoyed & greets her image there
Dashes of sunshine & a page of may
Live there a whole life long one summers day
A blossom in its witchery of bloom
There gathered dwells in beauty & perfume
The singing bird the brook that laughs along
There ceasless sing & never thirsts for song
A pleasing image to its page conferred
In living character & breathing word
Becomes a landscape heard & felt & seen
Sunshine & shade one harmonizing green
Where meads & brooks & forrests basking lie
Lasting as truth & the eternal sky
Thus truth to nature as the true sublime
Stands a mount atlas overpeering time
    Styles may with fashions vary—tawdry chaste
Have had their votaries which each fancied taste
From Donns old homely gold whose broken feet
Jostles the readers patience from its seat
To Popes smooth ryhmes that regularly play
In musics stated periods all the way
That starts & closes starts again & times
Its tuning gammut true as minster chimes

From these old fashions stranger metres flow
Half prose half verse that stagger as they go
One line starts smooth & then for room perplext
Elbows along & knocks against the next
& half its neighbour where a pause marks time
There the clause ends what follows is for ryhme
Yet truth to nature will in all remain
As grass in winter glorifies the plain
& over fashions foils rise proud & high
As lights bright fountain in a cloudy sky
    The man of sience in discoverys moods
Roams oer the furze clad heath leaf buried woods
& by the simple brook in rapture finds
Treasures that wake the laugh of vulgar hinds
Who see no further in his dark employs
Then village childern seeking after toys
Their clownish hearts & ever heedless eyes
Find nought in nature they as wealth can prize
With them self interest & the thoughts of gain
Are natures beautys all beside are vain
But he the man of science & of taste
Sees wealth far richer in the worthless waste
Where bits of lichen & a sprig of moss
Will all the raptures of his mind engross
& bright winged insects on the flowers of may
Shine pearls too wealthy to be cast away
His joys run riot mid each juicy blade
Of grass where insects revel in the shade
& minds of different moods will oft condemn
His taste as cruel such the deeds to them
While he unconsious gibbets butterflyes
& strangles beetles all to make us wise
Tastes rainbow visions own unnumbered hues
& every shade its sense of taste pursues
The heedless mind may laugh the clown may stare
They own no soul to look for pleasure there
Their grosser feelings in a coarser dress
Mock at the wisdom which they cant possess
    Some in recordless rapture love to breath
Natures wild Eden wood & field & heath
In common blades of grass his thoughts will raise
A world of beauty to admire & praise
Untill his heart oerflows with swarms of thought
To that great being who raised life from nought

The common weed adds graces to his mind
& gleams in beautys few beside may find
Associations sweet each object breeds
& fine ideas upon fancy feeds
He loves not flowers because they shed perfumes
Or butterflyes alone for painted plumes
Or birds for singing although sweet it be
But he doth love the wild & meadow lea
There hath the flower its dwelling place & there
The butterflye goes dancing through the air
He loves each desolate neglected spot
That seems in labours hurry left forgot
The warped & punished trunk of stunted oak
Freed from its bonds but by the thunder stroke
As crampt by straggling ribs of ivy sere
There the glad bird makes home for half the year
But take these several beings from their homes
Each beautious thing a withered thought becomes
Association fades & like a dream
They are but shadows of the things they seem
Torn from their homes & happiness they stand
The poor dull captives of a foreign land
Some spruce & delicate ideas feed
With them disorder is an ugly weed
& wood & heath a wilderness of thorns
Which gardeners shears nor fashions nor adorns
No spots give pleasure so forlorn & bare
But gravel walks would work rich wonders there
With such wild natures beautys run to waste
& arts strong impulse mars the truth of taste
Such are the various moods that taste displays
Surrounding wisdom in concentring rays
Where threads of light from one bright focus run
As days proud halo circles round the sun

STANZAS ON A CHILD

Times tide how swift its current flows
& mixed in every wave
That on its farewell errand goes
What pleasures find a grave

The happiest day that ever is
Is like a mourner gay
For where lives one that cannot miss
Some pleasure taen away

Theres not a hid or secret rout
That hope can take to joy
But grief in time will find it out
& every hope destroy

No no our sorrows grow extreme
Our griefs are often vain
When we in hopeless anguish seem
A hope doth yet remain

A few clouds gathered & were oer
A few cares troubled & were bye
& now thourt on a happier shore
To breath a milder sky

Thy pains are oer then why engross
The heart with thoughts of pain
When all we vainly count as loss
Proves thy eternal gain

Death like a friend did come to thee
As loath to make thee weep
Thou knew him not thine enemy
& sunk as if to sleep

So short thy life thy morning sun
Seemed but to rise in vain
Yet when it set—thy spirit won
A joy unknown to pain

& thou art blest & happy now
Aye more thou little child

Than even when thy sunny brow
Saw summer flowers & smiled

For thou art in a golden sky
Mid everlasting blooms
Where suns neer set hopes never die
& trouble never comes

A braided wreath—a golden crown
Paint exits such as thine
But vain to write such baubles down
Where memory grows divine

For low is fancys earthly eye
That heavenly light asumes
To think that mortal pagentry
Immortal life illumes

Crowns pearls & all though splendid now
With empty pride & show
Twere vain to think an angels brow
Wears aught from pomps below

No matter hopes are recconsiled
Thy little heads at rest
Deaths angel read thy name & smiled
To find thee with the blest

TO THE MEMORY OF AN ADMIRAL

Departed shade of lofty birth
Though proud & high thy pedigree
Thou wert the poor mans friend on earth
For thou wert one to me

& shall no tender chord be strung
No plaintive strain to honour thee
& shall no honest lay be sung
To grave thy memory

Though humble be the power I claim
Though mean & poor my dittys be
I care not though the muse I shame
To show my love to thee

The mourning that thy bier bedewed
The feeling that attends the brave
The "still small voice" of gratitude
Were all that blest thy grave

When great men die their deeds of fame
Around their scutcheoned hearse are hung
& thou wert great in birth & name
Yet not a lyre was strung

When heroes vanish honours breath
Bids fame their loud sung deeds reward
A heroe thou yet at thy death
Not een a dirge was heard

When good men go the muses skill
Wreaths memorys musings round the spot
& thou wert good though all were still
As if they knew thee not

& this poor theme that fain would bloom
Around the memory of the brave
Is all that wreaths a warriors tomb
& shrouds a good mans grave

& worth shall live when themes decay
Far brighter themes than mine
When earthly splendours pass away
The good mans deeds shall shine

DEATH

Why should mans high aspiring mind
Burn in him with so proud a breath
When all his haughty views can find
In this world yields to death
The fair the brave the vain the wise
The rich the poor & great & small
Are each but worms anatomys
To strew his quiet hall

Power may make many earthly gods
Where gold & briberys guilt prevails
But deaths unwelcome honest odds
Kicks oer the unequal scales
The flattered great may clamours raise
Of power & their own weakness hide
But death shall find unlooked for ways
To end the farce of pride

An arrow hurtled eer so high
From een a jiants sinewy strength
In times untraced eternity
Goes but a pigmy length
Nay whirring from the tortured string
With all its pomp of hurried flight
Tis by the skylarks little wing
Out measured in its height

Just so mans boasted strength & power
Shall fade before deaths lightest stroke
Laid lower than the meanest flower
Whose pride oertopt the oak
& he who like a blighting blast
Dispeopled worlds with wars alarms
Shall be himself destroyed at last
By poor despised worms

Tyrants in vain their power secure
& awe slaves murmurs with a frown
But unawed death at last is sure
To rap the babels down
A stone thrown upward to the sky
Will quickly meet the ground agen

138

So men gods of earths vanity
Shall drop at last to men

& power & pomp their all resign
Blood purchased thrones & banquet halls
Fate waits to sack ambitions shrine
As bare as prison walls
Where the poor suffering wretch bows down
To laws a lawless power hath past
& pride & power & king & clown
Shall be deaths slaves at last

Time the prime minister of death
Theres nought can bribe his honest will
He stops the richest tyrants breath
& lays his mischief still
Each wicked scheme for power all stops
With grandeurs false & mock display
As eves shades from high mountain tops
Fade with the rest away

Death levels all things in his march
Nought can resist his mighty strength
The pallace proud triumphal arch
Shall mete their shadows length
The rich the poor one common bed
Shall find in the unhonoured grave
Where weeds shall crown alike the head
Of tyrant & of slave

FAREWELL TO LOVE

Love & thy vain employs away
From this too oft deluded breast
No longer will I court thy stay
To be my bosoms teazing guest
Thou treacherous medicine reckoned pure
Thou quackery of the harrassed heart
That kills what thou pretendst to cure
Life mountebank thou art

With nostrum vain of boasted powers
That taen a worse disorder breeds
An asp hid in a group of flowers
That kills & slays when none percieves
Thou mock truce to the troubled mind
Leading it on in sorrows way
Freedom that leaves us more confined
I bid thee hence away

Dost taunt & deem my power beyond
The resolution reason gave
Tut—falsity hath snapt each bond
That made me once thy quiet slave
& made thy snares a spiders threads
Which een my breath can break in twain
Nor will I be like Sampson led
To trust thy wiles again

I took thee as my staff to guide
Me on the road I did pursue
& when my weakness most relied
Upon its strength it broke in two
I took thee as my friendly host
That council might in dangers show
But when I needed thee the most
I found thou wert my foe

So go thou folly painted toy
Thou plaything all display
I will at least outbrave the boy
& throw such idle toys away
Thou dream for follys idle hour
Which I have found a dream indeed

Thou distant seeming showey flower
That proves when near a weed

Go trump thy mystic lotterys
Elsewere—veiled neath deceptions blot
Holding out every draw a prize
Where worthless blanks are only got
& flourish with thy patron dame
Yclipt a goddess & her boy
That fills the world with empty fame
& lives in painted joy

Tempt me no more with rosey cheeks
Nor daze my reason with bright eyes
Im wearied with thy painted freaks
& sicken at such vanitys
Be roseys fine as eer they will
They with the meanest fade & dye
& eyes though thronged with darts to kill
Are doomed to like mortality

Feed the young bard that madly sips
His nectar draughts from follys flowers
Bright eyes fair cheeks & ruby lips
Till muses melt to honey showers
Lure him to thrum thy empty lays
While flattery listens to the chimes
Till words themselves grow sick with praise
& stops for want of ryhmes

Let such be still thy paramours
& chaunt loves old & idle tune
Robbing the spring of all her flowers
& heaven of its stars & moon
To guild with dazzling similies
Blind follys vain & empty lay
Im sobered from such phantacys
So get thee hence away

Nor bid me sigh for mine own cost
Nor count it loss for mine anoy
Nor say my stubbornness hath lost
A paradise of dainty joy
I ll not believe thee till I know

That sober reason turns an ape
Or acts the harlequin to show
That cares in every shape

Heart aching sighs & grief wrung tears
Shame blushes at betrayed distress
Dissembled smiles & jealous fears
Are nought but real happiness
Then will I mourn what now I brave
& suffer Celias quirks to be
Like a poor fate bewildered slave
The rulers of my destiny

I ll weep & sigh when eer she wills
To frown—& when she deigns to smile
It shall be cure for all my ills
& foolish still I ll laugh the while
But till that comes I ll bless the rules
Experience taught & deem it wise
To hold thee as the game of fools
& all thy tricks despise

THE VILLAGE DOCTRESS

"Bold to prescribe & busy to apply" Garth

The Hut that stands in unpretending pride
With mossy thatch the meanest in the street
& smoke stained chimney far afield descried
Where swallows come springs dewy morn to meet
& in its shelter find a snug retreat
Plain shed yet they that in its shelter dwell
A portion of lifes joys neer fail to meet
Though [cares] full thick & often round them fell
Full pleasant are the tales their chronicles can tell

Calm industry though scantily supplied
Toils with content & smiles at idle fears
Warm providence their deity & guide
Trims hopes sweet bark to stem the sea of years
That life spreads onward—beautiful appears
The seeming smiles of comforts painted sky
Though neer attained faith still witholds its tears
& cheers them onward with unwearied eye
Still hoping better luck when e'er the worst is bye

Here dwells the village doctress one that owns
The praise of half the village for her powers
In curing every ill save broken bones
With famous drinks & ointments made of flowers
Sought for & gathered in propitious hours
When the fast waxing moon with thrifty speed
Outgrows her slender horns & dewy showers
Quickens the earth & fattens every weed
& thus her skill for cures grows marvelous indeed

Charms for the ague wrapt with mystic care
From the too curious eye of prying wight
That shivering patients in their bosoms wear
For many a hopeful day & restless night
Untill at last with wondersome delight
They miss the shivering fit & pleased confess
The wonder working charm hath acted right
& grant her mickle fame for such success
& think her deeply skilled & who can fancy less

143

Thus famed she is for miles the village round
Though not the noisey travelled far & near
That water doctors gain from ways profound
Who sound without detection shaming fear
Quackerys loud trump in superstitions ear
She is contented with an humble claim
& thus her modest worth to all is dear
Strange is it thus to think that dainty fame
Should stoop at humble cots to notice such a dame

Culpeppers Herbal dark star reading wight
She as an helpmate to their skill possest
& Westleys Phisic which all dames delight
To read who fancy simple things the best
There in a corner cupboard she possest
Locked up for safetys sake as wisdom rare
From meddling child with mischief in its breast
Who as she turned her back might climb a chair
& pull the shelf books down a picture out to tear

Yet from the doctors stars she nought could learn
Puzzles indeed one easy might suppose
For wiser heads then grannys to discern
Yet fain their mighty mysterys to disclose
She often placed her glasses on her nose
To pore in study deep & earnest heed
Letting a hole grow bigger in her clothes
Neglecting toil his dark consciets to read
& when she d racked her brains she rose sore vexed indeed

Yet though so ignorant in signs & lures
That skill of conjuring quack so well commends
She with poor people did such morts of cures
That in their eyes & such like partial friends
Phisic seemed oozing from her finger ends
They nothing know of learnings pomp not they
That makes so great a mystery—she attends
Prescribes & plasters—all for little pay
Thus fame & patients too increase with every day

Each broken teacup she preserves with care
& morts of things that on her shelf abound
Bottles that do their former uses wear
"Daffeys" & "Godfreys Cordial" labeled round

Employed for drugs & uses less renowned
To hold unlabeled water for the eye
& oyster shells picked off the fallow ground
To hold the salve which woodmen come to buy
As oft their dangerous toils are needing fresh supply

& oft to hunt her herbs she hies abroad
Where she would meet birdnesting boys at play
Strewing the mossy nests about the road
& bearing in their hats the eggs away
She'd preach like parson oer their sinful play
& if they laughed her pitying plaints to hear
She'd shake her stick & threaten sore dismay
To make their rebel deeds grow kind in fear
For she in pitys cause was advocate severe

She had a tender heart as eer could be
& for live things aye she d a love for all
She would not let the children kill a bee
With beating hats beside her cottage wall
& if a spider in her cot did crawl
She d take her brush & sweep it to the door
& een when beetles neath her foot did fall
As bustling oer the footpath or the floor
It cost her many a sigh & grieved her heart full sore

That whasp that in her window light trepanned
Buzzes for pitys sake nor calls in vain
She instant wraps her apron round her hand
& guides the adventurer to the broken pane
To greet its freedom & its friends again
Nor living thing that ever flies or crawls
Hath reason of her malice to complain
Save felon mouse that mercys boon forestalls
& in the baited trap for nightly plunder falls

The herbs most famous in her skills esteem
Were such as herbal books the most commend
Herbs that in common eyes do only seem
As common weeds unskilled to comprehend
The virtues wisdom in their praise has penned
& but for her & such as her they'd grow
Their little lives away without a friend
One passing glance of notice to bestow

145

As when they come in bloom or out of bloom they go

Famed earthern tongue that sprouts on april baulks
& Mallows horseshoe leaves by every wall
& inner bark scraped from young eldern stalks
Of these she makes an ointment fit for all
Green wounds that eer to poor mans lot befall
& wormwood tufts that thrive in many a town
& stinking seeding burdock spreading tall
That plagues the maiden in her sunday gown
These in her matchless skill grew weeds of high renown

& self heal flowering in a russet husk
& scurvy grass that pursy grannys prize
With dwarf heath mallows smelling faint of musk
Bogbean too shining in its mozzly dyes
Brooklime that on the shallow water lies
With famous eyebrights slightly penciled flowers
Infallable for weak short sighted eyes
These strange to schoolboys in flower seeking hours
Who think them worthless all to her own mighty powers

Tormentil also with its yellow bloom
Thriving on wild uncultivated land
& creeping five leaved grass that maketh room
In every spot its tendrills to expand
These would she gather with right careful hand
& hang them up to dry in many a row
For drinks & teas & uses rightly scanned
& more she sought whose fames I must forego
Or my unlearned ryhmes will bulky herbals grow

In sooth she is an all accomplished dame
Not learned in herbs alone but all compact
In useful skill not taking note of fame
She turns her hand to every thing in fact
& though some errors now & then detract
Some little from the much she seems to know
Her knowledge doth full many brains distract
That of her thrift & fame right jealous grow
& struggles all how vain in the same steps to go

Bees much her head to study did invite
& with her musing hours doth well agree

146

It bringeth all both profit & delight
To study knowledge of the honey bee
& she by certain signs few else could see
Knew when they were in liklihood to swarm
From certain sounds that in the hive would be
For even to such signs she could conform
As if those sounds were words & language uniform

When round the hives in May they thickening flye
She seeks her new made hives to dress them well
With balm & hairy fennel scented high
That grow in monstrous bunches by the well
Mysterious problems of some learned spell
To make them in their new abode remain
& warming pan half loud as village bell
She rings their roving ears to entertain
As though they loved the sound nor rings she oft in vain

& when they swarm on plumb or eldern tree
She'll take them in the hive with naked hand
Not frit to bear the sting of rebel bee
Harmless as flies as if by choice trepanned
Or by her spells subjected to command
They spin about her ears on harmless wing
& though she close about their hives will stand
For hours on sabbath mornings in the spring
To watch them at their toil none ever shows his sting

Yet she did reverence to the sunday pay
& set her brush & mop behind the door
& all her dirty things & wheel away
Putting her house to rights the day before
Of labour she would dare to do no more
When sunday came—yet shes so passing clean
Folks vow they een could eat upon the floor
Which not one time in ten was ever seen
Unswept or grit the while to fill the bricks atween

She neer missed going to church or foul or fair
Loath as she is her good red cloak to spoil
She seeks her ancient prayerbook wrapt with care
In cotton covers lest her hands should soil
The gilded back full loath is she to spoil
A book of which her parents took such heed

For it hath grown in memorys sacred soil
An old esteem from sire to son decreed
& to ill use such book were sacrilidge indeed

& if she failed to hear the chiming bell
As much her hearing failed her—at the door
She ll watch some neighbour her mishap to tell
& sigh & undergo temptations sore
Thinking that God will heed her prayers no more
Thus to neglect her duty—yet the while
She ll read the prayers & good church lessons oer
Or "Bunyans Pilgrim" errors to beguile
& thus oer godly books her fears will recconsile

Two jobs there are which she feels bound to do
What ever rest the sabbath may require
& on a working day she'll cease to sew
& close her book how eer she may admire
The passage she is reading or desire
To finish—she must turn the leaf adown
& pull her glasses off to stir the fire
& turn her hour glass up in case of brown
Worm eat by heedless age & praised by many a clown

In wicker cage placed in the lilac bush
That hides the cottage door with flowers in may
Loud sings & long hath sung a merry thrush
Hung constant there to share the sunny day
Strangers oft turn to listen to the lay
& village boys full often & full long
Forgo their errands by that spot to play
While bawling mothers scold that thrushes song
& with unfeeling ears the powers of music wrong

A magpie too as tame as dunghill cock
Strays where it will & where it lists will flye
& every human voice it hears will mock
Sing whistle talk & mimic laugh & cry
& should some merry maid go dancing bye
Like wicked clown it will her worth defame
Holes in her stocking heels soon meets his eye
& fast he follows while she runs in shame
Calling her naughty names my ryhmes are loath to name

148

& she has bantum fowls few else will prize
Muffled with feathers to the very toe
Scarce bigger than a partridge in their size
To whom a dish of corn she'll daily throw
& proud the cock will stretch his wings & crow
Beside his dames—though sparrows on the tree
That overhang the well will let him know
They think their little selves as good as he
& peck the corn with him & see no fear to flee

& more of curious things to note & heed
The tasteful eye about her cot may see
That would be deemed right curious all indeed
Had Dr Solomon or such as he
Been born the tennant of her cot to be
Yet she as worthy honours neer procures
From colledge grants diploma or degree
While some thats gained them shameful sight endures
To see their drugs less prized & notified for cures

& when she dies no doubt fames latent spark
Will light up epitaph her powers to tell
& warm the muse of worthy parish clerk
To chime a stanza while he chimes the bell
& unto all the world her praises tell
If all the world would read her humble stone
For twere a burning shame & sin as well
That one who hath such cures & wonders shown
Should leave the world for aye & be for aye unknown

STANZAS

Though lifes rude floods with sudden roar
Drifts me on seas without a shore
While Gods my hope & anchor I
Can find a quiet place to lie

Mans heart may ache mans spirit fear
But thou my God when thou art near
I doubted once—I know it now
Thy smiles can cheer the saddest brow

Anoyed by envys bitter gibes
Beset with troubles evil tribes
I called on God he heard the call
& proved a friendship all in all

THE ANNIVERSARY
TO A FLOWER OF THE DESERT

March wakened in wildness
Or musing in glee
Thy tempest or sunshine
Is welcome to me
I found on thy bosom
A treasure of spring
A fairer & dearer
Than summer could bring

Ere the throstle had ventured
A song to the morn
Or the blackbird to build him
A nest in the thorn
On the wild hills of walkerd
All withered & bare
Had Eden existed
I had thought it was there

Hope long had been blighted
Love lingered in chains
Faith long had been plighted
To scorn & disdains
The road it was weary
That led me along
With no thought to cheer me
But the sorrows of song

I looked to the east twas
A sunrise in shrouds
I looked to the west there
Was nothing but clouds
In aching & sorrow
Hope lost her employ
She had grief for the morrow
But no day for joy

Here a sun burst a cloud where
I looked for a shower
Here a spot that seemed desert
Discovered a flower
Endowed in youths glory

Both blossom & stem
Was the model of beauty
& I worshiped the gem

For my heart it was neuter
To form & disguise
Nor like a freebooter
I looked on the prize
But with heart that felt friendless
I wanted a friend
On a way that seemed endless
& now met an end

I loved it & proved it
& down to this hour
I neer saw the beauty
I found in that flower
Summer lived in its blossom
Though winter was bye
Joy laughed in its bosom
Though sorrow was nigh

A pallace without it
A prison would be
& the cottage that owned it
Was a pallace to me
My heart it was weary
I sued as a guest
Love was all that could cheer me
& there I had rest

Twas the hope most bewitching
That beauty inspired
Twas the joy most enriching
That fancy admired
Twas the bloom of lifes fancys
To garland my brow
& though sick of romances
Tis my bosoms home now

A MORNING WALK

Ah sure it is a lovely day
As ever summers glory yields
& I will put my books away
& wander in the fields
Just risen is the red round sun
Cocks from the roost doth loudly bawl
& house bee busily begun
Hums round the mortered wall

& while I take my staff to start
Birds sing among the eldern leaves
& fighting sparrows glad at heart
Chirp in the cottage eaves
Nor can I help but turn & view
Ere yet I close the creaking door
The sunbeams eager peeping through
Upon the sanded floor

The twilight streaks of lightsome grey
Hath from the eastern summit gone
& clouds cloathed in the pride of day
Put golden liverys on
The creeping sun large round & red
Yet higher hastens up & higher
Till blazing oer its cloudy bed
It shines a ball of fire

Cows now their morning meals pursue
The carthorse to its labour's sped
& sheep shake off the nightly dew
Just risen from their bed
Tha maids are out & many a smile
Are left them by the passing swain
Who as they lightly skip the stile
Will turn & smile again

All nightly things are on the rout
By daylights burning smiles betrayed
& gnats retreating from the sun
Fly dancing to the shade
The snail is stealing from the light
Where grass a welcome shelter weaves

& white moths shrink in cool delight
Behind the bowering leaves

The hares their fearful morsels eat
Till by a snufling dog descried
Then hastening to their snug retreat
They waited eventide
The rabbit bustled out of sight
Nor longer cropt each thymy hill
But seeks his den where gloomy night
Is kept imprisoned still

The walks that sweetest pleasure yields
When things appear so fresh & fair
Are when we wander round the fields
To breath the morning air
The fields like spring seem young & gay
The dewy trees & painted sky
& larks as sweetly as in May
Still whistle as they fly

The woods that oft my steps recieves
I cannot search for resting bowers
For when I touch the sleepy leaves
Dews patter down in showers
But I can range the green & share
The charms the pasture scene displays
Crooking down sheep tracks here & there
That lead a thousand ways

Bowing dewdropping by the stream
The flowers glow lively on the sight
Awaking from nights summer dream
As conscious of delight
Nor could I crop them in such hours
Without regret that I'd destroyed
A joy in my companion flowers
As sweet as I enjoyed

The stinking finweeds blushing bloom
Their pea like flowers appear so fair
That bees will to their bosoms come
& hope for honey there
For bumble bees ere flowers are dry

Will wake & brush the trembling dew
& drone as mellancholy bye
When dreams are proved untrue

While waving rushbeds winding through
I idly swing my staff about
To free their tasseled tops from dew
The leveret startles out
& now the lark starts from its nest
But not to sing—on thistle nigh
It perks in fear & prunes its breast
Till I have journeyed bye

The resting cow just turns its head
To stare then chews its cud again
The colt more timid leaves its bed
& shakes its shaggy main
The shoy sheep flye & faster still
The wet grass smoaking neath their flight
When shepherds urged their whistles shrill
& dogs appear in sight

Still there is joy that will not cease
Calm hovering oer the face of things
That sweet tranquility & peace
That morning ever brings
The shadows by the sun portrayed
Lye basking in the golden light
Een little hillocks stretch their shade
As if they loved the sight

The brook seemed purling sweeter bye
As freshened from the cooling light
& on its breast the morning sky
Smiles beautiful & bright
The pools still depth as night was bye
Warmed as to life in curling rings
Stirred by the touch of water flye
Or zephers gentle wings

& cows did on its margin lie
As blest as morn would never cease
& knapping horse grazed slowly bye
That added to its peace

No flies disturbed the herding boys
Save flies the summer water breeds
That harmless shared the mornings joys
& hummed among the weeds

Birds fluttered round the waters brink
Then perched their dabbled wings to dry
& swallows often stooped to drink
& twittered gladly bye
& on the brook banks rushy ridge
Larks sat the morning sun to share
& doves where ivy hides the bridge
Sing soothing dittys there

The leaves of ash & elms & willows
That skirt the pastures wildered way
Heaved to the breeze in gentle billows
Of mingled green & grey
—The birds the breeze—the milkers call
The brook that in the sun did glisten
Told morns delight that smiled on all
As one that loves to listen

O who can shun the lovely morning
The calms the crowds of beautious things
O wheres the soul that treats with scorning
The beauty morning brings
With dewdrops braided round her hair
& opening flowers her breast adorning
O wheres the soul that cannot share
The lovliness of morning

By hedgerow side & field & brook
I love to be its partner still
To turn each leaf of natures book
Where all may read as will
& he who loves it not destroys
His quiet & makes life a slave
His soul is dead to loves & joys
His own heart is their grave

The very boys appear to share
The joy of mornings lovely hours
In rapture running here & there

To stick their hats with flowers
Some loll them by a resting stile
To listen pleasing things around
Dove lark & bee & try the while
To imitate the sound

The shepherd muses oer his hook
& quiet as the morning seems
Or reads some wild mysterious book
On "fortunes moles & dreams"
While by his side as blest as he
His dog in peaceful slumber lies
Unwakened as he used to be
To watch the teazing flies

Rapt in delight I long have stood
Gazing on scenes that seem to smile
& now to view far field & wood
I climb this battered stile
There sails the puddock still & proud
Assailed at first by swopping crows
But soon it meets the morning cloud
& scorns such humble foes

The mist that round the distance bent
By woodland side & slopeing hill
Fled as each minute came & went
More far & further still
& the blue tinge which night renewed
Round the horisons fairey way
More faster than the eye pursued
Shrank unpercieved away

By leaning trees beneath the swail
For pleasing things I love to look
Or loll oer oak brigs guarding rail
That strideth oer the brook
To mark above the willow row
The painted windmills peeping sails
Seeming in its journey slow
Pleased with the easy gentle gales

& oft I sit me on the ground
Musing upon a neighbouring flower

157

Or watch the church clocks humming sound
To count the passing hour
Or mark the brook its journey take
In gentle curves round many a weed
Or hear the soft wind first awake
Among the rustling reed

TO P + + + +

Fair was thy bloom when first I met
Thy summers maiden blossom
& thou art fair & lovely yet
& dearer to my bosom
O thou wast once a wildling flower
All garden flowers excelling
& still I bless the happy hour
That led me to thy dwelling

Though nursed by field & brook & wood
& wild in every feature
Spring neer unsealed a fairer bud
Nor formed a blossom sweeter
& of all flowers the spring has met
& it has met with many
Thou art to me the fairest yet
& lovliest of any

Though ripening summers round thee bring
Buds to thy swelling bosom
That wait the cheering smiles of spring
To ripen into blossom
These buds shall added blessings be
To make our love sincerer
For as their flowers resemble thee
Theyll make thy memory dearer

& though thy bloom shall pass away
By winter overtaken
Thoughts of the past will charms display
& many joys awaken
When time shall every sweet remove
& blight thee on my bosom
Let beauty fade—to me & love
Thoult neer be out of blossom

159

EMMONSALES HEATH

In thy wild garb of other times
I find thee lingering still
Furze oer each lazy summit climbs
At natures easy will

Grasses that never knew a scythe
Waves all the summer long
& wild weed blossoms waken blythe
That ploughshares never wrong

Stern industry with stubborn pride
& wants unsatisfied
Still leaves untouched thy maiden soil
In its unsullied pride

The birds still find their summer shade
To build their nests agen
& the poor hare its rushy glade
To hide from savage men

Nature its family protects
In thy security
& blooms that love what man neglects
Find peaceful homes in thee

The wild rose scents thy summer air
& woodbines weave in bowers
To glad the swain sojourning there
& maidens gathering flowers

Creations steps ones wandering meets
Untouched by those of man
Things seem the same in such retreats
As when the world began

Furze ling & brake all mingling free
& grass forever green
All seem the same old things to be
As they have ever been

The brook oer such neglected ground
Ones weariness to sooth

160

Still wildly threads its lawless bounds
& chafes the pebble smooth

Crooked & rude as when at first
Its waters learned to stray
& from their mossy fountain birst
It washed itself a way

O who can pass such lovely spots
Without a wish to stray
& leave lifes cares a while forgot
To muse an hour away

Ive often met with places rude
Nor failed their sweet to share
But passed an hour with solitude
& left my blessing there

He that can meet the morning wind
& oer such places roam
Nor leave a lingering wish behind
To make their peace his home

His heart is dead to quiet hours
No love his mind employs
Poesy with him neer shares its flowers
Nor solitude its joys

O there are spots amid thy bowers
Which nature loves to find
Where spring drops round her earliest flowers
Uncheckt by winters wind

Where cowslips wake the childs supprise
Sweet peeping ere their time
Ere april spreads her dappled skyes
Mid mornings powdered rime

Ive stretched my boyish walks to thee
When maydays paths were dry
When leaves had nearly hid each tree
& grass greened ancle high

& mused the sunny hours away
& thought of little things
That childern mutter oer their play
When fancy trys its wings

Joy nursed me in her happy moods
& all lifes little crowd
That haunt the waters fields & woods
Would sing their joys aloud

I thought how kind that mighty power
Must in his splendour be
Who spread around my boyish hour
Such gleams of harmony

Who did with joyous rapture fill
The low as well as high
& made the pismires round the hill
Seem full as blest as I

Hopes sun is seen of every eye
The haloo that it gives
In natures wide & common sky
Cheers every thing that lives

HYMN TO SPRING

Thou virgin bliss the seasons bring
Thou yet beloved in vain
I long to hail thee gentle spring
& meet thy face again
That rose bud cheek that lit eye
Those locks of fairest hue
Which zephers wave each minute bye
& show thy smiles anew

O how I wait thy reign begun
To gladden earth & skys
When threatened with a warmer sun
The sullen winter flies
When songs are sung from every tree
When bushes bud to bowers
When plains a carpet spread for thee
& strew thy way with flowers

Ah I do long that day to see
When neer a fountain side
I loiter hours away with thee
With beauty gratified
To look upon those eyes of blue
Whose light is of the sky
& that unearthly face to view
Which love might deify

I long to press that glowing breast
Whose softness might suffice
A pillow for an angels rest
& still be paradise
& o I wait those smiles to see
To me to nature given
Smiles stolen from joys eternity
When mortals taste of heaven

O urge the surley winter bye
Nor let him longer live
Whose suns creep shyly down the sky
& grudge the light they give
O bring thy suns & brighter days
Which lover like delight

To hasten on their morning ways
& loath retire at night

O hasten on thou lovely spring
Bid winter frown in vain
Thy mantle oer thy shoulders fling
& choose an early reign
Thy herald flower in many a place
The daisey joins with me
While chill winds nip his crimpled face
He smiles in hopes of thee

Then come & while my heart is warm
To sing thy pleasures new
Led onward by thy lovely arm
I ll high me through the dew
Or meet thy noondays sober wind
Thy rearing flowers to see
& weave a wreath of those I find
To nature & to thee

VALENTINE TO MARY

This visionary theme is thine
From one who loves thee still
Tis writ to thee a Valentine
But call it what you will
No more as wont thy beaming eye
To voilets I compare
Nor talk about the lilys dye
To tell thee thou art fair

The time is past when hopes sweet will
First linked thy name with mine
& the fond muse with simple skill
Chose thee its Valentine
Though some may yet their powers employ
To wreath with flowers thy brow
With me thy loves a withered joy
With hope thourt nothing now

The all that youths fond spring esteems
Its blossoms pluckt in May
Are gone like flowers in summer dreams
& thoughts of yesterday
The heavenly dreams of early love
Youths spell has broken there
& left the aching heart to prove
That earth owns nought so fair

Spring flowers were fitting hopes young songs
To grace loves earliest vow
But withered ones that autumn wrongs
Are emblems meetest now
Their perished blooms that once were green
Hopes faded tale can tell
Of shadows were a sun hath been
& suits its memory well

Then why should I on such a day
Address a song to thee
When withered hope hath died away
& love no more can be
When blinded fate that still destroys
Hath rendered all as vain

165

& parted from the bosom joys
Twill never meet again

The substance of our joys hath been
Their flowers have faded long
But memory keeps the shadow green
& wakes this idle song
Then let esteem a welcome prove
That can t its place resign
& friendship take the place of love
To send a valentine

VERSES

Tho winter comes dreary
In frost & in snow
A sun shall come cheery
& bid them all go
The spring it shall greet with
Its songs & its showers
The summer shall meet with
Its dancing & flowers

But alas for the lover
Thats loved not again
No art can discover
A cure for the pain
Full dark is the token
Of pleasures adieu
The heart that is broken
No hopes can renew

The star falls in darkness
To be no more seen
& leaves a blank markless
Where splendour hath been
On the shore speedy dying
Noughts seen of the wave
So the heart for love dying
Sinks into the grave

THE HOLIDAY WALK

Come Eliza & Anna lay bye top & ball
& Freddy boy throw away cart & toys all
Look about for your hats & dispence with your play
We'll seek for the fields & be happy to day
Do but hark at the shouts of the boys by the school
As noisey & merry as geese in a pool
While the master himself is so sick of his thrall
That he laughs like the merriest child of them all
While they race with their shadows he joins in the fray
& leaps oer the "cat gallows" nimble as they
As glad to get out of his school in the sun
As a captive would be from his prison to run
The morning invites us to walk come along
Tis so sweet that the sparrow een tries at a song
The dews are all gone save amid the dark glooms
Neath the woods crowded leaves were the sun never comes
Nor need we regret that the dews linger there
For brambles defye us to come if we dare
& doubtless each poor little bird in the end
Is glad to consider the bramble its friend
For girls even often its dwelling destroys
& boys are so cruel birds cannot like boys
So we'll be contented to roam far away
Through bean fields in blossom & closes of hay
Do but look at those ducks how delighted they seem
All plashing & cleaning themselves in the stream
& the swallow that loves in black chimneys to sing
Will scarcely dart oer without washing his wing
Now were out of the town see the fields how they smile
So sweet that the boy climbs astride on the stile
To gaze round about him as much as to say
I should like to go where it pleased me to day
But poor little fellow he wishes in spite
Of his toil—for his sheep they want tending till night
Look here as we come in this cool narrow lane
How close martins pass us & pass us again
Darting on by the side of the hedges they go
As swift as an arrow shot out of a bow
The dust is all past which we met in the street
& the grass like a carpet spreads under our feet
See theres a fine Butterflye sits on that leaf
Aye you may go creeping as still as a thief

It can hear you & see you—see there up it flies
With wings like the rain bow youve seen in the skies
Yes yes you may run there it crosses the stream
As far out of reach as a joy in a dream
Aye now it delights ye to look at the sky
Those are hawks sailing proud as the clouds & as high
See there ones at rest hanging still even now
As fixed in the air as a bird on a bough
These are sweet sights in sooth but the milking maid sees
The sky every morning wear sweeter than these
When she hies to her cows while the sun large & round
Starts up like a table of fire from the ground
& she sees it so often she gives it no praise
Though some never saw it not once all their days
This morning I marked in what splendour he rose
Like a king of the east ere his journey he goes
His bed in the skys any fancy might trace
With a curtain of scarlet half hiding his face
Then as he rose up to his throne for a seat
It changed to a carpet of gold at his feet
Then as a majicians wand touched it there came
A dye oer the east of all hues ye can name
A dappled profusion of gold blue & red
Like pavements of rubies where angels may tread
A shadow een now of its splendour remains
Like an old ruined tapestry all blotches & stains
Giving lessons of grandeur & earthly parade
To think even heaven hath glories that fade
Nay sigh not at all you shall see bye & bye
The sun rise as oft as the milkmaid & I
Stop theres a whasps nest what a bustle & hum
Like legions of armies where danger is come
There they rush one by one in their jackets of yellow
Not one offers fight but he's backed by his fellow
So come on nor reach at that rose on the bower
We'll hazard no wounds for the sake of a flower
Heres the snail with his fine painted shell at his back
& theres one without in his jacket of black
The paths even covered with insects—each sort
Flock by crowds in the smiles of the morning to sport
Theres the cricket in brown & his couzin in green
The Grasshopper dancing & oer them is seen
The lady bird dressed like a hunter in red
Creeping out from the blossoms with whom she went bed

So good little girls now disturb not their play
& you Freddy stop till they hop far away
For to kill them in sport as a many folks will
& call it a pastime tis cruel & ill
As their lives are as sweet of enjoyment as ours
& they doat like yourselves upon sunshine & flowers
See yonders some boys all at swee in the cool
On the wood riding gate playing truant from school
How gladly they seek the fields freedom to play
To swee creaking gates & to roll in the hay
Mocking loud the wood ecchoes that answer again
In musical haloos so soft & so plain
That they no longer dread them as jiants or elves
But think them all boys fond of sport as themselves
& they shout in their pastimes to coax them away
From the woods gloomy arbours to join in their play
Now loves ye are weary I see by your walk
Well well heres a sweet cock of hay on the baulk
An ash hung with ivy too leans from the stile
So sit you down here & we ll rest us awhile
But not on that molehill for see what a mass
Of pismires are nimbling about in the grass
If you had crumbs to throw them theyed haul them away
& never seem weary the whole summers day
& if you sit on them as small as they are
Theyll sting you & teaze you so prythee beware
Do but look how the fields slope away from our eyes
Till the trees in the distance seem clouds in the skyes
A map spreads about us in greens of all stains
Dark woods paler meadows & fields varied grains
& look oer the gap of yon hedge & behold
Yon turnip lands seeming as littered with gold
Tis the charlock in blossom a troublesome weed
Yet a beautiful sight in the distance indeed
They are nought for a nosegay yet still in fine weather
You see what a show they make growing together
Aye yonder are steeples that catch on the eye
Like jiants of stone stretching up the blue sky
& windmills are sweeping their sails up & down
& cottages peeping all sunny & brown
See the cows grazing yonder & less quiet sheep
Some at feed & some chewing their cuds till they sleep
Thus the prospect in varied profusions abound
& spreadeth a beautiful picture around

Though there shines no old ruins for artists to prize
Nor mountains to thrust up their heads to the skyes
Yet as like Dewints pictures as nature can be
For nature owns no sweeter painter than he
Nay dont be alarmed & start up from the hay
Thats nought but a little mouse running away
& now she finds out we're not foes to destroy
Do but hear in the grass how she chitters for joy
No doubt in the beans nigh at hand may sojourn
Her childern awaiting her mothers return
See there where the willow bends over the brook
At our feet like an old shepherd over his crook
Neath its boughs Gnats & midges are still at their play
Like ball rooms of faireys all dancing away
Aye there in rich dress goes the great dragon flye
Like another proud thing buzzing scornfully bye
He scarce turns his head on their dancing & glee
& theyre full as carless of notice as he
O dont you my Anna be cruel & vain
The smallest of things are not strangers to pain
That long legged shepherd youve caught let him go
For he knows naught at all what you threaten no no
Though you tell him you'll kill both his son & his daughter
If he will not afford you a small drop of water
Your threats & your language he cant understand
Though he sheds tears for freedom while shut in your hand
& heres little Freddy crying "click clocking clay"
Poh—Lady birds know not the time of the day
Of "one oclock two oclock" no such a thing
So give it its freedom & let it take wing
Well now if your rested we'll wander again
Here the path strides the brook over closes of grain
So who's first to venture—come never see fear
Though the plank bends beneath no danger is near
Well if you are fearful we ll turn back & go
Where stepping stones ford oer a shallow below
Dangers seldom my childern so near as we think
& often seems far when we stand on the brink
As the runlet in shallows bawls loud & in deeps
Decietfully sinks into silence & sleeps
Do but try how delicious those bean blossoms smell
No flower in the garden delights me so well
Perfuming the nest of the Partridge that lies
Basking safe in the shadows their forrest supplies

& the hare heres a beaten path tracks her retreat
Feels timidly safe in her corn covered seat
On this mown baulk no doubt she oft ventures to play
When a grasshoppers rustle might fright her away
How sweet & how happy such places appear
Well indeed may you wish that our cottage was here
With the wild bees for neighbours the whole summer long
& the Lark ever near us a piping his song
With the beans in full blossom close up to our door
& cows in the distance at feed on the moor
& grasshoppers singing wherere we might roam
& partridges calling at night by our home
Where we might sit at eve in our parlour & see
The rabbit bob out from that old hollow tree
& hear from yon thicket so gloomy & deep
The sweet little nightingale sing us to sleep
Which we heard tother night—dont you reccolect now
When I clomb the wood stile to get each one a bough
How one sung "jug jug" & you all sung amain
"Jug jug" & laughed loud as it answered again
Aye aye I knew well such a beautiful song
Would not be so quickly forgot come along
For the day gets so hot you may well wish again
To meet with the coolness we left in the lane
Do but [look] at our shadows what strangers weve got
Those jiants that came with us first from our cot
Stalking on stride for stride in a pomp stirring mood
Nigh as tall as the oaks that lay peeled by the wood
Whose long legs might cross a brook ever so wide
& leap oer a hedge nay a house at a stride
Theyve left us & shrunk from our sight by degrees
To childern & dwarfs scarce as high as our knees
That as we go on shrink so close to our feet
As if they were glad to get out of the heat
Come here is the foot path that leads to the town
Dont stop tis so hot loves we cannot sit down
O I see what delights ye—aye climb on the stile
& look round about as ye wish for awhile
Those things that go sweeing away to the wind
Though the willows scarce move that are growing behind
Are the sails of the Mill—& indeed as you say
They follow each other like things in their play
Now dropping then rising their wearisome round
& seem where you stand to spring out of the ground

172

Yon shepherd boy doubtless thinks so as he lies
Lolling oer the gate gazing in happy supprise
See now they move slower the winds nearly still
& there comes the miller—look—out of his mill
To peep at the weather with meal powderd oer
More white then the dog rose in bloom by the door
See there goes the mower a sweeping away
& yon folks in the nook see are stacking of hay
Some loading some forking the grounds are alive
With their labour as busy as bees in a hive
Theres no one seems idle but this little boy
Who runs after butterflyes bawling for joy
& now he has run like a fox in the wheat
If the farmer came bye he would surely get beat
The partridge whirs up frit away from her nest
& the hare with the morning dew yet on her breast
Jumps away from his hustle & bustle & noise
Which he makes in the midst of his rapture & joys
Now singing & tearing up weeds of all sorts
Showy corn poppys shining like foxhunters coats
& bluecaps & cockleflowers no matter what
To make a gay garland to stick in his hat
& now he struts out what a gesture he wears
As proud of his colours as soldiers of theirs
& why may he not be as vain as the rest
Of proud folk were the proudest are baubles at best
—Yes summer indeed bringeth pleasure to all
That colt feels its freedom now loosed from its stall
& even this wearisome wayfaring ass
Can find on the common his bunches of grass
While round the warped camp neath yon bushes & trees
The gipseys lie basking themselves at their ease
& the gipsey boys shaking their rags to the sun
Are head over ears in their frolic & fun
Chasing barefoot along with their dogs by their side
Barking loud as the rabbits bob by them to hide
See there sit the swath summer lovers at play
Neath the shade of those broad spreading maples all day
Those brown tawney lasses with lips like a cherry
& hair full as dark as the autumn blackberry
The mole hillocks make them soft cushions for love
& the hedges in harbours hang blooming above
As blest as the rich who on sofas reposes
They toy neath the shades of wild woodbines & roses

—Now look at the sky it grows muddy with showers
& black snails are creeping about in the flowers
The daisey too look tis a good weather glass
It seems even now half asleep in the grass
& other flowers too like the sun on the wane
Are shutting their eyes & seem dreaming of rain
While that shepherd boy yonder is startled from sleep
Peeping up at the sky as he bawls to his sheep
No doubt he is seeking his hut by the hedge
All wattled with willows & covered with sedge
To lie on his bed of cut brakes & be dry
While the threatened approach of the storm lessens bye
Now I see you are glad to get sight of the town
See theres the old spire & below it look down
Our cottage is peeping aye now you see't plain
As if it was happy to find us again
& happy am I we're so nigh to the door
So run in & take to your play as before
Or rest in your chairs from the toils of the day
By the oak bough that blooms in the chimney so gay
See there waining sunbeams they twitter & fall
Through the diamond paned window to dance on the wall
The pictures seem smiling its glitter to court
& up jumps the kitten to join in the sport
Aye well may you say you are glad weve got home
For sweeter it seemeth the farther we roam
So now we'll sit down & enjoy at our ease
The rest leisure gives us & do as we please
Take your toys or read lessons & chatter between
Of the walk we have had & the things we have seen
& while you are pleasing or resting yourselves
I ll reach down a poet I love from the shelves
My Thompson or Cowper like flowers in their prime
That set not in closets to study & ryhme
But roamed out of doors for their verses that yield
A freshness like that which we left in the field
That sing both at once to the ear & the eye
& breath of the air & the grass & the sky
A music so sweet while we're hid from the rain
That we even seem taking our rambles again

MARY LEE

I have traced the valleys fair
In may mornings dewy air
My bonny Mary Lee
Wilt thou deign the wreath to wear
Gathered all for thee
They are not flowers of pride
For they graced the dingle side
Yet they grew in heavens smile
My gentle Mary Lee
Can they fear thy frowns the while
Though offered all by me

Heres the lily of the vale
That perfumed the morning gale
My fairey Mary Lee
All so spotless & so pale
Like thine own purity
& might I make it known
Tis an emblem of my own
Love—if I dare so name
My esteem for thee
Surely flowers can bear no blame
My bonny Mary Lee

Heres the violets modest blue
That neath awthorns hides from view
My gentle Mary Lee
Would show whose heart is true
While it thinks of thee
Though they chuse each lowly spot
The sun disdains them not
I m as lowly too indeed
My charming Mary Lee
So Ive brought these flowers to plead
& win a smile from thee

Heres a wild rose just in bud
Springs beauty in its hood
My bonny Mary Lee
Tis the first in all the wood
I could find for thee
Though a blush is scarcely seen

175

Yet it hides its worth within
Like my love for Ive no power
My angel Mary Lee
To speak unless the flower
Can plead excuse for me

Though they deck no princely halls
In bouquets for glittering balls
My gentle Mary Lee
Richer hues than painted walls
Might make them dear to thee
For the blue & laughing sky
Spreads a grander canopy
Than all wealths golden skill
My charming Mary Lee
Love would make them dearer still
That offers them to thee

My wreath of flowers are few
Yet no fairer drank the dew
My bonny Mary Lee
& may seem as trifles too
Yet not I hope to thee
Some may boast a richer prize
Under pride & wealths disguise
None a fonder offering bore
Then mine to thee
& can true love wish for more
Surely not Mary Lee

THE COTTAGER

True as the church clock hand the hour pursues
He plods about his toils & reads the news
& at the blacksmiths shop his hour will stand
To talk of "Lunun" as a foreign land
For from his cottage door in peace or strife
He neer went fifty miles in all his life
His knowledge with old notions still combined
Is twenty years behind the march of mind
He views new knowledge with suspicious eyes
& thinks it blasphemy to be so wise
Oer steams almighty tales he wondering looks
As witchcraft gleaned from old blackletter books
Life gave him comfort but denied him wealth
He toils in quiet & enjoys his health
He smokes a pipe at night & drinks his beer
& runs no scores on tavern screens to clear
He goes to market all the year about
& keeps one hour & never stays it out
Een at St Thomas tide old Rovers bark
Hails dapples trot an hour before its dark
He is a simple worded plain old man
Whose good intents take errors in their plan
Oft sentimental & with saddend vein
He looks on trifles & bemoans their pain
& thinks the angler mad & loudly storms
With emphasis of speech oer murdered worms
& hunters cruel—pleading with sad care
Pitys petition for the fox & hare
Yet feels self satisfaction in his woes
For wars crushed myriads of his slaughterd foes
He is right scrupelous in one pretext
& wholesale errors swallows in the next
He deems it sin to sing yet not to say
A song a mighty difference in his way
& many a moving tale in antique ryhmes
He has for christmass & such merry times
When Chevy chase his masterpiece of song
Is said so earnest none can think it long
Twas the old Vicars way who should be right
For the late Vicar was his hearts delight
& while at church he often shakes his head
To think what sermons the old vicar made

Downright orthodox that all the land
Who had their ears to hear might understand
But no such mighty learning meets his ears
He thinks it greek or latin which he hears
Yet church recieves him every sabbath day
& rain or snow he never keeps away
All words of reverence still his heart reveres
Low bows his head when Jesus meets his ears
& still he thinks it blasphemy as well
Such names without a capital to spell
In an old corner cupboard by the wall
His books are laid—though good in number small
His bible first in place—from worth & age
Whose grandsires name adorns the title page
& blank leaves once now filled with kindred claims
Display a worlds epitome of names
Parents & childern & grandchildern all
Memorys affections in the lists recall
& Prayer book next much worn though strongly bound
Proves him a churchman orthodox & sound
The "Pilgrims Progress" too & "Death of Abel"
Are seldom missing from his reading table
& prime old Tusser in his homely trim
The first of bards in all the world with him
& only poet which his leisure knows
—Verse deals in fancy so he sticks to prose
These are the books he reads & reads again
& weekly hunts the almanacks for rain
Here & no further learnings channels ran
Still neighbours prize him as the learned man
His cottage is a humble place of rest
With one spare room to welcome every guest
& that tall poplar pointing to the sky
His own hand planted when an idle boy
It shades his chimney while the singing wind
Hums songs of shelter to his happy mind
Within his cot the "largest ears of corn"
He ever found his picture frames adorn
Brave Granbys head De Grasses grand defeat
He rubs his hands & tells how Rodney beat
& from the rafters upon strings depend
Beanstalks beset with pods from end to end
Whose numbers without counting may be seen
Wrote on the Almanack behind the screen

Around the corner upon worsted strung
Pootys in wreaths above the cupboards hung
Memory at trifling incidents awakes
& there he keeps them for his childerns sakes
Who when as boys searched every sedgey lane
Traced every wood & shattered cloaths again
Roaming about on raptures easy wing
To hunt those very pooty shells in spring
& thus he lives too happy to be poor
While strife neer pauses at so mean a door
Low in the sheltered valley stands his cot
He hears the mountain storm—& feels it not
Winter & spring toil ceasing ere tis dark
Rests with the lamb & rises with the lark
Content is helpmate to the days employ
& care neer comes to steal a single joy
Time scarcely noticed turns his hair to grey
Yet leaves him happy as a child at play

NATURES MELODYS

THE MUSIC OF THE STORM

All nature owns in glory
The Lord & power of all
With everlasting story
& never ceasing call
The great "I am" emblazoned
Is seen of every eye
On natures humblest blossom
On thunders grandest sky

Man nature all upbraids him
Who stands in terror bye
She lauds the God that made him
Her sounds are "glorify"
Hark how the tempest sounding
Wings music through the air
& clouds like whales are bounding
To own his presence there

The sun whose splendid glory
Shamed darkness into flight
& told morns noble story
From whence he borrowed light
& now in gloomy splendours
God bids the tempests lour
How meekly he surrenders
To a superior power

All natures shining splendour
Withdraws her light awhile
Right willing to surrender
Her light till God shall smile
The earth the sky the ocean
Sun moon & stars & all
Pay natures grand devotion
& own their makers call

The woods are like a[n] ocean
All moving at his breath
Praise spreads the wild commotion
Around above beneath

The mighty oak is bending
In worship to his power
& in submission blending
Soft trembles every flower

Morns sky in dappled livery
A sea of happy isles
Heard thunders noble reverie
& now no longer smiles
The sky has lost its glory
The clouds their hues resign
& storms in splendid story
Owns god is all divine

Hark how the tempest groaning
Extolls his majesty
& echo gladly owning
In worship makes reply
More proud & yet more proudly
The tempest dares along
More loud & yet more loudly
The thunder wakes his song

A song of mighty praises
To him who reigns alone
Whose power all nature raises
In unison as one
The mountains burning crater
The valleys crowded sod
The forrests leafy nature
Are all the voice of God

Man hears & heedeth nothing
Man sees & turns aside
His thoughts such interests loathing
Are bound to scorn & pride
All else of Gods adornings
Great small & weak & strong
Attend to natures warnings
& thousands greet her song

THE CALM

Beneath my feet the very dust
Up with the wirlwinds summonds flies
To tell the doubting & the just
That even dust shall greet the skys
Beside my path the flowers & grass
In trembling joy their praises pay
Yet unobserving man goes bye
Nor gleans a lesson in his way

Though nature breaths in quiet moods
& wooes the heart in gentle ways
A sterner power with time intrudes
Shall waken all to fear & praise
When death shall rise on every eye
& blend his voice with every call
When all but natures debt shall die
& man the debtor pay for all

That day shall come & mighty storms
Each year its coming typifyes
Yet what are thunders dread alarms
To that shall bid the dead to rise
The wind the water fire & all
As actors in that dreadful play
Make ready in their parts to fall
Rehearsing portions every day

Yet man ordained in every scene
To act the first & chiefest part
Neglects to feel the part he's in
Nor gets a single page by heart
Although the stage be worlds destroyed
The curtains torn unpillared skyes
The actor man by God employed
To do his part of smiles or sighs
Life everlastingly enjoyed
Or pains unceasing sacrifice
—& I by idle things employed
Dread what the finale typifyes

THE SUMMER SHOWER

I love it well oercanopied in leaves
Of crowding woods to spend a quiet hour
& where the woodbine weaves
To list the summer shower

Brought by the south west wind that balm & bland
Breaths luscious coolness loved & felt by all
While on the uplifted hand
The rain drops gently fall

Now quickening on & on the pattering woods
Recieves the coming shower birds trim their wings
& in a joyful mood
The little woodchat sings

& blackbird squatting on her mortared nest
Safe hid in ivy & the pathless wood
Pruneth her sooty breast
& warms her downy brood

& little Pettichap like hurrying mouse
Keeps nimbling near my arbour round & round
Aye theres her oven house
Built nearly on the ground

Of woodbents withered straws & moss & leaves
& lined with downy feathers saftys joy
Dwells with the home she weaves
Nor fears the pilfering boy

The busy falling rain increases now
& sopping leaves their dripping moisture pour
& from each loaded bough
Fast falls the double shower

Weed climbing hedges banks & meeds unmown
Where rushy fringed brooklet easy curls
Look joyous while the rain
Strings their green suit[with] pearls

While from the crouching corn the weeding troop
Run hastily & huddling in a ring

Where the old willows stoop
Their ancient ballads sing

& gabble over wonders ceasless tale
Till from the southwest sky showers thicker come
Humming along the vale
& bids them hasten home

With laughing skip they stride the hasty brook
That mutters through the weeds untill it gains
A clear & quiet nook
To greet the dimpling rain

& on they drabble all in mirth not mute
Leaving their footmarks on the elting soil
Where print of sprawling foot
Stirs up a tittering smile

On beautys lips who slipping mid the crowd
Blushes to have her anckle seen so high
Yet inly feeleth proud
That none a fault can spy

Yet rudely followed by the meddling clown
Who passes vulgar gibes—the bashful maid
Lets go her folded gown
& pauses half afraid

To climb the stile before him till the dame
To quarrel half provoked assails the knave
& laughs him into shame
& makes him well behave

Birdnesting boys oertaken in the rain
Beneath the ivied maple bustling run
& wait in anxious pain
Impatient for the sun

& sigh for home yet at the pasture gate
The molehill tossing bull with straining eye
Seemeth their steps to wait
Nor dare they pass him bye

Till wearied out high over hedge they scrawl
To shun the road & through the wet grass roam
Till wet & draggled all
They fear to venture home

The plough team wet & dripping plashes home
& on the horse the ploughboy lolls along
Yet from the wet grounds come
The loud & merry song

Now neath the leafy arch of dripping bough
That loaded trees form oer the narrow lane
The horse released from plough
Naps the moist grass again

Around their blanket camps the gipseys still
Heedless of showers while black thorns shelter round
Jump oer the pasture hills
In many an idle bound

From dark green clumps among the dripping grain
The lark with sudden impulse starts & sings
& mid the smoaking rain
Quivers her russet wings

A joy inspiring calmness all around
Breaths a refreshing sense of strengthening power
Like that which toil hath found
In sundays leisure hour

When spirits all relaxed heartsick of toil
Seeks out the pleasant woods & shadowy dells
& where the fountain boils
Lye listening distant bells

Amid the yellow furze the rabbits bed
Labour hath hid his tools & oer the heath
Hies to the milking shed
That stands the oak beneath

& there he wiles the pleasant shower away
Filling his mind with store of happy things
Rich crops of corn & hay
& all that plenty brings

185

The crampt horison now leans on the ground
Quiet & cool & labours hard employ
Ceases while all around
Falls a refreshing joy

TO CONTENT

Cheerful content thy home be mine
Do not my suit disdain
They who prefer the worlds to thine
Shall find it false & vain
From broken hopes & storms I fly
To hide me in thy peaceful sky

The flatterers meet with smiles
The cunning find their friends
Whoso without makes pilgrimage
Shall meet but small amends
As childern they who in the sun
Seek flowers in winter & find none

Some cringe to menial slaves
Some worship haughty power
Some bend the knee to knaves
The price of earthly dower
Which they who were not taught to pay
May see & empty turn away

Earths pleasure is to flatter
Lifes love is but to hate
To praise what they in heart abuse
Alas in church & state
& whoso makes not this their game
Shall keep their wants & shun the shame

Thus flattery findeth friends
In every grade & state
Thus telling truth offends
The lowly & the great
Yet truth at last shall bloom & rise
When flatterys folly fades & dies

Prides pomps are shadows all
Mere wealth is honours toys
Whose merits oft are small
Whose praise but empty noise
Rainbows upon the skys of May
Fade soon but scarce so soon as they

Then sweet content thy home be mine
If sorrows should pursue
Thoult shake them from those smiles of thine
As morning does the dew
& as thoughts broken hopes decay
My heart shall struggle & be gay

As hopes from earth shall dissapear
With thee I ll not despair
For thou canst look at heaven & hear
The vagrant calling there
& see her smile & sweetly see
The loss she met was gain to me

LOVE & MEMORY

Thou art gone the dark journey
That leaves no returning
Tis fruitless to mourn thee
But who can help mourning
To think of the life
That did laugh on thy brow
In the beautiful past
Left so desolate now

When youth seemed immortal
So sweet did it weave
Heavens haloo around thee
Earths hopes to decieve
Thou fairest & dearest
Where many were fair
To my heart thou art nearest
Though this name is but there

The nearer the fountain
More pure the stream flows
& sweeter to fancy
The bud of the rose
& now thourt in heaven
More pure is the birth
Of thoughts that wake of thee
Than ought upon earth

As a bud green in spring
As a rose blown in June
Thy beauty looked out
& departed as soon
Heaven saw thee too fair
For earths tennants of clay
& ere age did thee wrong
Thou wert summoned away

I know thou art happy
Why in grief need I be
Yet I am & the more so
To feel its for thee
For thy presence possest
As thy abscence destroyed

The most that I loved
& the all I enjoyed

So I try to seek pleasure
But vainly I try
Now joys cup is drained
& hopes fountain is dry
I mix with the living
Yet what do I see
Only more cause for sorrow
In loosing of thee

The year has its winter
As well as its May
So the sweetest must leave us
& the fairest decay
Suns leave us to night
& their light none may borrow
So joy retreats from us
Overtaken by sorrow

The sun greets the spring
& the blossom the bee
The grass the blea hill
& the leaf the bare tree
But suns nor yet seasons
As sweet as they be
Shall ever more greet me
With tidings of thee

The voice of the cuckoo
Is merry at noon
& the song of the nightingale
Gladdens the moon
But the gayest to day
May be saddest to morrow
& the loudest in joy
Sink the deepest in sorrow

For the lovely in death
& the fairest must die
Fall once & for ever
Like stars from the sky
So in vain do I mourn thee

I know its in vain
Who would wish thee from joy
To earths troubles again

Yet thy love shed upon me
Life more then mine own
& now thou art from me
My being is gone
Words know not my grief
Thus without thee to dwell
Yet in one I felt all
When life bade thee farewell

THE FALLEN ELM

Old elm that murmured in our chimney top
The sweetest anthem autumn ever made
& into mellow whispering calms would drop
When showers fell on thy many coloured shade
& when dark tempests mimic thunder made
While darkness came as it would strangle light
With the black tempest of a winter night
That rocked thee like a cradle to thy root
How did I love to hear the winds upbraid
Thy strength without—while all within was mute
It seasoned comfort to our hearts desire
We felt thy kind protection like a friend
& edged our chairs up closer to the fire
Enjoying comforts that was never penned
Old favourite tree thoust seen times changes lower
Though change till now did never injure thee
For time beheld thee as her sacred dower
& nature claimed thee her domestic tree
Storms came & shook thee many a weary hour
Yet stedfast to thy home thy roots hath been
Summers of thirst parched round thy homely bower
Till earth grew iron—still thy leaves was green
The childern sought thee in thy summer shade
& made their play house rings of sticks & stone
The mavis sang & felt himself alone
While in thy leaves his early nest was made
& I did feel his happiness mine own
Nought heeding that our friendship was betrayed
Friend not inanimate—though stocks & stones
There are & many formed of flesh & bones
Thou owned a language by which hearts are stirred
Deeper then by a feeling cloathed in words
& speakest now whats known of every tongue
Language of pity & the force of wrong
What cant assumes what hypocrites will dare
Speaks home to truth & shows it what they are
I see a picture which thy fate displays
& learn a lesson from thy destiny
Self interest saw thee stand in freedoms ways
So thy old shadow must a tyrant be
Thoust heard the knave abusing those in power
Bawl freedom loud & then opress the free

Thoust sheltered hypocrites in many a shower
That when in power would never shelter thee
Thoust heard the knave supply his canting powers
With wrongs illusions when he wanted friends
That bawled for shelter when he lived in showers
& when clouds vanished made thy shade amends
With axe at root he felled thee to the ground
& barked of freedom—O I hate the sound
Time hears its visions speak & age sublime
Had made thee a deciple unto time
—It grows the cant term of enslaving tools
To wrong another by the name of right
It grows the liscence of oerbearing fools
To cheat plain honesty by force of might
Thus came enclosure—ruin was its guide
But freedoms clapping hands enjoyed the sight
Though comforts cottage soon was thrust aside
& workhouse prisons raised upon the scite
Een natures dwellings far away from men
The common heath became the spoilers prey
The rabbit had not where to make his den
& labours only cow was drove away
No matter—wrong was right & right was wrong
& freedoms bawl was sanction to the song
—Such was thy ruin music making elm
The rights of freedom was to injure thine
As thou wert served so would they overwhelm
In freedoms name the little that is mine
& there are knaves that brawl for better laws
& cant of tyranny in stronger powers
Who glut their vile unsatiated maws
& freedoms birthright from the weak devours

193

THE OLD SHEPHERD

Tis pleasant to bear reccolections in mind
Of joys that time hurrys away
To look back on smiles that have past like the wind
& compare them with frowns of to day
Twas the joy of old Robin forsooth
Oer the past with fond pleasure to dwell
To recount the fond loves of his joys & his youth
& days of lost pleasures to tell

"Tis now many years" like a child he would say
"Since I joined in the sports of the green
Since I tied up the flowers for the garlands of may
& danced with the holiday queen
Reccolections look backward in sorrowful pride
Reccolections look forward in tears
To the past when my happiness withered & died
& the present dull desolate years"

"I love to be counting while sitting alone
With many a heart aching sigh
How many a season has rapidly flown
& springs with their summers gone bye
Since Susan the pride of the village was deemed
To whom youths affections I gave
Whom I led to the church & beloved & esteemed
& followed in grief to the grave

Lifes changes for many hours musings supply
How the past & the present appear
To mark how a few passing years hurry bye
When nothing is left as it where
The youth that with me to mans summer did bloom
Have dwindled away to old men
& maidens like flowers of the spring have made room
For many new blossoms since then

I have lived to see all but lifes sorrows pass bye
Leaving changes & pains & decay
Where nought is the same but the wide spreading sky
& the sun that awakens the day
The green where I tended my sheep when a boy
Has yielded its pride to the plough

& the shades where my infancy revelled in joy
The axe has left desolate now

Yet a bush lingers still that invites me to stop
What heart can such whimsies withstand
Where Susan once saw a birds nest in its top
& I reached her the eggs with my hand
& so long since the day I remember it well
It has stretched to a sizable tree
& the birds yearly come in its branches to dwell
As far from a jiant as me

On a favourite spot by the side of a brook
When Susan was just in her prime
A ripe bunch of nutts from her apron she took
& planted them close by my side
It has grown up with years & on many a bough
Groweth nutts like its parent agen
Where shepherds no doubt have oft sought them ere now
To please other susans since then

The joys that I knew when my youth was in prime
Like a dream thats half ended is oer
& the faces I knew in that changable time
Are seen with the living no more
I have lived to see friends that I loved pass away
With the pleasures their company gave
I have lived to see love with my susan decay
& the grass growing green on her grave

Poor Rover the mate of my youths summer day
That came to my whistle with pride
That shared the first years of my labour & play
Grew old in my friendship & died
& this old friend that now lyeth down by my feet
Looks as old as his master to be
Yet when the past scenes of my life I repeat
He even seems a new comer to me

Thus oft oer his staff the old shepherd would bend
Recounting in sorrowful pride
The things of his youth while some young shepherd friend
Stood to listen the tales by his side—
The pleasures of youth when too late we esteem

When its follys no longer engage
When the beautiful past like a midsummer dream
Looks green through the winter of age

NAPOLEON

The heroes of the present & the past
Were puny vague & nothingness to thee
Thou grasped a span almighty to the last
& strained for glory when thy die was cast
That little island on the mighty sea
Was but a dust spot in a lake thy mind
Swept space as shoreless as eternity
Thy jiant powers outstript this gaudy age
Of heroes & as looking at the sun
Gazing upon thy greatness made them blind
To merits that had adoration won
In olden times—for leaving kings behind
The world was but a comma on thy page
Of victorys—& fame a crowded mind
That found no room such greatness to presage
Thy prophets now are a superior kind
To friends or enemies—for natures eye
Sweeps over space great shadows to reclaim
& time—thy fate thy monument & fame
Links thee with names that cannot fade or die

SPORT IN THE MEADOWS

Maytime is to the meadows coming in
& cowslap peeps have gotten eer so big
& water blobs & all their golden kin
Crowd round the shallows by the striding brig
Daisys & buttercups & lady smocks
Are all abouten shining here & there
Nodding about their gold & yellow locks
Like morts of folken flocking at a fair
The sheep & cows are crowding for a share
& snatch the blossoms in such eager haste
That basket bearing childern running there
Do think within their hearts theyll get them all
& hoot & drive them from their gracless waste
As though there wa'n't a cowslap peep to spare
—For they want some for tea & some for wine
& some to maken up a cuckaball
To throw accross the garlands silken line
That reaches oer the street from wall to wall
—Good gracious me how merrily they fare
One sees a fairer cowslap then the rest
& off they shout—the foremost bidding fair
To get the prize—& earnest half & jest
The next one pops her down—& from her hand
Her basket falls & out her cowslaps all
Tumble & litter there—the merry band
In laughing friendship round about her fall
To helpen gather up the littered flowers
That she no loss may mourn—& now the wind
In frolic mood among the merry hours
Wakens with sudden start & tosses off
Some untied bonnet on its dancing wings
Away they follow with a scream & laugh
& aye the youngest ever lags behind
Till on the deep lakes very brink it hings
They shout & catch it & then off they start
To chase for cowslaps merry as before
& each one seems so anxious at the heart
As they would even get them all & more
One climbs a molehill for a bunch of may
One stands on tiptoe for a linnets nest
& pricks her hand & throws her flowers away
& runs for plantin leaves to have it drest

198

So do they run abouten all the day
& teaze the grass hid larks from getting rest
—Scarce give they time in their unruly haste
To tie a shoestring that the grass unties
& thus they run the meadows bloom to waste
Till even comes & dulls their phantasys
When one finds losses out to stifle smiles
Of silken bonnet strings—& uthers sigh
Oer garments renten clambering over stiles
Yet in the morning fresh afield they hie
Bidding the last days troubles all good bye
When red pied cow again their coming hears
& ere they clap the gate she tosses up
Her head & hastens from the sport she fears
The old yoe calls her lamb nor cares to stoop
To crop a cowslap in their company
Thus merrily the little noisey troop
Along the grass as rude marauders hie
For ever noisey & forever gay
While keeping in the meadows holiday

WILD BEES

These childern of the sun which summer brings
As pastoral minstrels in her merry train
Pipe rustic ballads upon busy wings
& glad the cotters quiet toils again
The white nosed bee that bores its little hole
In mortared walls & pipes its symphonies
& never absent couzin black as cole
That indian like bepaints its little thighs
With white & red bedight for holiday
Right earlily a morn do pipe & play
& with their legs stroke slumber from their eyes
& aye so fond they of their singing seem
That in their holes abed at close of day
They still keep piping in their honey dreams
& larger ones that thrum on ruder pipe
Round the sweet smelling closen & rich woods
Where tawney white & red flushed clover buds
Shine bonnily & beanfields blossom ripe
Shed dainty perfumes & give honey food
To these sweet poets of the summer field
Me much delighting as I stroll along
The narrow path that hay laid meadow yields
Catching the windings of their wandering song
The black & yellow bumble first on wing
To buzz among the sallows early flowers
Hiding its nest in holes from fickle spring
Who stints his rambles with her frequent showers
& one that may for wiser piper pass
In livery dress half sables & half red
Who laps a moss ball in the meadow grass
& hurds her stores when april showers have fled
& russet commoner who knows the face
Of every blossom that the meadow brings
Starting the traveller to a quicker pace
By threatening round his head in many rings
These sweeten summer in their happy glee
By giving for her honey melodie

THE NIGHTINGALES NEST

Up this green woodland ride lets softly rove
& list the nightingale—she dwelleth here
Hush let the wood gate softly clap—for fear
The noise might drive her from her home of love
For here Ive heard her many a merry year
At morn & eve nay all the live long day
As though she lived on song—this very spot
Just where that old mans beard all wildly trails
Rude arbours oer the rode & stops the way
& where that child its blue bell flowers hath got
Laughing & creeping through the mossy rails
There have I hunted like a very boy
Creeping on hands & knees through matted thorns
To find her nest & see her feed her young
& vainly did I many hours employ
All seemed as hidden as a thought unborn
& where these crimping fern leaves ramp among
The hazels underboughs—Ive nestled down
& watched her while she sung—& her renown
Hath made me marvel that so famed a bird
Should have no better dress then russet brown
Her wings would tremble in her extacy
& feathers stand on end as'twere with joy
& mouth wide open to release her heart
Of its out sobbing songs—the happiest part
Of summers fame she shared—for so to me
Did happy fancies shapen her employ
But if I touched a bush or scarcely stirred
All in a moment stopt—I watched in vain
The timid bird had left the hazel bush
& at a distance hid to sing again
Lost in a wilderness of listening leaves
Rich extacy would pour its luscious strain
Till envy spurred the emulating thrush
To start less wild & scarce inferior songs
For cares with him for half the year remain
To damp the ardour of his speckled breast
While nightingales to summers life belongs
& naked trees & winters nipping wrongs
Are strangers to her music & her rest
Her joys are evergreen her world is wide
—Hark there she is as usual lets be hush

For in this black thorn clump if rightly guest
Her curious house is hidden—part aside
These hazel branches in a gentle way
& stoop right cautious neath the rustling boughs
For we will have another search to day
& hunt this fern strown thorn clump round & round
& where this seeded woodgrass idly bows
We'll wade right through it is a likely nook
In such like spots & often on the ground
Theyll build where rude boys never think to look
Aye as I live her secret nest is here
Upon this white thorn stulp—I've searched about
For hours in vain—there put that bramble bye
Nay trample on its branches & get near
—How subtle is the bird she started out
& raised a plaintive note of danger nigh
Ere we were past the brambles & now near
Her nest she sudden stops—as choaking fear
That might betray her home—so even now
We'll leave it as we found it—safetys guard
Of pathless solitudes shall keep it still
See there shes sitting on the old oak bough
Mute in her fears—our presence doth retard
Her joys & doubt turns every rapture chill
   Sing on sweet bird may no worse hap befall
Thy visions then the fear that now decieves
We will not plunder music of its dower
Nor turn this spot of happiness to thrall
For melody seems hid in every flower
That blossoms near thy home—these harebells all
Seems bowing with the beautiful in song
& gaping cuckoo with its spotted leaves
Seems blushing of the singing it has heard
How curious is the nest no other bird
Uses such loose materials or weaves
Their dwellings in such spots—dead oaken leaves
Are placed without & velvet moss within
& little scraps of grass—& scant & spare
Of what seems scarce materials down & hair
For from mans haunts she seemeth nought to win
Yet nature is the builder & contrives
Homes for her childerns comfort even here
Where solitudes deciples spend their lives
Unseen save when a wanderer passes near

That loves such pleasant places—Deep adown
The nest is made an hermits mossy cell
Snug lies her curious eggs in number five
Of deadened green or rather olive brown
& the old prickly thorn bush guards them well
& here we'll leave them still unknown to wrong
As the old woodlands legacy of song

VASCO NUNEZ ON HIS ENEMIES
AFTER READING WASHINGTON IRVINGS
LIVES OF THE EARLY NAVIGATORS

A cloud is cast about me & the spell
Of evil tongues gloom round me like a hell
& shall their falshoods triumph & shall I
See fames sun wither in its summer sky
If so so be it—the eternal doom
of wrath & vengance on my side shall come
& for the truths compared to lies though few
Fate give them credit—hell should have its due
& for their lies in numberless array
That eat the heart hopes of my fame away
Time curse them with the curses of thy powers
Till pains eternitys grow out of hours
& hell itself in anguish so untried
Cries out time spare them—hell is satisfied
Yet spare their memories like a thunder sky
Wrap them in living flames & never let them die

INSECTS

Thou tiney loiterer on the barleys beard
& happy unit of a numerous herd
Of playfellows the laughing summer brings
Mocking the sunshine in their glittering wings
How merrily they creep & run & flye
No kin they bear to labours drudgery
Smoothing the velvet of the pink hedge rose
& where they flye for dinner no one knows
The dewdrops feed them not—they love the shine
Of noon whose sun may bring them golden wine
All day theyre playing in their sunday dress
Till night goes sleep & they can do no less
Then in the heath bells silken hood they flie
& like to princes in their slumber lie
From coming night & dropping dews & all
In silken beds & roomy painted hall
So happily they spend their summer day
Now in the cornfields now the new mown hay
One almost fancys that such happy things
In coloured hoods & richly burnished wings
Are fairy folk in splendid masquerade
Disguised through fear of mortal folk affraid
Keeping their merry pranks a mystery still
Lest glaring day should do their secrets ill

OLD FEELINGS

It did delight me—& delights me still
To make a summer seat upon a hill
Shielded from sun & wind by little bush
To list the song & not to start the thrush
Then rested down a pleasant path to roam
Through fields where peace is never found from home
& woods where woodbines dangle in the boughs
Daring the boys to reach them tending cows
Who often aided by a treacherous stile
Climb & destroy them in their idle toil
Dragging them down & spoiling hedgrow bowers
Singing more loud when they possess the flowers
& roads where clover bottles swarm full blown
Both red & white as thick as they were sown
Round which the bees go buzzing with delight
Following rich joy thats never out of sight
Then mark a clump of sheep & bye & bye
A brindled cow among the rushes lie
Now fresh ploughed lands seen through the gappy lane
Where peeps the spire that beckons home again
While oer the wooden brig that starts supprise
A footstep hastens & a morehen flies
& then a tripping maiden skips the stiles
Who speaks in blushes & represses smiles
So sweet—one turns half round to look agen
To see if she be handsome fair or plain
& if she be a woman in her mind
She must be fair—& though a savage kind
& thus we turn to praise—who questions why
Ask thine own heart when beauty passes bye

BUSHY CLOSE

There is a thicket of familiar face
A little thicket green on summers morn
Soon as the largest—tis a quiet place
Thick set with foulroyce privet & blackthorn
So thickly set that birdboys cannot trace
Its mysterys or climb its little trees
Unless they creep upon their hands & knees
As I have crept full many hours away
To hunt for nests & wood flowers—for in these
My boyish heart was living—woods & vales
Made up my being—all the live long May
When leisure left me did I list the tales
Of shepherds & go nesting far away
& in this little spot the nightingales
Did sing so many all the night & day
I thought that all did to this thicket come
& on through mossy roots so eager on
I crept—the fox rushed up & left his lair
The first time danger seemed so near his home
But as for nightingales there seemed not one
All stopt their song as if no bird was there
& when I left my teazing search as vain
They teazed me with their singing all again
& for the sake of feelings witnessed then
I often in the summer morning fare
To see that little "bushy close" agen
& walk its little riding full of sloughs
& elting footmarks of the pastoral cows
Who through the hedges broken gaps intrude
& in the woodlands browze in happy mood
Seeming as they themselves loved melody
& the sweet woodland shadows well as me
So in these spots that memory makes divine
I dream of happiness & call it mine

THE MOORHENS NEST

O poesys power thou overpowering sweet
That renders hearts that love thee all unmeet
For this rude world its trouble & its care
Loading the heart with joys it cannot bear
That warms & chills & burns & bursts at last
Oer broken hopes & troubles never past
I pay thee worship at a rustic shrine
& dream oer joys I still imagine mine
I pick up flowers & pebbles & by thee
As gems & jewels they appear to me
I pick out pictures round the fields that lie
In my minds heart like things that cannot die
Like picking hopes & making friends with all
Yet glass will often bear a harder fall
As bursting bottles loose the precious wine
Hopes casket breaks & I the gems resign
Pain shadows on till feelings self decays
& all such pleasures leave me is their praise
& thus each fairy vision melts away
Like evening landscapes from the face of day
Till hope returns with aprils dewy reign
& then I start & seek for joys again
& pick her fragments up to hurd anew
Like fancy-riches pleasure loves to view
& these associations of the past
Like summer pictures in a winter blast
Renews my heart to feelings as the rain
Falls on the earth & bids it thrive again
Then een the fallow fields appear so fair
The very weeds make sweetest gardens there
& summer there puts garments on so gay
I hate the plough that comes to dissaray
Her holiday delights—& labours toil
Seems vulgar curses on the sunny soil
& man the only object that distrains
Earths garden into deserts for his gains
Leave him his schemes of gain—tis wealth to me
Wild heaths to trace—& not their broken tree
Which lightening shivered—& which nature tries
To keep alive for poesy to prize
Upon whose mossy roots my leisure sits
To hear the birds pipe oer their amorous fits

Though less beloved for singing then the taste
They have to choose such homes upon the waste
Rich architects—& then the spots to see
How picturesque their dwellings make them be
The wild romances of the poets mind
No sweeter pictures for their tales can find
& so I glad my heart & rove along
Now finding nests—then listening to a song
Then drinking fragrance whose perfuming cheats
Tinges lifes sours & bitters into sweets
That heart stirred fragrance when the summers rain
Lays the road dust & sprouts the grass again
Filling the cracks up on the beaten paths
& breathing insence from the mowers swaths
Insence the bards & prophets of old days
Met in the wilderness to glad their praise
& in these summer walks I seem to feel
These bible pictures in their essence steal
Around me—& the ancientness of joy
Breath from the woods till pleasures even cloy
Yet holy breathing manna seemly falls
With angel answers if a trouble calls
& then I walk & swing my stick for joy
& catch at little pictures passing bye
A gate whose posts are two old dotterel trees
A close with molehills sprinkled oer its leas
A little footbrig with its crossing rail
A wood gap stopt with ivy wreathing pale
A crooked stile each path crossed spinny owns
A brooklet forded by its stepping stones
A wood bank mined with rabbit holes—& then
An old oak leaning oer a badgers den
Whose cave mouth enters neath the twisted charms
Of its old roots & keeps it safe from harms
Pickaxes spades & all its strength confounds
When hunted foxes hide from chasing hounds
—Then comes the meadows where I love to see
A floodwashed bank support an aged tree
Whose roots are bare—yet some with foothold good
Crankle & spread & strike beneath the flood
Yet still its leans as safer hold to win
On tother side & seems as tumbling in
While every summer finds it green & gay
& winter leaves it safe as did the may

209

Nor does the morehen find its safety vain
For on its roots their last years homes remain
& once again a couple from the brood
Seek their old birth place & in safetys mood
Lodge there their flags & lay—though danger comes
It dares & tries & cannot reach their homes
& so they hatch their eggs & sweetly dream
On their shelfed nests that bridge the gulphy stream
& soon the sutty brood from fear elopes
Where bulrush forrests give them sweeter hopes
Their hanging nest that aids their wishes well
Each leaves for water as it leaves the shell
& dive & dare & every gambol trie
Till they themselves to other scenes can fly

PEWITS NEST

Accross the fallow clods at early morn
I took a random track where scant & spare
The grass & nibbled leaves all closely shorn
Leaves a burnt flat all bleaching brown & bare
Where hungry sheep in freedom range forlorn
& neath the leaning willow & odd thorn
& molehill large that vagrant shade supplies
They batter round to shun the teazing flies
Trampling smooth places hard as cottage floors
Where the time-killing lonly shepherd boys
Whose summer homes are ever out of doors
Their chockholes form & chalk their marble ring
& make their clay taws at the bubbling spring
&in their rangling sport & gambling joys
They straine their clocklike shadows—when it cloys
To guess the hour that slowly runs away
& shorten sultry turmoil with their play
Here did I roam while veering overhead
The Pewet whirred in many whewing rings
& "chewsit" screamed & clapped her flapping wings
To hunt her nest my rambling steps was led
Oer the broad baulk beset with little hills
By moles long formed & pismires tennanted
As likely spots—but still I searched in vain
When all at once the noisey birds were still
& on the lands a furrowed ridge between
Chance found four eggs of dingy dirty green
Deep blotched with plashy spots of jockolate stain
Their small ends inward turned as ever found
As though some curious hand had laid them round
Yet lying on the ground with nought at all
Of soft grass withered twitch & bleached weed
To keep them from the rain storms frequent fall
& here she broods on her unsavory bed
When bye & bye with little care & heed
Her young with each a shell upon its head
Run after their wild parents restless cry
& from their own fears tiney shadows run
Neath clods & stones to cringe & snugly lie
Hid from all sight but the all seeing sun
Till never ceasing danger seemeth bye

THE YELLOW WAGTAILS NEST

Upon an edding in a quiet nook
We double down choice places in a book
& this I noted as a pleasant scene
Hemmed in all round with barleys juicey green
While in its clover grass at holiday
A broken plough as leisures partner lay
A pleasant bench among the grass & flowers
For merry weeders in their dinner hours
From fallow fields released & hot turmoil
It nestled like a thought forgot by toil
& seemed so picturesque a place for rest
I een dropt down to be a minutes guest
& as I bent me for a flower to stoop
A little bird cheeped loud & fluttered up
The grasses tottered with their husky seeds
That ramped beside the plough with ranker weeds
I looked— & there a snug nest deep & dry
Of roots & twitches entertained my eye
& six eggs sprinkled oer with spots of grey
Lay snug as comforts wishes ever lay
The yellow wagtail fixed its dwelling there
Sheltered from rainfalls by the shelving share
That leaned above it like a sheltering roof
From rain & wind & tempest comfort proof
Such safety-places little birds will find
Far from the cares & help of human kind
For nature is their kind protector still
To chuse their dwellings furthest off from ill
So thought I—sitting on that broken plough
While evenings sunshine gleamed upon my brow
So soft so sweet—& I so happy then
Felt life still eden from the haunts of men
& in the brook-pond waters spread below
Where misty willows wavered too & fro
The setting sun shed such a golden hue
I almost felt the poets fables true
& fashioned in my minds creating eye
Dryads & nymphs like beautys dreams go bye
From the rich arbours of the distant wood
To taste the spring & try its golden flood
Thus pleasures to the fancy often shine
Truest when false when fables most divine

& though each sweet consception soon decays
We feel such pleasures after many days

TO + + + + ON NEWYEARS DAY

A new years welcome lovely maid
Awakes the poets song
Be not of moral truths afraid
Nor deem the lesson wrong
Though newyears still their welcomes bring
& hails thy blooming hour
& on the green lap of the spring
Leaves thee its fairest flower

The withered year had youth & pride
As thy unclouded joy
But the today though deified
To morrow shall destroy
& sweet as is thy lovely bloom
Of mingled white & red
A days in waiting yet to come
Shall find that beauty fled

Bind not thy heart to things so frail
A worshipher of pride
Let choice of better things prevail
& meaner ones deride
As fair as is that lovely bloom
Thy witching youth puts on
A frowning year is yet to come
Shall find its blossom gone

The withered year saw many flowers
As fair as thou art seen
That now are lost to suns & showers
With blossoms that have been
Then live from pride & folly free
& wear an angels bosom
& when the last new year shall be
Live an unfading blossom

ON SEEING A BEAUTIFUL STATUE

Thou lovely shade of heavenly birth
Aught else thou cannot be
The copy of the loves on earth
Were never types of thee
Where is the face can looks impart
So heavenly born as thine
Rude nature tamed with studied art
Owns nothing so divine

Thou type of beautys reigning flower
To form thee thus was given
A soul that spurned at earthly power
& grasped the fire of heaven
Of faded Greece the Goddess still
Formed from eternity
T'were hard to deem it heathen-ill
To worship such as thee

For love might yet with bended knee
Urge its promethian prayer
& worship in its extacy
The soul thought kindles there
Beautys the type of heaven above
Where sinless praise is given
Nor is it vain for earth to love
Aught that resembles heaven

THE FLITTING

Ive left mine own old home of homes
Green fields & every pleasant place
The summer like a stranger comes
I pause & hardly know her face
I miss the hazels happy green
The bluebells quiet hanging blooms
Where envys sneer was never seen
Where staring malice never comes

I miss the heath its yellow furze
Molehills & rabbit tracts that lead
Through beesom ling & teazle burrs
That spread a wilderness indeed
The woodland oaks & all below
That their white powdered branches shield
The mossy paths—the very crow
Croaks music in my native field

I sit me in my corner chair
That seems to feel itself from home
& hear bird-music here & there
From awthorn hedge & orchard come
I hear but all is strange & new
—I sat on my old bench in June
The sailing puddocks shrill "peelew"
Oer royce wood seemed a sweeter tune

I walk adown the narrow lane
The nightingale is singing now
But like to me she seems at loss
For royce wood & its shielding bough
I lean upon the window sill
The trees & summer happy seem
Green sunny green they shine—but still
My heart goes far away to dream

Of happiness & thoughts arise
With home bred pictures many a one
Green lanes that shut out burning skies
& old crooked stiles to rest upon
Above them hangs the maple tree
Below grass swells a velvet hill

& little footpaths sweet to see
Goes seeking sweeter places still

With bye & bye a brook to cross
Oer which a little arch is thrown
No brook is here I feel the loss
From home & friends & all alone
—The stone pit with its shelvy sides
Seemed hanging rocks in my esteem
I miss the prospect far & wide
From Langley bush & so I seem

Alone & in a stranger scene
Far far from spots my heart esteems
The closen with their ancient green
Heaths woods & pastures sunny streams
The awthorns here were hung with may
But still they seem in deader green
The sun een seems to loose its way
Nor knows the quarter it is in

I dwell on trifles like a child
I feel as ill becomes a man
& still my thoughts like weedlings wild
Grow up to blossom where they can
They turn to places known so long
& feel that joy was dwelling there
So home fed pleasures fill the song
That has no present joys to heir

I read in books for happiness
But books are like the sea to joy
They change—as well give age the glass
To hunt its visage when a boy
For books they follow fashions new
& throw all old esteems away
In crowded streets flowers never grew
But many there hath died away

Some sing the pomps of chivalry
As legends of the ancient time
Where gold & pearls & mystery
Are shadows painted for sublime
But passions of sublimity

Belong to plain & simpler things
& David underneath a tree
Sought when a shepherd Salems springs

Where moss did into cushions spring
Forming a seat of velvet hue
A small unnoticed trifling thing
To all but heavens hailing dew
& Davids crown hath passed away
Yet poesy breaths his shepherd skill
His palace lost—& to this day
The little moss is blooming still

Strange scenes mere shadows are to me
Vague unpersonifying things
I love with my old home to be
By quiet woods & gravel springs
Where little pebbles wear as smooth
As hermits beads by gentle floods
Whose noises doth my spirits sooth
& warms them into singing moods

Here every tree is strange to me
All foreign things where eer I go
Theres none where boyhood made a swee
Or clambered up to rob a crow
No hollow tree or woodland bower
Well known when joy was beating high
Where beauty ran to shun a shower
& love took pains to keep her dry

& laid the shoaf upon the ground
To keep her from the dripping grass
& ran for stowks & set them round
Till scarce a drop of rain could pass
Through—where the maidens they reclined
& sung sweet ballads now forgot
Which brought sweet memorys to the mind
But here no memory knows them not

There have I sat by many a tree
& leaned oer many a rural stile
& conned my thoughts as joys to me
Nought heeding who might frown or smile

Twas natures beauty that inspired
My heart with raptures not its own
& shes a fame that never tires
How could I feel myself alone

No—pasture molehills used to lie
& talk to me of sunny days
& then the glad sheep resting bye
All still in ruminating praise
Of summer & the pleasant place
& every weed & blossom too
Was looking upward in my face
With friendship welcome "how do ye do"

All tennants of an ancient place
& heirs of noble heritage
Coeval they with adams race
& blest with more substantial age
For when the world first saw the sun
There little flowers beheld him too
& when his love for earth begun
They were the first his smiles to woo

There little lambtoe bunches springs
In red tinged & begolden dye
For ever & like china kings
They come but never seem to die
There may-blooms with its little threads
Still comes upon the thorny bowers
& neer forgets those pinky threads
Like fairy pins amid the flowers

& still they bloom as on the day
They first crowned wilderness & rock
When abel haply crowned with may
The firstlings of his little flock
& Eve might from the matted thorn
To deck her lone & lovely brow
Reach that same rose the heedless scorn
Misnames as the dog rosey now

Give me no highflown fangled things
No haughty pomp in marching chime
Where muses play on golden strings

& splendour passes for sublime
Where citys stretch as far as fame
& fancys straining eye can go
& piled untill the sky for shame
Is stooping far away below

I love the verse that mild & bland
Breaths of green fields & open sky
I love the muse that in her hand
Bears wreaths of native poesy
Who walks nor skips the pasture brook
In scorn—but by the drinking horse
Leans oer its little brig to look
How far the sallows lean accross

& feels a rapture in her breast
Upon their root-fringed grains to mark
A hermit morehens sedgy nest
Just like a naiads summer bark
She counts the eggs she cannot reach
Admires the spot & loves it well
& yearns so natures lessons teach
Amid such neighbourhoods to dwell

I love the muse who sits her down
Upon the molehills little lap
Who feels no fear to stain her gown
& pauses by the hedgrow gap
Not with that affectation praise
Of song to sing & never see
A field flower grow in all her days
Or een a forests aged tree

Een here my simple feelings nurse
A love for every simple weed
& een this little "shepherds purse"
Grieves me to cut it up—Indeed
I feel at times a love & joy
For every weed & every thing
A feeling kindred from a boy
A feeling brought with every spring

& why—this "shepherds purse" that grows
In this strange spot—In days gone bye

Grew in the little garden rows
Of my old home now left—And I
Feel what I never felt before
This weed an ancient neighbour here
& though I own the spot no more
Its every trifle makes it dear

The Ivy at the parlour end
The woodbine at the garden gate
Are all & each affections friend
That rendered parting desolate
But times will change & friends must part
& nature still can make amends
Their memory lingers round the heart
Like life whose essence is its friends

Time looks on pomp with careless moods
Or killing apathys disdain
—So where old marble citys stood
Poor persecuted weeds remain
She feels a love for little things
That very few can feel beside
& still the grass eternal springs
Where castles stood & grandeur died

THE SUMMER GONE

The summer she is gone her book is shut
That did my idle leisure so engage
Her pictures were so many—some I put
On memorys scroll—Of some I turned the page
Adown for pleasures after heritage
But I have stayed too long—& she is gone
Decay her stormy strife begins to wage
Scenes flit & change & new scenes hurry on
Till winters hungry maw shall gorge them every one

The cleanly maiden down the village streets
In pattens clicks oer causways never dry
While eves drop on her cap—& oft she meets
The laughing urchin with mischevious eye
Who tryes to plash her as she hurrys bye
The swains afield right early seek their ploughs
& to the maids right vulgar speech applies
Yet gentler shepherd pleads & she alows
His proffered aid to help her over sloughs

The hedger soaked with the dull weather chops
On at his toils which scarcely keep him warm
At every stroke he takes—large swarms of drops
Patter about him like an april storm
The sticking dame with cloak upon her arm
To guard against the storm—walks the wet leas
Of willow groves—or hedges round the farms
Picking up aught her splashy wandering sees
Een withered kecks—& sticks winds shake from off the trees

Boys often clamber up a sweeing tree
To see the scarlet hunter hurry bye
& fain would in their merry uproar be
But sullen labour hath its tethering tie
Crows swop around & some on bushes nigh
Watch for a chance when eer he turns away
To settle down their hunger to supply
From morn to eve bird scaring claims his stay
Save now & then an hour which leisure steals for play

Gaunt greyhounds now the coursers sports impart
With long legs stretched on tiptoe for the chace

& short loose ear & eye upon the start
swift as the winds their motions they unlace
When bobs the hare up from her hiding place
Who in its furry coat of fallow stain
Squats on the lands or with a dodging pace
Trys its old coverts of wood grass to gain
& oft by cunning ways makes all their speed in vain

The pigeon with its breast of many hues
That spangles to the sun—turns round & round
About his timid paramour & coos
Upon the cottage ridge—while oer them wews
The puddock & below the clocking hen
Calls loud her chickens out of dangers way
That skulk & scuttle neath her wings agen
Nor peeps again till dangers far away
& one bye one they peep & hardly dare to stray

So summer went & so the autumn goes
Hedge orchard wood to red & yellow turn
The lark becrowding field a desert grows
The brooks that sung do nothing else but mourn
For company—there long necked cranes sojourn
Unstartled by the groups that summer gave
When reapers shepherds all with thirst did burn
& thronged its stream—aye life need little crave
For such will winter be in the unnoticed grave

THE PROGRESS OF RYHME

O soul enchanting poesy
Thoust long been all the world with me
When poor [thy] presence grows my wealth
When sick thy visions gives me health
When sad thy sunny smile is joy
& was from een a tiney boy
When trouble was & toiling care
Seemed almost more than I could bear
While threshing in the dusty barn
Or squashing in the ditch to earn
A pittance that would scarce alow
One joy to smooth my sweating brow
Where drop by drop would chace & fall
—Thy presence triumphed over all
The vulgar they might frown & sneer
Insult was mean but never near
Twas poesys self that stopt the sigh
& malice met with no reply
So was it in my earlier day
When sheep to corn had strayed away
Or horses closen gaps had broke
Ere suns had peeped or I awoke
My masters frowns might force the tear
But poesy came to check & cheer
It glistened in my shamed eye
But ere it fell the swoof was bye
I thought of luck in future days
When even he might find a praise
I looked on poesy like a friend
To cheer me till my life should end
Twas like a parents first regard
& love when beautys voice was heard
Twas joy twas hope & maybe fear
But still twas rapture everywhere
My heart were ice unmoved to dwell
Nor care for one I loved so well
Through rough & smooth through good & ill
That led me & attends me still
It was an early joy to me
That joy was love & poesy
& but for thee my idle lay
Had neer been urged in early day

224

The Harp imagination strung
Had neer been dreamed of—but among
The flowers in summers fields of joy
I d lain an idle rustic boy
No hope to think of fear or care
& even love a stranger there
But poesy that vision flung
Around me as I hummed or sung
I glowered on beauty passing bye
Yet hardly turned my sheepish eye
I worshiped yet could hardly dare
To show I knew the goddess there
Lest my presumptious stare should gain
But frowns ill humour & disdain
My first ambition was its praise
My struggles aye in early days
Had I by vulgar boldness torn
That hope when it was newly born
By rudeness gibes & vulgar tongue
The curse of the unfeeling throng
Their scorn had frowned upon the lay
& hope & song had dyed away
& I with nothing to attone
Had felt myself indeed alone
But promises of days to come
The very fields would seem to hum
Those burning days when I should dare
To sing aloud my worship there
When beautys self might turn its eye
Of praise—what could I do but try
Twas winter then—but summers shone
From heaven when I was all alone
& summer came & every weed
Of great or little had its meed
Without its leaves there wa'n't a bower
Nor one poor weed without its flower
Twas love & pleasure all along
I felt that I'd a right to song
& sung—but in a timid strain
Of fondness for my native plain
For everything I felt a love
The weeds below the birds above
& weeds that bloomed in summers hours
I thought they should be reckoned flowers

They made a garden free for all
& so I loved them great & small
& sung of some that pleased my eye
Nor could I pass the thistle bye
But paused & thought it could not be
A weed in natures poesy
No matter for protecting wall
No matter though they chance to fall
Where sheep & cows & oxen lie
The kindly rain when they're adry
Falls on them with as plenteous showers
As when it waters garden flowers
They look up with a blushing eye
Upon a tender watching sky
& stifl enjoy the kindling smile
Of sunshine though they live with toil
As garden flowers with all their care
For natures love is even there
& so it cheered me while I lay
Among their beautiful array
To think that I in humble dress
Might have a right to happiness
& sing as well as greater men
& then I strung the lyre agen
& heartened up oer toil & fear
& lived with rapture everywhere
Till dayshine to my themes did come
Just as a blossom bursts to bloom
& finds itself in thorny ways
So did my musings meet with praise
& though no garden care had I
My heart had love for poesy
A simple love a wild esteem
As heartfelt as the linnets dream
That mutters in its sleep at night
Some notes from extacys delight
Thus did I dream oer joys & lie
Muttering dream-songs of poesy
—The night dislimned & waking day
Shook from wood leaves the drops away
Hope came—storms calmed—& hue & cry
With her false pictures herded bye
With tales of help when help was not
Of friends who urged to write or blot

226

Whose taste were such that mine were shame
Had they not helped it into fame.
Poh—let the idle rumour ill
Their vanity is never still
My harp though simple was my own
When I was in the fields alone
With none to help & none to hear
To bid me either hope or fear
The bird & bee its chords would sound
The air hummed melodys around
I cought with eager ear the strain
& sung the music oer again
Or love or instinct flowing strong
Fields were the essence of the song
& fields & woods are still as mine
Real teachers that are all divine
So if my song be weak or tame
Tis I not they who bear the blame
But hope & cheer through good & ill
They are my aids to worship still
Still growing on a gentle tide
Nor foes could mar or friends could guide
Like pasture brooks through sun & shade
Crooked as channels chance hath made
It rambles as it loves to stray
& hope & feeling leads the way
—Aye birds no matter what the tune
Or "croak" or "tweet"—twas natures boon
That brought them joy—& music flung
Its spell oer every mattin sung
& een the sparrows chirp to me
Was song in its felicity
When grief hung oer me like a cloud
Till hope seemed even in her shroud
I whispered poesys spells till they
Gleamed round me like a summers day
When tempests oer my labour sung
My soul to its responses rung
& joined the chorus till the storm
Fell all unheeded void of harm
& each old leaning shielding tree
Where princely palaces to me
Where I would sit me down & chime
My unheard rhapsodies to ryhme

All I beheld of grand—with time
Grew up to beautifuls sublime
The arching groves of ancient Limes
That into roofs like churches climb
Grain intertwisting into grain
That stops the sun & stops the rain
& spreads a gloom that never smiles
Like ancient halls & minster aisles
While all without a beautious screen
Of summers luscious leaves is seen
While heard that everlasting hum
Of insects haunting where they bloom
As though twas natures very place
Of worship where her mighty race
Of insect life & spirits too
In summer time were wont to go
Both insects & the breath of flowers
To sing their makers mighty powers
Ive thought so as I used to rove
Through burghley park that darksome grove
Of Limes where twilight lingered grey
Like evening in the midst of day
& felt without a single skill
That instinct that would not be still
To think of song sublime beneath
That heaved my bosom like my breath
That burned & chilled & went & came
Without or uttering or a name
Untill the vision waked with time
& left me itching after ryhme
Where little pictures idly tells
Of natures powers & natures spells
I felt & shunned the idle vein
Laid down the pen & toiled again
But spite of all through good & ill
It was & is my worship still
No matter how the world approved
Twas nature listened—I that loved
No matter how the lyre was strung
From my own heart the music sprung
The cowboy with his oaten straw
Although he hardly heard or saw
No more of music than he made
Twas sweet—& when I pluckt the blade

Of grass upon the woodland hill
To mock the birds with artless skill
No music in the world beside
Seemed half so sweet—till mine was tried
So my boy-worship poesy
Made een the muses pleased with me
Untill I even danced for joy
A happy & a lonely boy
Each object to my ear & eye
Made paradise of poesy
I heard the blackbird in the dell
Sing sweet could I but sing as well
I thought untill the bird in glee
Seemed pleased & paused to answer me
—& nightingales O I have stood
Beside the pingle & the wood
& oer the old oak railing hung
To listen every note they sung
& left boys making taws of clay
To muse & listen half the day
The more I listened & the more
Each note seemed sweeter then before
& aye so different was the strain
She'd scarce repeat the note again
—"Chew-chew chew-chew" & higher still
"Cheer-cheer cheer-cheer" more loud & shrill
"Cheer-up cheer-up cheer-up"—& dropt
Low "Tweet tweet jug jug jug" & stopt
One moment just to drink the sound
Her music made & then a round
Of stranger witching notes was heard
As if it was a stranger bird
"Wew-wew wew-wew chur-chur chur-chur
"Woo-it woo-it"—could this be her
"Tee-rew tee-rew tee-rew tee-rew
"Chew-rit chew-rit"—& ever new
"Will-will will-will grig-grig grig-grig"
The boy stopt sudden on the brig
To hear the "tweet tweet tweet" so shrill
The "jug jug jug" & all was still
A minute—when a wilder strain
Made boys & woods to pause again
Words were not left to hum the spell
Could they be birds that sung so well—

229

I thought & may be more then I
That musics self had left the sky
To cheer me with its majic strain
& then I hummed the words again
Till fancy pictured standing bye
My hearts companion poesy
　　No friends had I to guide or aid
The struggles young ambition made
In silent shame the harp was tried
& raptures guess the tune applied
Yet oer the songs my parents sung
My ear in silent musings hung
Their kindness wishes did regard
They sung & joy was my reward
All else was but a proud decree
The right of bards & nought to me
A title that I dare not claim
& hid it like a private shame
I whispered aye & felt a fear
To speak aloud though none was near
I dreaded laughter more then blame
& dare not sing aloud for shame
So all unheeded lone & free
I felt it happiness to be
Unknown obscure & like a tree
In woodland peace & privacy
No not a friend on earth had I
But my own kin & poesy
Nor wealth—& yet I felt indeed
As rich as anybody need
To be—for health & hope & joy
Was mine although a lonely boy
& what I felt—as now I sing
Made friends of all & everything
Save man the vulgar & the low
The polished t'was not mine to know
Who paid me in my after days
& gave me even more than praise
Twas then I found that friends indeed
Where needed when I d less to need
—The pea that independant springs—
When in its blossom hails & clings
To every help that lingers bye
& I when classed with poesy

Who stood unbrunt the heaviest shower
Felt feeble as that very flower
& helpless all—but beautys smile
Is harvest for the hardest toil
Whose smiles I little thought to win
With ragged coat & downy chin
A clownish silent haynish boy
Who even felt ashamed of joy
So dirty ragged & so low
With nought to reccomend or show
That I was worthy een a smile
—Had I but felt amid my toil
That I in days to come should be
A little light in minstrelsy
& in the blush of after days
Win beautys smile & beautys praise
My heart with lonely fancy warm
Had even bursted with the charm
& Mary thou whose very name
I loved—whose look was even fame
From those delicious eyes of blue
In smiles & rapture ever new
Thy timid step thy fairy form
Thy face with blushes ever warm
When praise my schoolboy heart did move
I saw thy blush & thought it love
& all ambitious thee to please
My heart was ever ill at ease
I saw thy beauty grow with days
& tried song-pictures in thy praise
& all of fair or beautiful
Where thine akin—nor could I pull
The blossoms that I thought divine
Lest I should injure aught of thine
So where they grew I let them be
& though I dare not look to thee
Of love—to them I talked aloud
& grew ambitious from the crowd
With hopes that I should one day be
Beloved Mary een by thee
But I mistook in early day
The world—& so our hopes decay
Yet that same cheer in after toils
Was poesy—& still she smiles

231

As sweet as blossoms to the tree
& hope love joy are poesy

THE ENTHUSIAST
A DAY DREAM IN SUMMER

"Daydreams of summers gone["] White

Wearied with his lonely walk
Hermit like with none to talk
& cloyed with often seen delight
His spirits sickened at the sight
Of lifes realitys & things
That spread around his wanderings
Of wood & heath in brambles clad
That seemed like him in silence sad
The lone enthusiast weary worn
Sought shelter from the heats of morn
& in a cool nook by the stream
Beside the bridge wall dreamed a dream
& instant from his half closed eye
Reality seemed fading bye
Dull fields & woods that round him lay
Like curtains to his dreaming play
All slided by & on his sight
New scenes appeared in fairy light
The skys lit up a fairer sun
The birds a cheery song begun
& flowers bloomed fair & wildly round
As ever grew on dreaming ground
& mid the sweet enchanting view
Created every minute new
He swooned at once from care & strife
Into the poesy of life
A stranger to the thoughts of men
He felt his boyish limbs again
Revelling in all the glee
Of lifes first fairy infancy
Chasing by the rippling spring
Dragon flyes of purple wing
Or setting mushroom-tops afloat
Mimmicing the sailing boat
Or vainly trying by supprise
To catch the settling butterflyes
& oft with rapture driving on
Where many partner boys had gone
Wading through the rustling wheat

Red & purple flowers to meet
To weave & trim a wild cockade
& play the soldiers gay parade
Then searched the ivy haunted dell
To seek the pootys painted shell
& scaled the trees with burning breast
Mid scolding crows to rob their nest
Heart bursting with unshackled joys
The only heritage of boys
That from the haunts of manhood flye
Like song birds from a winter sky
& now tore through the clinging thorns
Seeking kecks for bugle horns
Thus with the schoolboys heart again
He chased & halooed oer the plain
Till the old church clock counted one
& told us freedoms hour was gone
In its dull humming drowsy way
It called us from our sports & play
How different did the sound appear
To that which brought the evening near
That lovely humming happy strain
That brought them liberty again
—The desk the books were all the same
Marked with each well known little name
& many a cover blotched & blurred
With shapless forms of beast & bird
& the old master white with years
Sat there to waken boyish fears
While the tough scepter of his sway
That awed to silence all the day
The peeled wand acting to his will
Hung oer the smoak stained chimney still
—The church yard still its trees possest
& jackdaws sought their ancient nest
In whose old trunks they did acquire
Homes safe as in the mossy spire
The school they shadowed as before
With its white dial oer the door
& bees hummed round in summers pride
In its time-crevised walls to hide
The gravestones childhood eager reads
Peeped oer the rudely clambering weeds
Where cherubs gilt [that] represent

234

The slumbers of the innoscent
Smiled glittering to the slanting sun
As if deaths peace with heaven was won
All all was blest & peace & plays
Brought back the enthusiasts fairy days
& leaving childhood unpercieved
Scenes sweeter still his dream relieved
Lifes calmest spot that lingers green
Manhood & infancy between
When youths warm feelings have their birth
Creating angels upon earth
& fancying woman born for joy
With nought to wither & destroy
That picture of past youths delight
Was swimming now before his sight
& loves soft thrills of pleasant pain
Was whispering its deciets again
& Mary pride of pleasures gone
Was at his side to lead him on
& on they went through field & lane
Haunts of their loves to trace again
Clung to his arm she skipt along
With the same music on her tongue
The self-same voice as soft & dear
As that which met his youthful ear
The sunny look the witching grace
Still blushed upon her angel face
As though one moments harmless stay
Had never stole a charm away
That self-same bloom & in her eye
That blue of thirteen summers bye
She took his hand to climb the stiles
& looked as wont her winning smiles
& as he met her looks divine
More tender did their blushes shine
Her small hand peeped within his own
Thrilled pleasures life hath never known
His heart beat as it once had done
& felt as love had just begun
As they'd neer told their minds before
Or parted long to meet no more
The pleasant spots where they had met
All shone as nought had faded yet
The sun was setting oer the hill

The thorn bush it was blooming still
As it was blooming on the day
When last he reached her boughs of may
& pleased he clumb the thorny grain
To crop its firstling buds again
& claimed in eager extacys
Loves favours as he reached the prize
Marking her hearts uneasy rest
The while he placed them on her breast
& felt warm loves oerbounding thrill
That it could beat so tender still
& all her artless winning ways
Where with her as of other days
Her fears such fondness to reveal
Her wishes struggling to consceal
Her cheeks loves same warm blushes burned
& smiled when he its warmth returned
O he did feel as he had done
When Marys bosom first was won
& gazed upon her eyes of blue
& blest her tenderly & true
As she sat by his side to rest
Feeling as then that he was blest
The talk the whisper met his ears
The same sweet tales of other years
That as they sat or mused along
Melted like music from her tongue
Objects of summer all the same
Where nigh her gentle praise to claim
The lark was rising from his nest
To sing the setting sun to rest
& her fair hand was oer her eyes
To see her favourite in the skies
& oft his look was turned to see
If love still felt that melody
& blooming flowers were at her feet
Her bending lovely looks to meet
The blooms of spring & summer days
Lingering as to wait her praise
& though she showed him weeds the while
He praised & loved them for a smile
The cuckoo sung in soft delight
Its ditty to departing light
& murmuring childern far away

Mockt the music in their play
& in the ivied tree the dove
Breathed its soothing song to love
& as her praise she did renew
He smiled and hoped her heart as true
She blushed away in maiden pride
Then nestled closer to his side
He loved to watch her wistful look
Following white moths down the brook
& thrilled to mark her beaming eyes
Brightening in pleasure & surprise
To meet the wild mysterious things
That evenings soothing presence brings
& stepping [on] with gentle feet
She strove to shun the larks retreat
& as he near the bushes prest
& scared the linnet from its nest
Fond chidings from her bosom fell
Then blessed the bird & wished it well
His heart was into rapture stirred
His very soul was with the bird
He felt that blessing by her side
As only to himself applied
Tis womans love makes earth divine
& life its rudest cares resign
& in his raptures gushing whim
He told her it was meant for him
She neer denied but looked the will
To own as though she blest him still
Yet he had fearful thoughts in view
Joy seemed too happy to be true
He doubted if twas Mary bye
Yet could not feel the reason why
He loitered by her as in pain
& longed to hear her voice again
& called her by her witching name
She answered—twas the very same
& looked as if she knew his fears
Smiling to cheer him through her tears
& whispering in a tender sigh
"Tis youth & Mary standing bye"
His heart revived yet in its mirth
Felt fears that they were not of earth
That all were shadows of the mind

237

Picturing the joys it wished to find
Yet he did feel as like a child
& sighed in fondness till she smiled
Vowing they neer would part no more
& act so foolish as before
She nestled closer by his side
& vowed "we never will" & sighed
He grasped her hand it seemed to thrill
& whispered "no we never will"
& thought in raptures mad extream
To hold her though it proved a dream
& instant as that thought begun
Her presence seemed his love to shun
& deaf to all he had to say
Quick turned her [tender] face away
When her small waist he strove to clasp
She shrunk like water from his grasp
He woke—all lonely as before
He sat beside the rilling streams
& felt that aching joy once more
Akin to thought & pleasant dreams

THE YELLOWHAMMERS NEST

Just by the wooden brig a bird flew up
Frit by the cowboy as he scrambled down
To reach the misty dewberry—let us stoop
& seek its nest—the brook we need not dread
Tis scarcely deep enough a bee to drown
So it sings harmless oer its pebbly bed
—Aye here it is stuck close beside the bank
Beneath the bunch of grass that spindles rank
Its husk seeds tall & high—tis rudely planned
Of bleached stubbles & the withered fare
That last years harvest left upon the land
Lined thinly with the horses sable hair
—Five eggs pen-scribbled over lilac shells
Resembling writing scrawls which fancy reads
As natures poesy & pastoral spells
They are the yellowhammers & she dwells
A poet-like—where brooks & flowery weeds
As sweet as Castaly to fancy seems
& that old molehill like as parnass hill
On which her partner haply sits & dreams
Oer all his joy of song—so leave it still
A happy home of sunshine flowers & streams
Yet in the sweetest places cometh ill
A noisome weed that burthens every soil
For snakes are known with chill & deadly coil
To watch such nests & seize the helpless young
& like as though the plague became a guest
Leaving a housless home a ruined nest
& mournful hath the little warblers sung
When such like woes hath rent its little breast

THE PETTICHAPS NEST

Well in my many walks I rarely found
A place less likely for a bird to form
Its nest close by the rut gulled waggon road
& on the almost bare foot-trodden ground
With scarce a clump of grass to keep it warm
& not a thistle spreads its spears abroad
Or prickly bush to shield it from harms way
& yet so snugly made that none may spy
It out save accident—& you & I
Had surely passed it on our walk to day
Had chance not led us by it—nay e'en now
Had not the old bird heard us trampling bye
& fluttered out—we had not seen it lie
Brown as the roadway side—small bits of hay
Pluckt from the old propt-haystacks pleachy brow
& withered leaves make up its outward walls
That from the snub-oak dotterel yearly falls
& in the old hedge bottom rot away
Built like a oven with a little hole
Hard to discover—that snug entrance wins
Scarcely admitting e'en two fingers in
& lined with feathers warm as silken stole
& soft as seats of down for painless ease
& full of eggs scarce bigger e'en then peas
Heres one most delicate with spots as small
As dust—& of a faint & pinky red
—We'll let them be & safety guard them well
For fears rude paths around are thickly spread
& they are left to many dangers ways
When green grass hoppers jump might break the shells
While lowing oxen pass them morn & night
& restless sheep around them hourly stray
& no grass springs but hungry horses bite
That trample past them twenty times a day
Yet like a miracle in safetys lap
They still abide unhurt & out of sight
—Stop heres the bird that woodman at the gap
Hath put it from the hedge—tis olive green
Well I declare it is the pettichaps
Not bigger than the wren & seldom seen
Ive often found their nests in chances way
When I in pathless woods did idly roam

But never did I dream untill to day
A spot like this would be her chosen home

THE WILD BULL

Upon the common in a motely plight
Horses & cows claim equal common right
Who in their freedom learn mischiveous ways
& driveth boys who thither nesting strays
& schoolboys leave their path in vain to find
A nest—when quickly on the threatening wind
The noisey bull lets terror out of doors
To chase intruders from the cowslap moores
& though a thousand blooms where he runs on
He dare not in his terror stoop for one
& when they see the urchins run away
Will toss the ground like savages at play
The schoolboy runs & whines & pants for breath
Like fear heart bursting from the chase of death
& through the hedge he tears for safetys lap
While the bull roars on t'other side the gap
He sees a nest but dare not stop to see
If eggs or birds within the dwelling be
—E'en skewish poneys show their teeth & kick
If leisure stirs a hand or bears a stick
& at the pointed fingure scream & run
Till mischiefs self the danger's forced to shun
& birds are all that whistle where they come
The[y] bite the bush but never hurt their home
& if a larks nest happens where they stray
They'll snuff't—& sturt—& turn another way
So birds are all that make such neighbours friends
& for such faith snug safety makes amends
There on a dotterel oak from year to year
The magpie builds her dwelling void of fear
Which danger guards around—& daring boys
Are seldom found to mar her quiet joys
For though tis easy clomb & far from high
Here many a year she trains her broods to flye
& there upon the awthorn easy seen
The linnet builds in plumage half as green
Yet safe she lives as in a pathless wood
& lays her eggs & rears her little brood
Till from the nest they flye—at ease reclined
On some projecting branches while the wind
Fans by the feathers of each downy breast
As soft as slumbers whispers into rest

While the hoarse bull lord of the pasture reigns
& lives like terror on the rushy plains
& there as soon as pleasure seeking boys
Hear the hoarse noise they startle from their joys
Drop down the rushes which they pulled to tie
The cowslip bunsh & leave the nest to flye
For safer scenes where they at peace can find
Their nests & flowers & leave their fears behind
Reading made easy such life pictures own
That still delight from pleasures they have known
I read such little books at leisures will
& joy though broken feels the picture still
I still look oer the cuts of boys at play
Among old hugh tree trunks or meadow hay
& read me of bird nesters bursting full
Of terror running from a roaring bull
& feel delight as boys with joy can be
To see him safety-pictured on a tree
Upon whose top he hides—while at its foot
The bulls bent head tears at each stubborn root
& then to read the reading just to see
How safety led the climber from the tree
& how the bull rage-weary went away
& left his prisoner pining after play
Who crept from grain to grain—& ventured down
& ran like lightening to the very town
& told on corner stool his dangers oer
& heard his parents cautions—never more
To hurt young birds or venture in the way
Of firey bulls but stay at home to play
& in my stolen walks on after years
The wild bulls dangers murmured in my ears
& now I feel by safetys side a joy
From memorys fears—delightful as a boy

THE SKY LARK

The rolls & harrows lie at rest beside
The battered road & spreading far & wide
Above the russet clods the corn is seen
Sprouting its spirey points of tender green
Where squats the hare to terrors wide awake
Like some brown clod the harrows failed to break
While neath the warm hedge boys stray far from home
To crop the early blossoms as they come
Where buttercups will make them eager run
Opening their golden caskets to the sun
To see who shall be first to pluck the prize
& from their hurry up the skylark flies
& oer her half formed nest with happy wings
Winnows the air—till in the clouds she sings
Then hangs a dust spot in the sunny skies
& drops & drops till in her nest she lies
Where boys unheeding past—neer dreaming then
That birds which flew so high—would drop agen
To nests upon the ground where any thing
May come at to destroy had they the wing
Like such a bird themselves would be too proud
& build on nothing but a passing cloud
As free from danger as the heavens are free
From pain & toil—there would they build & be
& sail about the world to scenes unheard
Of & unseen—O where they but a bird
So think they while they listen to its song
& smile & fancy & so pass along
While its low nest moist with the dews of morn
Lye safely with the leveret in the corn

THE EVENING STAR

How blest Ive felt on summer eves
When resting on a stile
Half hid in hazels moistening leaves
So weary after toil

& gazing on the evening star
That shed its ruddy light
Like joys which something came to mar
Retreating out of sight

Oer the wood corners somber brown
The lamp of dewy eve
No sooner up then sloping down
Seemed always taking leave

Yet tis a lovely sight to see
& beautiful the time
It shines in heavens canophy
As evenings gentle prime

Akin to images & things
That glad the quiet mind
A calmness oer the heart it flings
That poets love to find

It shines oer sheep within the fold
Oer shepherds whistling home
The plough lies in the fallow mould
The horse is free to roam

Tis welcome to the weary breast
It sweetens lifes employ
It sees the labourer to his rest
The lover to his joy

The wanderer seeks his easy chair
The light is in his cot
His evening star is shining there
& troubles are forgot

It looks on many a happy place
Where lovers steal to meet

It gilds the milkmaids ruddy face
While on her rustic seat

Upon the old tree in the glen
That by the hovel lay
The shepherd he had set the pen
& whistled on his way

It shines oer many a whispered pledge
By fondness told again
In cowsheds by the woodland hedge
Neath awthorns by the lane

It brings the balm to summer nights
Like insense from afar
& every musing mind delights
To see the evening star

THE ETERNITY OF NATURE

Leaves from eternity are simple things
To the worlds gaze whereto a spirit clings
Sublime & lasting—trampled underfoot
The daisy lives & strikes its little root
Into the lap of time—centurys may come
& pass away into the silent tomb
& still the child hid in the womb of time
Shall smile & pluck them when this simple ryhme
Shall be forgotten like a churchyard stone
Or lingering lie unnoticed & alone
When eighteen hundred years our common date
Grows many thousands in their marching state
Aye still the child with pleasure in his eye
Shall cry the daisy a familiar cry
& run to pluck it—in the self same state
As when time found it in his infant date
& like a child himself when all was new
Wonder might smile & make him notice too
—Its little golden bosom frilled with snow
Might win een eve to stoop adown & show
Her partner Adam in the silky grass
This little gem that smiled where pleasure was
& loving eve from eden followed ill
& bloomed with sorrow & lives smiling still
As once in eden under heavens breath
So now on blighted earth & on the lap of death
It smiles for ever—Cowslaps golden blooms
That in the closen & the meadow comes
Shall come when kings & empires fade & die
& in the meadows as times partners lie
As fresh two thousand years to come as now
With those five crimson spots upon its brow
& little brooks that hum a simple lay
In green unnoticed spots from praise away
Shall sing—when poets in times darkness hid
Shall lie like memory in a pyramid
Forgetting yet not all forgot though lost
Like a threads end in ravelled windings crost
& the small humble bee shall hum as long
As nightingales for time protects the song
& nature is their soul to whom all clings
Of fair or beautiful in lasting things

247

The little robin in the quiet glen
Hidden from fame & all the sons of men
Sings unto time a pastoral & gives
A music that lives on & ever lives
Both spring & autumn years rich bloom & fade
Longer then songs that poets ever made
& think ye these times play things pass proud skill
Time loves them like a child & ever will
& so I worship them in bushy spots
& sing with them when all else notice not
& feel the music of their mirth agree
With that sooth quiet that bestirreth me
& if I touch aright that quiet tone
That soothing truth that shadows from their own
Then many a year shall grow in after days
& still find hearts to love my quiet lays
Yet cheering mirth with thoughts sung not for fame
But for the joy that with their utterance came
That inward breath of rapture urged not loud
—Birds singing lone flye silent past a crowd
—So in these pastoral spots which childish time
Makes dear to me I wander out & ryhme
What time the dewy mornings infancy
Hangs on each blade of grass & every tree
& sprents the red thighs of the bumble bee
Who 'gins by times unwearied minstrelsy
Who breakfasts dines & most divinely sups
With every flower save golden buttercups
On their proud bosoms he will never go
But passes bye with scarcely "how do ye do"
So in their showy gaudy shining cells
May be the summers honey never dwells
—Her ways are mysterys all yet endless youth
Lives in them all unchangable as truth
With the odd number five strange natures laws
Plays many freaks nor once mistakes the cause
& in the cowslap peeps this very day
Five spots appear which time neer wears away
Nor once mistakes the counting—look within
Each peep & five nor more nor less is seen
& trailing bindweed with its pinky cup
Five lines of paler hue goes streaking up
& birds a many keep the rule alive
& lay five eggs nor more nor less then five

& flowers how many own that mystic power
With five leaves ever making up the flower
The five leaved grass trailing its golden cups
Of flowers—five leaves make all for which I stoop
& briony in the hedge that now adorns
The tree to which it clings & now the thorns
Own five star pointed leaves of dingy white
Count which I will all make the number right
& spreading goosegrass trailing all abroad
In leaves of silver green about the road
Five leaves make every blossom all along
I stoop for many none are counted wrong
Tis natures wonder & her makers will
Who bade earth be & order owns him still
As that superior power who keeps the key
Of wisdom power & might through all eternity

THE ROBINS NEST

Come luscious spring come with thy mossy roots
Thy weed strown banks—young grass—& tender shoots
Of woods new plashed sweet smells of opening blooms
Sweet sunny mornings & right glorious dooms
Of happiness—to seek & harbour in
Far from the ruder worlds inglorious din
Who see no glory but in sordid pelf
& nought of greatness but its little self
Scorning the splendid gift that nature gives
Where natures glory ever breaths & lives
Seated in crimping ferns uncurling now
In russet fringes ere in leaves they bow
& moss as green as silk—there let me be
By the grey powdered trunk of old oak tree
Buried in green delights to which the heart
Clings with delight & beats as loath to part
The birds unbid come round about to give
Their music to my pleasures—wild flowers live
About as if for me—they smile & bloom
Like uninvited guests that love to come
Their wild fragrant offerings all to bring
Paying me kindness like a throned king
Lost in such extacys in this old spot
I feel that rapture which the world hath not
That joy like health that flushes in my face
Amid the brambles of this ancient place
Shut out from all but that superior power
That guards & glads & cheers me every hour
That wraps me like a mantle from the storm
Of care & bids the cold[est] hope be warm
That speaks in spots where all things silent be
In words not heard but felt—each ancient tree
With lickens deckt—times hoary pedigree
Becomes a monitor to teach & bless
& rid me of the evils cares possess
& bids me look above the trivial things
To which prides mecenary spirit clings
The pomps the wealth & artificial toys
That men call wealth beleagued with strife & noise
To seek the silence of their ancient reign
& be my self in memory once again
To trace the path of briar entangled holt

Or bushy closen where the wanton colt
Crops the young juicey leaves from off the hedge
In this old wood where birds their passions pledge
& court & build & sing their under song
In joys own cue that to their hearts belong
Having no wish or want unreconsiled
But spell bound to their homes within the wild
Where old neglect lives patron & befriends
Their homes with safetys wildness—where nought lends
A hand to injure—root up or disturb
The things of this old place—there is no curb
Of interest industry or slavish gain
To war with nature so the weeds remain
& wear an ancient passion that arrays
Ones feelings with the shadows of old days
The rest of peace the sacredness of mind
In such deep solitudes we seek & find
Where moss grows old & keeps an evergreen
& footmarks seem like miracles when seen
So little meddling toil doth trouble here
The very weeds as patriarchs appear
& if a plant ones curious eyes delight
In this old ancient solitude we might
Come ten years hence of trouble dreaming ill
& find them like old tennants peaceful still
Here the wood robin rustling on the leaves
With fluttering step each visitor recieves
Yet from his ancient home he seldom stirs
In heart content on these dead teazle burs
He sits [&] trembles oer his under notes
So rich—joy almost choaks his little throat
With extacy & from his own heart flows
That joy himself & partner only knows
He seems to have small fear but hops & comes
Close to ones feet as if he looked for crumbs
& when the woodman strinkles some around
He leaves the twig & hops upon the ground
& feeds untill his little daintys cloy
Then claps his little wings & sings for joy
& when in woodland solitudes I wend
I always hail him as my hermit friend
& naturally enough whenere they come
Before me search my pockets for a crumb
At which he turns his eye & seems to stand

251

As if expecting somthing from my hand
& thus these feathered heirs of solitude
Remain the tennants of this quiet wood
& live in melody & make their home
& never seem to have a wish to roam
Beside this ash stulp where in years gone bye
The thrush had built & taught her young to flye
Where still the nest half filled with leaves remains
With moss still green amid the twisting grains
Here on the ground & sheltered at its foot
The nest is hid close at its mossy root
Composed of moss & grass & lined with hair
& five brun-coloured eggs snug sheltered there
& bye & bye a happy brood will be
The tennants of this woodland privacy

THE EVERGREEN ROSE

Delightful flower tis seldom mine
Such lasting smiles to win
To see thee through the window shine
Each morning looking in

& laughing at the window pane
Right merry at all hours
No matter wether wind or rain
Thourt never lost to flowers

Autumn takes summer leaves away
& strips them like a thief
But shake thy green locks as he may
He cannot steal a leaf

As glossy as the ivys blooms
That round the oak is seen
No matter how the weather comes
Thou'rt still an evergreen

Birds scarce believe their eyes to meet
A rose tree still in bloom
The wren he cocks his tail to see't
& whistles when he comes

The Robin with his nimble eye
Looks sidling on the flower
& sings home bits of melody
& warms the winter hours

Then need I dread the winter more
Or think my dwelling drear
With evergreens agen the door
& roseys all the year

253

THE SHEPHERDS LODGE

There are unnoticed spots of earth
That the world but seldom sees
That know the sweetest joys & mirth
—The poets reveries
Are shadows to the sunny rays
That visits their untroubled days

In hidden spots surrounded close
With hedges woods & upland swells
There snug in solitudes repose
A cottage circle dwells
The world has never seen before
The pathway to that happy door

When merry children rich in joy
Play summers longest sunshine down
As fearless in their minds employ
As dwellers in a crowded town
Though stranger faces scarce appear
At their lone dwelling once a year

& but for some few straggling flowers
Some roseys nailed against the wall
Strangers might pass in silent hours
Close bye & never dream at all
That human life was living near
So hidden doth the place appear

The chamber windows huddled up
With vine leaves scarce let daylight in
A tall man he must double stoop
Ere he the door can enter in
The eaves so low when sparrows dare
To build—boys reach them with a chair

A little dyke runs by the door
With ozier bushes by the side
The winter waters hasty roar
Makes little places deep & wide
That when the brook has done its song
Hold water all the summer long

254

The little wooden brig would make
A strangers courage feel at loss
That seeming ever on the shake
Bends double when they walk accross
But custom makes it safetys way
& crosses scores of times a day

The place is such a lonely place
Hidden the seasons circling years
They look upon a strangers face
As cities when a king appears
& nothing human passes bye
But they his very foot can spy

Which gives them thinkings for the week
To wonder who had gone that way
The very gates unfrequent creak
Calls up the children from their play
To see whats coming—yet tis plain
Noughts coming—so they play again

The pathway by a stranger guest
By accident may lead him bye
Like startling groundlark from its nest
Where nest could scarce be thought to lie
Noises he hears & then he feels
The trees some human home consceals

The lonely hedges hips & awes
They search for on a sabbath day
No wishes their attention draws
For company—they never stray
To neighbouring town—& some there are
That never saw a feast or fair

It is a shepherds cot & he
Has hardly seen a market town
But so much used to bush & tree
Not grows but he has noted down
Around that spot he loves to range
& never feels a wish to change

He notes the seasons year by year
Clouds birds & flowers to ear & eye

Are almanacks that tell him clear
When change of weather cometh nigh
When some by almanacks have guest
He smiles & thinks his own the best

Upon the lands the pimpernell
With crimson rim & golden eye
Smiles in his look & shows him well
Showers yet are absent from the sky
That little sky that like a dome
Surrounds his hedgrow fields & home

Oft in his rounds he'll hasten home
His little hay to cover down
Though skys ne'er token rain to come
With white rack moving up & down
Yet in the willow fringed vale
Pipes "wet my foot" the lonely quail

Right full upon the southwest gale
He hears the tempests murmurs come
Long ere the village in the vale
Thinks danger is so near its home
Long use foretells its coming near
Ere distant thunder meets his ear

The southwest often gathers up
A troop of clouds upon his eye
Till distant woods appear to stoop
Beneath the burthen of the sky
& sure as clouds approach that way
He prophecys a rainy day

To books unknown he never knows
What they to thinking minds supply
& yet his simple knowledge shows
Much wiser men may profit bye
A calm content that never strays
From providence in all his days

That never errs in sense of right
Though simple reasons mark his ways
He never rambles out of sight
From what he deems his makers praise

Though all the sermons which he hears
Are his own thoughts & humble fears

The poets page he never knew
Though Thompsons eye could hardly scan
The seasons with such truth or view
Their features closer as they ran
Familiar from his earliest day
He tracked the year from may to may

Some few old books in dissaray—
Though he is not the man to scoff
Good books—about the cottage lay
A Bunyan with the covers off
A Crusoe wanting some few leaves
That wonder for the winter eves

& one might marvel half a day
To see a book in such a spot
& wonder how they found the way
In places which the world knows not
& careful in a cupboard lay
The Bible for the Sabbath day

The poets sing of joy but he
With lifes right simple feelings strung
Feels joy in its rich melody
A page of happiness unsung
So sweet could kings see through their cares
How shepherds live they'd wish it theres

THE PRIMROSE BANK

Tis spring day roams with flowers
Down every little lane
& the night is hardly night
But a round of happy hours

Yes nights are happy nights
The sky is full of stars
Like worlds in peace they lye
Enjoying one delight

The dew is on the thorn
& the primrose underneath
Just agen the mossy root
Is smiling to the morn

With its little brunny eye
& its yellow rim so pale
& its crimp & curdled leaf
Who can pass its beautys bye

Without a look of love
When we tread the little path
That skirts the woodland side
Who can pass—nor look above

To him who blesses earth
With these messengers of spring
& decorates the fields
For our happiness & mirth

I cannot for I go
In my fancy once again
In the woods & little holts
Where the primrose used to grow

The wood bank seemed so fair
& the hedgrow in the lane
Seemed so sweet that scores of times
Have I wished my cottage there

& felt that lovely mood
As a birthright God had given

To muse in the green woods
& meet the smiles of heaven

& though no culture comes
To the places where they grow
Every spring finds more & more
Till the woods all yellow blooms

The woodmans guessing way
Oft tramples many down
But theres not a blossom missing
When he comes another day

The woods have happy guests
& the birds sing twice as loud
When they [see] such crowds of blossoms
Underneath their little nests

As beautys for the spring
Their maker sends them forth
That man may have his mirth
& nature laugh & sing

For when roaming where they flower
They seemed to make woods happy
& amid the green light round them
I've spent many a happy hour

But since I used to stray
In their hazel haunts for joy
The world has found the happy spots
& took the charm away

It has tracked the pleasant springs
Like armys on their march
Till dearest spots that used to be
Are nought but common things

Save that their sights employ
Balm gales & sunny blooms
The mind in shaping heavens
As one continued joy

THE WOODS

I love to roam the woods
Oft patted by the boughs
That meet from either side
& form an arch of leaves
Till hidden as it where from all the world
I stand & muse upon the pleasant scene

I seem to be myself
The only one that treads
The earth at such a time
So vacant is the mass
That spreads around me one hugh sea of leaves
& intertwining grains of thickest shades

No human eye is visible
No human sound attracts
The ear—but musing solitude
One unembodied thought
Thinks the heart into stillness as the world
Was left behind for somthing green & new

& lonely—& Ive thought
In such a spot to build
An hermitage or hut
With books & leisure left
How sweet t'would be but then again
I've turned to my old home & felt it vain

Yet sure a hut close thatched
Chafed by oerleaning boughs
In such a place when night
Dark on the crowd of trees
Found us locked in beside a blazing fire
Might give us happiness & pleasing fears

Fear books can give us
When we read strange tales
Of dwellers in the depths
Of earths untrodden shades
Where woods surround lone huts impassable
& nought lives near them but the hope of heaven

FEARS

Beside the little fire at night
I think of dismal things
Of lonely spots where pale affright
Hides neath nights sooty wings
Where nothing hides at such a time
But what the fancy finds in rhyme

Save some oertaken traveller
That night hath led astray
Who listens to all sounds that stir
Lest thieves should cross his way
So lone his lot I feel it joy
That other houses are so nigh

I think upon the pleasant spots
I met beneath the sun
& feel how lone the scene has got
Now mellow day is done
Where nothing but the sheep & cow
Lyes resting in their darkness now

I feel lone thoughts untill I feel
The force of home delights
Where snuggest safety doth consceal
Our homes on lonely nights
Yet outside noises oft will start
A fear of somthing in the heart

Of listening robbers lurking nigh
While darkness in the window throws
A blackness on the musing eye
A dismal vacancy that grows
& would grow to a mighty fear
Where not another cottage near

The watch dog he is barking nigh
Right pleasant notes in safetys ear
& smiling upon vacancy
The cottage windows blazes near
So thus fears fancys I employ
& from its pictures gather joy

261

FANCYS

I sit & think of distant hills
Of fair famed places strange & fair
& pleasant moods my fancy fills
& wishes for a journey there
I picture mountain scenes that lye
Above the sunsets painted brow
Near neighbours to the painted sky
So high grass hardly dares to grow

Yet mid the rocks & danger spots
I picture many a little nest
Where human dwellers live forgot
The undisturbing eagles nest
I think what sights they daily share
Whose windows over look the rocks
Whose very thresholds higher are
Then highest steeples weathercocks

Where clouds like mists below them give
Rain to the valleys dropping round
& thunders war & yet they live
So high as not to hear the sound
I read of dwellings such as these
Hung in the mountain steeps so high
That birds who cross the deepest seas
Find not the courage there to flye

I read untill I fancy care
That bramble in the ways of men
Like birds dares not to venture there
& then I wish to start again
To climb the mountain sides & mark
Those little plots of dwelling ground
& feel like faith in noahs ark
More safe with danger all around

To trace the woods that hang in air
& oaks their dark bold foliage throw
Where weeds if weeds were only there
Would seem in dangers way to grow
I long to climb the toppling blocks
Of stone like castles rising high

Where shepherds with their daring flocks
Find paths & feel no danger bye

I long to reach their cloudy tops
& fancy what a many fears
Would make my daring rambles stop
Till terror tinkles in my ears
Yet fancy climbs by rocks deterred
Less difficult their shadows grow
& where no footing seemed for birds
Trees will from out the fissures grow

So up I climb—a branch assists
Me like a staff up steeper ways
& still the tops are hid in mist
& so my foolish fancy strays
Untill she feels a fairy view
Spread to the days unbounded smiles
Mountains & vales & citys new
A circle of a thousand miles

Yet up & up & higher still
The circling landscapes stretch away
Above the clouds—my pliant will
Seems mounting to a brighter day
While underneath my feet I leave
The fallen clouds & lowly wind
& still my fancys so decieve
The world itself is left behind

Till like the sun I seem to see
The world at once—& so I long
With travels pleasant groups to be
To trace the land of prose & song
With mountain shepherds once to try
Those heights that fancy paints so fine
& tread where mountains touch the sky
& look where danger grows divine

From rocky heights & glorious hills
Dashed with days shades of every hue
Till all the heart with rapture fills
& grows a jiant at the view
I feel a stretch of rapture caught

Above the reach of care & pain
Till fancy wearys with the thought
& meets the common earth again

THE SKY LARK LEAVING HER NEST

Right happy bird so full of mirth
Mounting & mounting still more high
To meet morns sunshine in the sky
Ere yet it smiles on earth

How often I delight to stand
Listening a minutes length away
Where summer spreads her green array
By wheat or barley land

To see thee with a sudden start
The green & placid herbage leave
& in mid air a vision weave
For joys delighted heart

Shedding to heaven a vagrant mirth
When silence husheth other themes
& woods in their dark splendour dreams
Like heaviness on earth

My mind enjoys the happy sight
To watch thee to the clear blue sky
& when I downward turn my eye
Earth glows with lonely light

Then nearer comes thy happy sounds
& downward drops thy little wing
& now the valleys hear thee sing
& all the dewy grounds

Gleam into joy now from the eye
Thourt dropping sudden as a stone
& now thourt in the wheat alone
& still the circle of the sky

& abscent like a pleasure gone
Though many come within the way
Thy little song to peeping day
Is still remembered on

For who that crosses fields of corn
Where sky larks start to meet the day

But feels more pleasure on his way
Upon a summers morn

Tis one of those heart cheering sights
In green earths rural chronicles
That upon every memory dwells
Among home fed delights

THE LANDRAIL

How sweet & pleasant grows the way
Through summer time again
While landrails call from day to day
Amid the grass & grain

We hear it in the weeding time
When knee deep waves the corn
We hear it in the summers prime
Through meadows night & morn

& now I hear it in the grass
That grows as sweet again
& let a minutes notice pass
& now tis in the grain

Tis like a fancy everywhere
A sort of living doubt
We know tis something but it ne'er
Will blab the secret out

If heard in close or meadow plots
It flies if we pursue
But follows if we notice not
The close & meadow through

Boys know the note of many a bird
In their birdnesting rounds
But when the landrails noise is heard
They wonder at the sounds

They look in every tuft of grass
Thats in their rambles met
They peep in every bush they pass
& none the wiser yet

& still they hear the craiking sound
& still they wonder why
It surely can t be under ground
Nor is it in the sky

& yet tis heard in every vale
An undiscovered song

& makes a pleasant wonder tale
For all the summer long

The shepherd whistles through his hands
& starts with many a whoop
His busy dog accross the lands
In hopes to fright it up

Tis still a minutes length or more
Till dogs are off & gone
Then sings & louder then before
But keeps the secret on

Yet accident will often meet
The nest within its way
& weeders when they weed the wheat
Discover where they lay

& mowers on the meadow lea
Chance on their noisey guest
& wonder what the bird can be
That lays without a nest

In simple holes that birds will rake
When dusting in the ground
They drop their eggs of curious make
Deep blotched & nearly round

A mystery still to men & boys
Who knows not where they lay
& guess it but a summer noise
Among the meadow hay

THE MEADOW GRASS

Delicious is a leisure hour
Among the sweet green fields to be
So sweet indeed I have no power
To tell the joys I feel & see
See here the meadows how they lie
So sunny level & so green
The grass is waving ancle high
A sweeter rest was never seen

I look around & drop me down
& feel delight to be alone
Cares hardly dare to show a frown
While mays sweet leisure is my own
Joy half a stranger comes to me
& gives me thoughts to profit bye
I think how happy worlds must be
That dwell above that peaceful sky

That happy sky with here & there
A little cloud that would express
By the slow motions that they wear
They live with peace & quietness
I think so as I see them glide
Thoughts earthly tumults can t destroy
So calm so soft so smooth they ride
Im sure their errands must be joy

The sky is all serene & mild
The sun is gleaming far away
So sweet so rich—the very child
Would feel its maker brought the may
For heavens ways are pleasant ways
Of silent quietness & peace
& he who musing hither strays
Finds all in such a scene as this

Where no strife comes but in the songs
Of birds half frantic in their glee
Hid from the rude worlds many wrongs
How can they else but happy be
In places where the summer seems
Entirely out of troubles way

Where joy oer out door leisure dreams
As if twas sunday every day

For nature here in self delight
Bestows her richest gifts—the green
Luxuriance all around—the light
Seems more then any common scene—
& yet appears no looker on
Left to herself & solitude
I seem myself the only one
Intruding on her happy mood

Intruding as of wont to meet
That joyousness she throws around
To feel the grass beneath my feet
Heart cheered to hear its brushing sound
Pit patting at ones legs to feel
Their seeded heads then bounce away
Theres somthing more then joy to steal
A walk oer meadows in the may

A noise now comes on joys repose
That mays right welcome visit brings
Up from the bush the blackbird goes
The fanned leaves dance beneath his wings
& up with yet a louder noise
Woodpiegons flusker—roadway cows
Brouze there—& soon the herdboy shows
His head amid the shaking boughs

Theres somthing more to fill the mind
Then words can paint to ears & eyes
A calmness quiet loves to find
In these green summer reveries
A freshness giving youth to age
A health to pain & troubles drear
The world has nought but wars to wage
Peace comes & makes her dwelling here

I feel so calm I seem to find
A world I never felt before
& heaven fills my clouded mind
As though it would be dull no more
An endless sunshine glows around

A meadow like a waveless sea
Glows green in many a level ground
A very paradise to me

Tis sweeter than the sweetest book
That ever met the poets eye
To read in this delightful nook
The scenes that round about me lie
& yet they are but common things
Green hedges bowering oer the grass
& one old tree that stoops & flings
Its boughs oer water smooth as glass

& on a ledge of gravel crags
Those golden blooms so nobly towers
Though but the yellow water flags
Theyre fine enough for garden flowers
& over head the breadth of sky
Goes spreading gladness everywhere
Yet on this meadow grass to lie
No where so happy seems as here

THE WOODPIEGONS NEST

Roaming the little path neath dotterel trees
Of some old hedge or spinney side I've oft
Been startled [pleasantly] from musing ways
By frighted dove that suddenly aloft
Sprung through the many boughs with cluttering noise
Till free from such restraints above the head
They smacked their clapping wings for very joys
& in a curious mood I've oft been led
To climb the twig surrounded trunk & there
On some few bits of sticks two white eggs lie
As left by accident—all lorn & bare
Almost without a nest yet bye & bye
Two birds in golden down will leave the shells
& hiss & snap at wind blown leaves that shake
Around their home where green seclusion dwells
Till fledged & then the young adventurers take
The old ones timid flights from oak to oak
Listening the pleasant sutherings of the shade
Nor startled by the woodmans hollow stroke
Till autumns pleasant visions pine & fade
Then they in bolder crowds will sweep & flye
& brave the desert of a winter sky

THE RAVENS NEST

Upon the collar of an hugh old oak
Year after year boys mark a curious nest
Of twigs made up a faggot near in size
& boys to reach it try all sorts of schemes
But not a twig to reach with hand or foot
Sprouts from the pillared trunk & as to try
To swarm the massy bulk tis all in vain
They scarce one effort make to hitch them up
But down they sluther soon as ere they try
So long hath been their dwelling there—old men
When passing bye will laugh & tell the ways
They had when boys to climb that very tree
& as it so would seem that very nest
That ne'er was missing from that selfsame spot
A single year in all their memorys
& they will say that the two birds are now
The very birds that owned the dwelling then
Some think it strange yet certaintys at loss
& cannot contradict it so they pass
as old birds living the woods patriarchs
Old as the oldest men so famed & known
That even men will thirst into the fame
Of boys [&] get at schemes that now & then
May captivate a young one from the tree
With iron clamms & bands adventuring up
The mealy trunk or else by waggon ropes
Slung over the hugh grains & so drawn up
By those at bottom one assends secure
With foot rope stirruped—still a perrilous way
So perrilous that one & only one
In memorys of the oldest men was known
To wear his boldness to intentions end
& reach the ravens nest—& thence acchieved
A theme that wonder treasured for supprise
By every cottage, hea[r]th the village through
Nor yet forgot though other darers come
With daring times that scale the steeples top
& tye their kerchiefs to the weather cock
As trophys that the dangerous deed was done
Yet even now in these adventureous days
Not one is bold enough to dare the way
Up the old monstrous oak where every spring

273

Finds the two ancient birds at their old task
Repairing the hugh nest—where still they live
Through changes winds & storms & are secure
& like a landmark in the chronicles
Of village memorys treasured up yet lives
The hugh old oak that wears the ravens nest

ON VISITING A FAVOURITE PLACE

There is a breath—indeed there is
Of eden left—I feel it now
Of somthing more then earthly bliss
That falls & cheers my sullen brow
I gaze about upon the trees
I view the sweep of distant hills
More high then sources such as these
Comes joy that in my heart distills
I view the sky—away despair
There falls the joy tis only there

Health greets me for I hear her voice
Hope—peace are comrades once again
Joy stoops for flowers that say rejoice
& shall such friendship cheer in vain
When last I roamed these bleachy swells
Of hills & hollows all was here
Oer which the heart in rapture dwells
Peace love & quiet everywhere
& nought is changed since last I came
Then can I help but be the same

With verses dancing on my tongue
The raptures of a heart at ease
A fondness & a taste for song
& love for places such as these
A mind oerflowing with excess
Of joys that spring from solitude
That sees all nature spring to bless
The heart away from noises rude
So did its sunshine warm my brow
& sure it gleams as lovely now

Tis full as still the grazing kine
Make but sweet music in their noise
The sweetest flowers it owns are mine
Free gifts & so are all its joys
The trees their friendly arms extend
& bid me welcome to their shade
The old molehills their welcomes lend
As if for rest on purpose made

The little pismires only care
To mark me an intruder there

Am I athirst a little brook
Down the corn crowded hollow runs
That guggling hides in many a nook
Cool draughts from summers sultry suns
Although it wants the spreading shade
That once oerhung its little pool
The bramble here & there hath made
A bower accross to keep it cool
& cool it runs & clear as wine
Where toil in harvest loves to dine

In every place in every land
Bird beast & all are well supplied
They greet it from their makers hand
Are happy & are satisfied
& shall that masterpiece of mind
Man in his makers image live
The only thing of earthly kind
Doubt him who owneth all to give
No God forgive it cannot be
Content be all I ask from thee

When last I paid a visit here
The book I brought for leisures way
Was useless for a volume dear
In crowds of pictures round me lay
The woods the heath the distant field
In strips of green & russet dye
Did such delicious pleasure yield
I shut & put the volume bye
The book at home was sweet indeed
But there I felt I could not read

I felt from all the world away
But old affections & esteems
While on the short brown sward I lay
& joys as somthing more then dreams
I viewed the trees & bushes near
& distance till it grew to grey
A power divine seemed everywhere
& joys own rapture where I lay

The furzeclumps in their golden flowers
Made edens in these golden hours

& more they made me feel a sense
Of lovliness that dwells above
Earth thoughts—when on lifes voyage hence
We go to that eternal love
That trys to make us happy here
By spreading beautys where we roam
To cheat us out of earthly fear
Till doubts frail pinnace harbours home
& pains frail life & cloudy sky
Like morning when she opes her eye

From night & darkness into day
When all its cares & pains are bye
& doubt throws all its foils away
& meets with joys reality
Such scenes will make the mind divine
Earth grows a prophet to the eye
In such a mood Gods love be mine
It were a pleasant thing to die
& when our thoughts that aid forgoes
O God how dull the journey grows

Tis care & dullness all the year
Tis sunless in the summer sun
Tis cold & cheerless everywhere
& o how dark when day is done
But hope & joy of such a friend
Our poverty becomes a wealth
A wealth too rich for life to spend
& pain it even turns to health
From ills & pains & troubles free
How rich that rising sun will be

ON SEEING SOME MOSS IN FLOWER
EARLY IN SPRING

Wood walks are pleasant every day
Where thought so full of talk
Through autumn brown & winter grey
Meets pleasure in the walk

O natures pleasant moods & dreams
In every journey lies
Gladding my heart with simple themes
& cheers & gratifyes

Though poesys woods & vales & streams
Grow up within the mind
Like beauty seen in pleasant dreams
We no where else can find

Yet common things no matter what
Which nature dignifyes
If happiness be in their lot
They gratifye our eyes

Some value things for being new
Yet nature keeps the old
She watches oer the humblest too
In blessings manifold

The common things of every day
However mean or small
The heedless eye may throw away
But she esteems them all

The common things in every place
Display their sweets abroad
The daisey shows a happy face
On every common road

When winters past & snows are gone
It is the first to bring
A merry happy hastener on
The coming of the spring

& violets—many sorts are known
But the sweetest yet that grows
Is that which every hedgrow owns
& every body knows

This moss upon the sallow roots
Of this secluded spot
Finds seasons that its station suits
& blossoms unforgot

This common moss so hid from view
To heedless crowd unknown
By nature made as happy too
Finds seasons of its own

It peeps among the fallen leaves
On every stoven grows
Sufficient sun its shade recieves
& so it buds & blows

Thus common things in every place
Their pleasing lessons give
They teach my heart lifes good to trace
& learn me how to live

They feed my heart with one consent
That humble hope & fear
That quiet peace & calm content
Are blessings every where

WALKS IN THE WOODS

O I do love to force away
Through woods where lone the woodman goes
Through all the matted shades to stray
The brambles tearing at my cloaths
& it may tear I love the noise
& hug the solitary joys

The woodman he from top to toe
In leathern doublet brushes on
He cares not where his rambles go
Thorns briars he beats them every one
Their utmost spite his armour foils
Unhurt he dares his daily toils

Knee deep in fern he daily stoops
& loud his bill or hatchet chops
As snug he trims the faggots up
Or gaps in mossy hedges stops
While echo chops as he hath done
As if she counted every one

Through thickest shades I love to go
Where stovens foiled to get above
Cramp crook & form so thick below
Fantastic arbours—O I love
To sit me there till fancy weaves
Rich joys beneath a world of leaves

Its moss stump grows the easiest chair
Agen its grains my back reclines
& woodbines twisted fragrance there
In many a yellow cluster shines
The lonesome bees that hither stray
Seem travellers that loose their way

The speedy awthorn first of all
To show the spring its tender green
Here in the way—where branches fall
Thornless & smooth is vulgar seen
Yet in its roots of safety sure
The rabbit burrow lies secure

A quiet comes accross the mind
With every ruffled thought subdued
When fields & light are left behind
& twilight leadeth through the wood
Parting the branches as we go
We sometimes [meet] a path below

A little path that shadows plain
That other feet hath gone before
Yet through such boughs it creeps again
As if no feet could find it more
Yet trodden on till nearly bare
It shows that feet oft trample there

Where stickers stroll from day to day
& gather loads of rotten wood
& poachers left in safety stray
When midnight wears its darkest mood
When badgers howl & foxes bark
Then plops the gun—the thicket dark

Seems frighted at unwonted sounds
That echo scarcely dares again
To call but mutters slowly round
What day would answer loud & plain
She seems in fear & dread to lie
When by their dens the badgers cry

But day has nought to do with fears
The green light every sound enjoys
Boys on the woodside gate she hears
& echo shouts as well as boys
They tumble down & laugh amain
& wonder who can laugh again

I brush along—the rustling sound
Makes jay birds scream & swop away
A warning to the birds around
That danger rustles in the way
The blackbird answers but the rest
Start silent from each mossy nest

So many—up one starts agen
A blackbird with its spotted breast

From hazels oer a badgers den
Heres five warm eggs within the nest
With spots of brown & bluish gray
No boys will find them out to day

Where open spots can meet the sky
Sweet resting places seldom found
Wild strawberrys entertain the eye
With crimson berrys shining round
Uncropt unlooked for & unknown
So birds have gardens of their own

Hid round with taper ashen poles
Where deep in earth the stoven shoots
There grunting badgers burrow holes
& bare the twisted mossy roots
In the fresh moulds are plainly seen
Footmarks when daylight hurried in

A noise in oaks above the head
Keeps tapping on from day to day
Woodpeckers nests are nearly made
& patient carpenters are they
In hardest oak their whimbles go
& dust like sawdust lies below

Where ashen stovens taper grow
The squirrels nest upon the top
Is seen—& if one shakes below
From branch to branch they out & hop
& up the oak trunks mealy white
They're in a moment out of sight

Those sweet excesses oft will start
When happy feelings cross the mind
That fill with calmness all the heart
When all around one boughs are twined
When nought but green leaves fill the eye
When brushing ash & hazel bye

Cornel & thorn & spindle tree
& hazel with the nuts in bud
& crab & lime that well agree
To make a host of underwood

It doth ones spirits good to go
Through beds of fern that fan below

The rustle that the branches make
While giving way to let me through
The leaves that for a moment shake
As out a blackbird hasty flew
O there is stillness in the noise
That brings to quiet many joys

Yes as the bouncing branches start
& backward hurry to their place
A rapture rushes at the heart
A joy comes flushing in the face
I feel so glad I can t explain
My joy & on I rush again

& now I meet a stoven full
Of clinging woodbines all in flower
They look so rich & beautiful
Though loath to spoil so sweet a bower
My fingers hitch to pull them down
To take a handful to the town

So then I mix their showy blooms
With many pleasant looking things
& fern leaves in my poesy comes
& then so beautifully clings
The heart leaved briony round the tree
It too must in a poesy be

Enchanters nightshade some few sprigs
So sweet a spot it blossoms in
& within reach the leafiest twigs
Of oak—if such my reach can win
& still unwilling to give oer
I stoop till I can hold no more

Then by the sun I homeward stray
& then the woodman at his toil
I hear him chop & guess the way
Who when I reach the side will smile
& wonder why a man should roam
& take such childish trifles home

SABBATH BELLS

Ive often on a sabbath day
Where pastoral quiet dwells
Lay down among the new mown hay
To listen distant bells
That beautifully flung the sound
Upon the quiet wind
While beans in blossom breathed around
A fragrance oer the mind

A fragrance & a joy beside
That never wears away
The very air seems deified
Upon a sabbath day
So beautiful the flitting wrack
Slow pausing from the eye
Earths music seemed to call them back
Calm settled in the sky

& I have listened till I felt
A feeling not in words
A love that rudest moods would melt
When those sweet sounds was heard
A melancholly joy at rest
A pleasurable pain
A love a rapture of the breast
That nothing will explain

A dream of beauty that displays
Ima[g]inary joys
That all the world in all its ways
Finds not to realize
All idly stretched upon the hay
The wind-flirt fanning bye
How soft how sweetly swept away
The music of the sky

The ear it lost & caught the sound
Swelled beautifully on
A fitful melody around
Of sweetness heard & gone
I felt such thoughts I yearned to sing
The humming airs delight

That seemed to move the swallows wing
Into a wilder flight

The butterflye in wings of brown
Would find me where I lay
Fluttering & bobbing up & down
& settling on the hay
The waving blossoms seemed to throw
Their fragrance to the sound
While up & down & loud & low
The bells were ringing round

A BEAUTIFUL SUNSET IN NOVEMBER

Behind the distant spire the sun
Sinks beautiful—& rolled
In smoky folds cloud-mountains run
All edged with peaks of gold

& now an orange splendour comes
& looses all the blue
Again a grove of roses bloom
& splendid is the view

Now crimson lines awhile remain
& cut new mountains high
They leave us when we look again
& all is like the sky

Yes that red bar that stretched for miles
& through such splendid crowds
Of hills is gone like favours smiles
& turned to common clouds

RYHMES IN THE MEADOWS

To day with summer out of doors
Ive had some happy rounds
In trailing up the meadow banks
& oer the meadow grounds

Theres pastoral pleasures out of books
Well suiting every taste
Tis met in labours merry looks
We feel it in his haste

When swinging on the meadow path
Down to the meadow hay
The beans in blossom hemmed him in
& patted all the way

His flaggon basket on a stick
Accross his shoulder hung
& the hugh bottle doubtless urged
The merry tune he sung

Still brushing on the narrow way
That to the meadow led
The sky lark fluttered from his feet
& whistled oer his head

Delightful was the meadow scene
Its summer toils begun
Brought half the village in the hay
Loud laughing in the sun

The merry water rippled
Aye a merry pace it ran
Till the bullrush reeled & staggered
Like any drunken man

Aye the water laughed & travelled
& the bulrush danced away
& the lark sung pastoral ballads
Oer the folks among the hay

The sunshine danced & glittered
Like a blaze the wrinkles shone

Oer & oer the swallow twittered
Took a sup & hurried on

The standing pools were covered
With a sort of hairy moss
& the little nodding wagtail
Printed many paths accross

The hay all oer the meadows lay
In shocks & some in swaths
Smelling sweeter far than blossoms there
All about the little paths

The burnets tawny knopples
Like little honey combs
Bees seeking honey dinners
With many passing hums

Would come & set them bowing
& their sweets would so detain
They'd hurry as if going on
& turn & try again

Aye summer in that happy place
Did so their flight detain
Full twenty times in little space
They'd stop & start again

The weeds beside the hedge[s] danced
Like lots of drunken men
Then rested till a breeze ran bye
& off they went agen

The meadowsweet in darksome green
Shone in the merry light
Till winds turned up their lappet leaves
& then they changed to white

So turns the maidens face to hear
The mellancholy song
That comes with full as sad a tune
From old dames merry tongue

She cannot bear to see the men
Where men had done the wrong
Laugh out at grief—& turns away
In trouble from the song

She thinks tears in her happy eyes
& there her sorrow keeps
Smiles on her lips her thoughts disguise
She never owns she weeps

With an awthorn bush above them
& the short sward underfoot
They sit them down at dinner time
On the green bank at its root

Near the lake where water lilies
White & yellow are in bloom
& the maiden from the hurry oft
In the burning weather comes

To sip from out her hands & hide
Her modestys disguise
Unowning she dislikes to kneel
Before so many eyes

She hears [the] buzzing dragon flye
& startles from the place
& soon the joke of laughing men
Burns red upon her face

They say she fears the proffered ale
Should turn her beauty brown
& there is one say what he will
That never meets a frown

She sometimes sips to drink a health
She keeps within her mind
All think her silence pride—but one
Says nought & thinks her kind

& so she is—when evil eyes
Are turned another way
She from her bosom steals the fruit
There hurded half the day

& he as fearful turns unseen
& eats the gift by stealth
& when the beavering comes again
He thinks her double health

The mower sees the sun get up
With visage roozy red
& then the laughing hay folks come
& sing him down to bed

& there they leave a measured track
With every swath cut down
& soon the hot & thirsty sun
Turns mornings green to brown

Till wearied with the haste at last
He hides beneath a shower
They wait awhile to see his face
& sweeten toil an hour

& so they sit beneath the shocks
Singing pastoral songs & tales
& when the rain had wet the hay
It sweetened all the vales

PASTORAL POESY

True poesy is not in words
But images that thoughts express
By which the simplest hearts are stirred
To elevated happiness

Mere books would be but useless things
Where none had taste or mind to read
Like unknown lands where beauty springs
& none are there to heed

But poesy is a language meet
& fields are every ones employ
The wild flower neath the shepherds feet
Looks up & gives him joy

A language that is ever green
That feelings unto all impart
As awthorn blossoms soon as seen
Give may to every heart

The pictures that our summer minds
In summers dwellings meet
The fancys that the shepherd finds
To make his leisure sweet

The dustmills that the cowboy delves
In banks for dust to run
Creates a summer in ourselves
He does as we have done

An image to the mind is brought
Where happiness enjoys
An easy thoughtlessness of thought
& meets excess of joys

The world is in that little spot
With him—& all beside
Is nothing all a life forgot
In feelings satisfied

& such is poesy its power
May varied lights employ

291

Yet to all mind it gives the dower
Of self creating joy

& wether it be hill or moor
I feel where e'er I go
A silence that discourses more
Then any tongue can do

Unruffled quietness hath made
A peace in every place
& woods are resting in their shade
Of social lonliness

The storm from which the shepherd turns
To pull his beaver down
While he upon the heath sojourns
Which autumn bleaches brown

Is music aye & more indeed
To those of musing mind
Who through the yellow woods proceed
& listen to the wind

The poet in his fitful glee
& fancys many moods
Meets it as some strange melody
& poem of the woods

It sings & whistles in his mind
& then it talks aloud
While by some leaning tree reclined
He shuns a coming cloud

That sails its bulk against the sun
A mountain in the light
He heeds not for the storm begun
But dallys with delight

& now a harp that flings around
The music of the wind
The poet often hears the sound
When beauty fills the mind

The morn with safforn strips & grey
Or blushing to the view
Like summer fields when run away
In weeds of crimson hue

Will simple shepherds' hearts imbue
With natures poesy
Who inly fancy while they view
How grand must heaven be

With every musing mind she steals
Attendance on their way
The simplest thing her heart reveals
Is seldom thrown away

The old man full of leisure hours
Sits cutting at his door
Rude fancy sticks to tye his flowers
—They're sticks & nothing more

With many passing by his door
But pleasure has its bent
With him 'tis happiness & more
Heart satisfied content

Those box edged borders that imprint
Their fragrance near his door
Hath been the comfort of his heart
For sixty years & more

That mossy thatch above his head
In winters drifting showers
To him & his old partner made
A music many hours

It patted to their hearts a joy
That humble comfort made
A little fire to keep them dry
& shelter over head

& such no matter what they call
Each all are nothing less
Then poesys power that gives to all
A cheerful blessedness

So would I my own mind employ
& my own heart impress
That poesy's self's a dwelling joy
Of humble quietness

So would I for the biding joy
That to such thoughts belong
That I lifes errand may employ
As harmless as a song

BALLADS & SONGS

THE SHEPHERDS SONG

Mary now let us love employ
Among the happy smiles of may
& let us bind the wings of joy
& keep him captive for a day
Nature in love doth now disclose
Her flowers in full ripe smiles to thee
Twill be too late to seek the rose
When autumn leaves have left the tree
So let us wreath joys brows to day
To morrow he may speed away

While on this meadow bank we sit
Mark thou the sights that might thee move
How that the winds in amorous fit
Woo things inanimate to love
The bulrush bows in graceful art
To kiss the rivers lesser weeds
& flags in many a merry start
Rustling whisper to the reeds
Shall things inanimate agree
To love unmoving thee & me

See yonder skylark from the corn
Rises to sing his wedding lay
For he was wed at early morn
& twilight gave the bride away
The church above the trees doth climb
Love promise & we ll soon be there
Tis best to borrow haste from time
If time has present joys to spare
Nor leave loves lot unto the morrow
Who oft pays backward debts in sorrow

THE MOTHERS ADVICE

Come come my boy Robin be wise lad & value
An old womans counsil that wishes ye well
Neer play with your watch chain nor stand 'shill I shall I'
Make your mind up at once boy & win Kitty Fell
Neer let the abscence of beauty prevent ye
That birdlime that catches at charm-smitten men
Shes horses & cows boy & money in plenty
To make a face tempting at three score & ten

Aye cows on the pasture & sheep at the fold
& horses to yoke at the waggon or plough
& land that would even grow guineas of gold
& better the crow never flies over now
Her yards never empty of poultry & swine
Of the flitch & the ham boy her walls never bare
—When the grist bag is torn—theres the bottom of twine
& the best of all beauty is much & to spare

What pucker your brow boy & will ye be scorning
A mothers good counscil—well take ye a wife
As fine as ye please but hear this as a warning
That love without money brings winter for life
Fine wenches I know in the springs sunny weathers
Look sweet as the glad singing linnets in spring
But birds are not valued for fine painted feathers
The sweet singing larks wears a plain russet wing

What still are ye silent O fie on ye Robin
To scoff at a mother that wishes ye well
Where I in your place I would saddle old dobbin
& not loose a moment to win Kitty Fell
But thourt won by show & its no use advising
Yet Robin beware how things glitter & shine
An old fashioned guinea is more worth the prizing
Than a new minted penny though ever so fine

Those fine dressy dames though so gay & bewitching
That show their fine hues as a peacock his tail
Are just as much use in a cottagers kitchen
As plumbs in a piecrust & sugar in ale
So take your own trundle—I ll sit & content me
To think that Ive told ye the best in my power

& do as ye please since theres nought to prevent ye
But mind that ye dont pluck a weed for a flower

Theres many a fop taen by dazzel & dressing
That turns up his nose at a girl getting old
Still the proverb is true that might learn ye a lesson
Always creep neath an old hedge to get from the cold
The pie trusts her dwelling on trees high & airy
Just as week chances & storms may agree
But larks Robin heark ye right cautious & wary
Ensure a snug home at the root of the tree

WOMAN

They may boast as they will over pleasures repast
Tracing bliss to false sources in idle employ
Yet still they acknowledge that woman at last
Is the fount from whence flows the worlds essence of joy
They may boast about flowers of the summers perfume
But when alls said & done can a blossom compare
To the cheeks of a lovely young maiden in bloom
O where is the rose found so luscious as there

They may talk about pleasure in lifes solitude
But when alls said & done & its silence is tried
They will soon wish again in the world to intrude
Where the heart aching charms of a woman abide
They may sing about wine & applaud in their glee
The glass that a moment of trouble beguiles
But folly reflecting soon wishes to be
In the sunlight of joy where a sweet woman smiles

Every pleasure on earth let them laud to the skies
While under gay bacchus's idle controul
They shall all find in reason that woman supplies
The relish & savour that sweeten the whole
Beauty dwells in the fragrance & colour of flowers
Beauty sparkles in wine & the pomp of the hall
But love in a desert will challange his powers
—There the beauty of woman surpasses them all

SONG

O the voice of womans love
What a bosom stirring word
Was a sweeter ever uttered
Was a dearer ever heard
    Than womans love

How it melts upon the ear
How it nourishes the heart
Cold ah cold must his appear
Who hath never shared a part
    Of womans love

Tis pleasure to the mourner
Tis freedom to the thrall
The pilgrimage of many
& the resting place of all
    Is womans love

Tis the gem of beautys birth
It competes with joys above
What were angels upon earth
If without a womans love
    A womans love

FIRST LOVES RECOLLECTIONS

First love will with the heart remain
When all its hopes are bye
As frail rose blossoms still retain
Their fragrance till they die
& joys first dreams will haunt the mind
With shades from whence they sprung
As summer leaves the stems behind
On which springs blossoms hung

Mary I dare not call thee dear
Ive lost that right so long
Yet once again I vex thine ear
With memorys idle song
Had time & change not blotted out
The love of former days
Thou wert the last that I should doubt
Of pleasing with my praise

When honied tokens from each tongue
Told with what truth we loved
How rapturous to thy lips I clung
Whilst nought but smiles reproved
But now methinks if one kind word
Were whispered in thine ear
Thoudst startle like an untamed bird
& blush with wilder fear

How loath to part how fond to meet
Had we too used to be
At sunset with what eager feet
I hastened on to thee
Scarce nine days passed ere we met
In spring nay wintry weather
Now nine years suns have risen & set
Nor found us once together

Thy face was so familiar grown
Thyself so often bye
A moments memory when alone
Would bring thee to mine eye
But now my very dreams forget
That witching look to trace

Though there thy beauty lingers yet
It wears a stranger face

I felt a pride to name thy name
But now that pride hath flown
My words een seem to blush for shame
That own I love thee on
I felt I then thy heart did share
Nor urged a binding vow
But much I doubt if thou couldst spare
One word of kindness now

& what is now my name to thee
Though once nought seemed so dear
Perhaps a jest in hours of glee
To please some idle ear
& yet like counterfeits with me
Impressions linger on
Though all the gilded finery
That passed for truth is gone

Ere the world smiled upon my lays
A sweeter meed was mine
Thy blushing look of ready praise
Was raised at every line
But now methinks thy fervent love
Is changed to scorn severe
& songs that other hearts approve
Seem discord to thine ear

When last thy gentle cheek I prest
& heard thee feign adieu
I little thought that seeming jest
Would prove a word so true
A fate like this hath oft befell
Een loftier hopes than ours
Spring bids full many buds to swell
That neer can grow to flowers

BALLAD

There is a tender flower
Yet found in every clime
That decks the rudest bower
Nor stays for place or time
In caves or desert sands
Unblest with sun or shower
Wherever life expands
Is found this tender flower

Where storms with keenest breath
Bid stronger flowers decay—
Where suns een shun its birth
It is content to stay
In sunshine & in gloom
As if 'twere sorrows dower
In griefs lap it will bloom
Or die a lovely flower

Within lifes wilderness
This fond & tender flower
Doth every bosom bless
& garlands sorrows bower
Rude falsehood may despise
Its bloom when in its power
& idle themes devise
To mock this injured flower

Yet truth hath long agreed
To call it first of flowers
Though treated like a weed
Too oft in follys bowers
On earth it loves to dwell
Though blest with heavenly power
& sure I need not tell
That loves the lauded flower

THE MAID OF THE HALL

Of all the fine lasses Ive led down the dance
Ive neer seen her equal at all
If ye search all the towns between London & France
Theres none like the maid of the Hall

Deckd out like a lady above all the rest
She looked like the queen of the ball
& all the young ploughmen that saw her confest
Twas a beauty that came from the Hall

Her feet stept so graceful so airy & gay
& so true to the fiddle did fall
To see but her dancing twould win ye to say
Theres none like the maid of the Hall

Her speech is so proper so fine & polite
Not a word in her talk she ll miscall
The clowns all concieted who saw her that night
Twas the Lady herself from the Hall

I feign would have begged her my sweetheart to be
But I feared that my chance would be small
So many agreed in opinion with me
That the finest lass came from the Hall

She shewed such good humour & prattled so free
We fancied she loved but us all
We knew not behaviour from courtship not we
Which distinguished the maid of the Hall

I once thought on paper my suit to appeal
& to send her a letter withall
But ignorance then would my meaness reveal
& disgrace the fair maid of the Hall

I once thought of telling my passion outright
But then if a word I d let fall
So vulgar it would have been sport for the night
& ashamed the fair maid of the Hall

& as I do love her & win her I can t
I ll entice her with nothing at all

305

As to come at her love all beside it I want
Heres adieu to the maid of the Hall

BALLAD

I dreamt not what it was to woo
& felt my heart secure
Till Robin dropt a word or two
Last evening on the moor
Though with no flattering words the while
His suit he urged to move
Fond ways informed me with a smile
How sweet it was to love

He left the path to let me pass
The dropping dews to shun
& walked himself among the grass
I deemed it kindly done
& when his hand was held to me
As oer each stile we went
I deemed it rude to say him nay
& manners to consent

He saw me to the town & then
He sighed but kissed me not
& whispered 'we shall meet agen'
But did'n't say for what
Yet on my breast his cheek hed lain
& though it gentle press'd
It bruised my heart & left a pain
That robs it of its rest

BALLAD

Where is the heart thou once hast won
Can cease to care about thee
Where is the eye thou'st smiled upon
Can look for joy without thee
Lorn is the lot one heart hath met
Thats lost to thy caressing
Cold is the hope that loves thee yet
Now thou art past possessing
  Fare thee well

We met we loved weve met the last
The farewell word is spoken
O Mary canst thou feel the past
& keep thy heart unbroken
To think how warm we loved & how
Those hopes should blossom never
To think how we are parted now
& parted oh for ever
  Fare thee well

Thou wert the first my heart to win
Thou art the last to wear it
& though another claims akin
Thou must be one to share it
Oh had we known when hopes were sweet
That hopes would once be thwarted
That we should part no more to meet
How sadly we had parted
  Fare thee well

THE MILKMAID

Three seasons have gone—sin' my shepherd did leave me
To go for a soldier in wars far away
His red coat became him—he ll never decieve me
Yet I grieved & this puts me in mind of the day
The cow pasture buttercups paved it with gold
The hedges about it were smothered in may
& the sheep by a stranger let out of the fold
Seemed to sorrow like me for his going away

Beside this old thorn I remember't as well
As though it was milking time but yesterday
His old dog that with a new master did dwell
Saw his red coat & feather & hurried away
He called him by name & he came at his call
For he knew his voice well but in terror & fear
He stared at his red coat & feather & all
& dropt on his haunches & wouldnt come near

Though the sound of his voice made him prick up his ear
He could not believe him in such a disguise
My old dogs forgot me he said—& the tear
Of regret though a soldier I saw in his eyes
I took it for granted & why disbelieve him
Twas me that occasioned a moment of pain
Though he doubted my soldier I ll never decieve him
If they keep him for life I shall know him again

& three years have gone sin' this thorn was in blossom
I never pass bye but I think on the day
By the side of a hill stood a cowslap in blossom
I cropt it—& he got a branch of the may
& when we had talked the last moment to parting
My heart while I think ont half doubtfully burns
He held it to me & he said just a starting
Jane take this & keep it till Jemmy returns

I sighed—but he laughed & said dont be fainthearted
Twas only to hide deeper trouble from me
For he lingered I thought that we couldnt have parted
& turned to look back far as eer we could see
A keepsake so odd could he mean to abuse me
& give me the thorn that his slight I might see

Tis foolish to think ont—he ll never ill use me
For he rubbed off the pricks ere he gave it to me

THE MILKING HOUR

The sun had grown on lessening day
A table large & round
& in the distant vapours grey
Seemed leaning on the ground
When Mary like a lingering flower
Did tenderly agree
To stay beyond her milking hour
& talk awhile with me

We wandered till the distant town
Had silenced nearly dumb
& lessened on the quiet ear
Small as a beetles hum
She turned her buckets upside & down
& made us each a seat
& there we talked the evening brown
Beneath the rustling wheat

& while she milked her breathing cows
I sat beside the streams
In musing oer our evening joys
Like one in pleasant dreams
The bats & owls to meet the night
From hollow trees had gone
& een the flowers had shut for sleep
& still she lingered on

We mused in rapture side by side
Our wishes seemed as one
We talked of times retreating tide
& sighed to find it gone
& we had sighed more deeply still
Oer all our pleasures past
If we had known what now we know
That we had met the last

SONG

Come give us the health to the dearest on earth
To the fairest the first & the best
The comfort of joy & the sunlight of mirth
From the south & the east to the west
Then heres to the suns that illumine the earth
To the flowers that in winter are blooming
To the gems that are found above purchase & worth
The love & the beauty of woman

Then give us the health to the dearest on earth
To the gem of all climates & soils
To the heart stirring pulse that enlivens our mirth
& the comfort that sweetens our toils
Then heres to the flowers in the desert of care
That in calms & in tempests are blooming
& heres to the angels of earth—so they are
The love & the beauty of woman

The charm that gives sweetness to wine & to mirth
& the balm of our anguish & thrall
The welcome & wealth of the cottagers hearth
& the gem of both palace & hall
What ist but our health to the dearest on earth
To the flowers that in winter are blooming
The eden where joy is indebted for birth
The love & the beauty of woman

Then heres to the health of the dearest on earth
& the treasures of cottage & hall
Then heres to our very existance & birth
Life without them were nothing at all
Theyre the joy of our sorrow the rest of our pain
Theyre the flowers that in deserts are blooming
Then fill up the glass & we ll give it again
To the love & the beauty of woman

312

LOVE

Love though it is not chill & cold
But burning like eternal fire
It is not of approaches bold
Which gay dramatic tastes admire
O timid love more fond then free
In dareing song is ill pourtrayed
Where as in war the devotee
By valour wins each captive maid

Where hearts are prest to hearts in glee
As they could tell each others minds
Where ruby lips are kissed as free
As flowers are by the summer winds
—No gentle love that timid dream
Whose hopes & fears at foil & play
Work like a skiff against the stream
Where it loves most finds least to say

It lives in blushes & in sighs
In hopes for which no words are found
Thoughts dare not look but in the eyes
The tongue is left without a sound
The pert & forward things that dare
Their whispers in each others ear
Feel no more then their shadows there
Mere things of form with nought of fear

True passion that so burns within
Is timid as the doves disguise
Tis for the murder aiming hawk
To dart at every bird that flies
True love it is no daring bird
But like the little timid wren
That in the new leaved thorns of spring
Shrinks further from the sight of men

The idol of its musing mind
The worship of its lonely hour
Love wooes her in the summer wind
It tells her name to every flower
But in her sight no open word
Escapes Loves passion to declare

The sighs by beautys majic stirred
Are all that speak its passion there

BALLAD

The spring returns the pewet screams
Loud welcomes to the dawning
Though harsh & ill as now it seems
Twas music last may morning
The grass so green—the daisy gay
Wakes no joy in my bosom
Although the garland last mayday
Wore not a finer blossom

For by this bridge my Mary sat
& praised the screaming plover
As first to hail the day—when I
Confessed myself her lover
& at that moment stooping down
I pluckt a daisy blossom
Which smilingly she called her own
May garland for her bosom

& in her heart she hid it there
As true loves happy omen
Gold had not claimed a safer care
I thought loves name was woman
I claimed a kiss she laughed away
I sweetly sold the blossom
I thought myself a king that day
My throne was beautys bosom

& little thought an evil hour
Was bringing clouds around me
& least of all that little flower
Would turn a thorn to wound me—
She showed me after many days
Though withered—how she prized it
& then she leaned to wealthy praise
& my poor love despised it

Aloud the whirring pewet screams
The daisy blooms as gaily
But where is Mary—absence seems
To ask that question daily
No where on earth where joy can be
To glad me with her pleasure

Another name she owns—to me
She is as stolen treasure

When lovers part—the longest mile
Leaves hope of some returning
Though mines close bye—no hope the while
Within my heart is burning
One hour would bring me to her door
Yet sad & lonely hearted
If seas between us both should roar
We were not further parted

Though I could reach her with my hand
Ere suns the earth goes under
Her heart from mine—the sea & land
Are not more far asunder
The wind & clouds now here now there
Hold not such strange dominion
As womans cold perverted will
& soon estranged opinion

THE OLD MANS SONG

Youth has no fear of ill by no cloudy days anoyed
But the old mans all hath fled & his hopes have met their doom
The bud hath burst to bloom & the flower been long destroyed
The root too is withered & no more can look for bloom
So I have said my say & I have had my day
& sorrow like a young storm creeps dark upon my brow
Hopes like to summer winds they have all blown away
& the worlds sunny side is turned over with me now
& left me like a lame bird upon a withered bough

I look upon the past tis as black as winter days
But the worst it is not over there is blacker days to come
O would I had but know[n] of the wide worlds many ways
But futurity is blind so I een must share my doom
Joy once reflected brightly of prospects overcast
But now like a looking glass thats turned to the wall
Life is nothing but a blank & the sunny shining past
Is overspread with glooms that doth every hope enthrall
While troubles daily thicken in the wind ere they fall

Life smiled upon me once as the sun upon the rose
My heart so free & open guessed every face a friend
Though the sweetest flower must fade & the sweetest season close
Yet I never gave it thought that my happiness would end
Till the warmest seeming friends grew the coldest at the close
As the sun from lonely night hides its haughty shining face
Yet I could not think them gone for they turned not open foes
While memory fondly mused former favours to retrace
& I turned but only found that my shadow kept its place

& this is nought but common life what every body finds
As well as I or mores the luck of those that better speed
I ll mete my lot to bear with the lot of kindred minds
& grudge not those who say they for sorrow have no need
Why should I when I know that it will not aid a nay
For summer is the season even then the little flye
Finds friends enew indeed both for leisure & for play
But on the winter window why they crawl alone to die
Such is life & such am I a wounded & a winter stricken flie

317

SALLY GREEN

I cannot bethink me the matter
Of the anguish thats got in my breast
Where my heart like a bird pitter patter
Will not let me get any rest
Ive neer drank no ale to be teazing
My head—yet right sick have I been
& my ills have been daily increasing
Ever since I first saw Sally Green

Folks talk about one little cupid
As how a heart robber is he
But to think he stole mine why its stupid
When he can t reach so high as my knee
No no Im aware of whose got it
Yet the robber no robber has been
We cannot steal gifts—so odd rot it
How can I go blame Sally Green

& to call her a thief would be loathing
For beauty like hers cannot steal
'Sides she might have a score hearts for nothing
Their praises folks cannot consceal
They stare in her face for her beauty
But she neer looks to know what they mean
If they think to have that as their booty
They already mistake Sally Green

She smiled at me over her shoulder
Though I'd never danced with her before
—Had the king ha' been there to behold her
He d never forgot her no more
She looked so delightful & blooming
No pack of cards own such a queen
Good dear if the king had been coming
He'd ha' thought her his own Sally Green

The parson in last sundays sermon
Often turned a hard look in my face
Though Im sure I did nought there was harm in
Nor slept een a wink in my place
—I know that while prayers are a reading
No other guess things should be seen

& though he my thoughts was a heeding
Pray who could forget Sally Green

I reached her a rose yester morning
The best I could find on the tree
& to hurt her Im sure I d be scorning
Who neer thought a thing to hurt me
So I rubbed off the thorns from the blossom
& I sighed though it could not be seen
When I offered the gift for her bosom
As the best I could give Sally Green

I set up the dance at the shearing
& I quaked like a bird in the snow
Though the people all said in my hearing
They were melting like ice in a thaw
But just like a blossom at mayday
There sat betwixt me & the screen
—Good dear need I tell ye the lady
Did ye know how I love Sally Green

Ive been six years in service come may day
& but six weeks in love overseen
For in truth though I thought her a lady
Folks call her a child of sixteen
But let them be laughing & humming
Folks often say more then they mean
For believe me I neer saw a woman
So charming as young Sally Green

I loved her too dearly to linger
Though they talked of such out o way things
& ashamed to examine her finger
I made a guess start for the ring
Says the Goldsmith says he Mr Ploughman
Now seek out the size that ye mean
Gosh—I sighd I could hardly tell how mun
But the smallest will fit Sally Green

The man laughing loud when I said so
Bore me down that I pickt it too small
But if dame Tibbs had been at my elbow
She d have seen he knew nothing at all
—Aye—she d one Mr Goldsmith to pleaze ye

319

The big finger size that ye mean
But she saw one get two in it easy
& that was my sweet Sally Green

So I brought her the ring at a venture
& I shall go see bye & bye
But I dont wish that fools should torment her
& I know she is timid & shy
Like a rosebud that blushes in may so
& seems half afraid to be seen
I know who she loves— & wont say so
So why need I plague Sally Green

When I meet her at milking o mornings
& offer her help over stiles
I never meet none of her scornings
For she pays me in blushes & smiles
Though she seems always willing to linger
She colours wheneer we are seen
Yet when the ring graces her finger
She ll soon forget shoy Sally Green

But I know when the parson comes near her
She ll wish his big book on the shelf
& be ready to faint—but I ll cheer her
& speak both for her & myself
For I know that she'll stick to her duty
Though a bible vow never had been
& if truth as folks tell ye be beauty
Ive no cause to doubt Sally Green

BALLAD—THE BACKWARD SPRING

The day waxes warmer
The winters far gone
Then come out my charmer
& bring summer on
Thy beauty is gleaming
So sweet where ye be
Tis summer & sunshine
To be only with thee

Tardy spring came so loathing
I thought that the spring
Had took winters cloathing
But no such a thing
For the snow neath the hedges
Hath packt up & gone
& mays little pledges
For summer comes on

The flowers on the awthorn
—Oak balls on the tree
& the blackbird is building
Loves pallace in glee
Then come out my charmer
& lead summer on
Where e'er thou art smiling
Care & winter are gone

—Even snows neath thy feet
I could fancy to be
A carpet of daiseys
—The rime on the tree
Would bloom in thy smiling
& quickly appear
Like blossoms beguiling
The prime of the year

The ice on the water
O I could agree
That winter had changed to
A pallace for thee
Turning pools into mirrors
& silence to glee

321

Reflecting the image
Of rapture in thee

Then come forth my charmer
Thy presence can charm
Into summer the winter
To sunshine the storm
I can think how delightful
The prospect would be
In summer or winter
That blest me with thee

But the place of thy absence
All language is lost
I cannot imagine
What pain it would cost
Though without thee I feel
Where a desert would be
& all in thy presence
Grows eden with me

NUTTING

Right rosey gleamed the autumn morn
Right golden shone the autumn sun
The mowers swept the bleached corn
While long their early shades did run
The leaves were burnt to many hues
The hazel nuts were ripe & brown
My Marys kindness could but chuse
To pluck them when I bore them down

The shells her auburn hair did show
A zemblance faint yet beautiful
She smiled to hear me tell her so
Till I forgot the nuts to pull
I looked up on ash & thorn
For nuts—my wits was all astray
She laughed so rich that autumn morn
All all but love was wide away

& soon the day was on its wane
Ere joy had thought one hour away
Who could but wish them back again
When love was so inclined to stay
She started at each little sound
The branches made—yet would her eye
Regret the gloom encroaching round
That told her night was in the sky

I helped her through the hedge row gap
& thought the very thorns unkind
As not to part—while in her lap
She sought the ripest bunch to find
Then on a hill beneath a tree
We leamed her nuts—as lover spells
She often threw the nuts at me
& blushed to see me hurd the shell

Love tokens for an after day
Passports a blushing kiss to claim
Soon went that autumn eve away
& never more its fellow came
The west was in a glorious trim
Of colours mixed in endless thrall

323

& on the dark woods distant rim
The sun hung like a golden ball

Right luscious was those nutting bowers
Impulses sweet for many a day
Joy never smiled on sweeter hours
Or sighed oer sweeter passed away
Twas Marys smiles & sweet replies
That gave the sky so sweet a stain
So bright I never saw him rise
Nor ever set so sweet again

THE GIPSEY SONG

The Gipseys life is a merry life
& happy boys we be
We pay no rent nor tax to none
& live untythed & free
None cares for us for none care we
& where we list we roam
& merry boys we gipseys be
Though the wild woods are our home

& come what will brings no dismay
We're with few cares perplext
For if to days a swaily day
We meet with luck the next
& thus we sing & kiss our mates
While our chorus still shall be
Bad luck to tyrant majistrates
& the gipseys dwelling free

To mend old pans & bottom chairs
Around the towns we tramp
When a day or two our purse repairs
& plenty fills our camp
& our songs we sing & our fiddles sound
Their catgut harmony
While echo fills the woods around
With gipsey liberty

The green grass is our softest bed
The sun our clock we call
The nightly sky hangs over head
Our curtains house & all
Though housless while the wild winds blow
Our joys are uncontrouled
We barefoot dance through winters snow
When others die with cold

Our maidens they are fond & free
& lasting are their charms
Brown as the berry on the tree
No suns their beauty harms
Their beautys are no garden blooms
That fade before they flower

Unsheltered where the tempest comes
They smile in sun & shower

& they are wild as the woodland hare
That feeds on the evening lea
& what care we for ladys fair
Since ours are fond & free
False hearts hide in a lily skin
But ours are coarse & fond
No parsons fetters link us in
Our hearts a stronger bond

Though the wild woods are our house & home
Tis a home of liberty
Free as the summer clouds we roam
& merry boys we be
We dance & sing the year along
& loud our fiddles play
& no day goes without a song
With us all months are may

The hare that haunts the fallow grounds
& round the common feeds
The fox that tracks the woodland bounds
& in the thicket breeds
These are the neighbours were we dwell
& all the guests we see
That share & love the quiet well
Of gipsey liberty

The elements have grown our friends
& leave our huts alone
The thunder bolt that rocks & rends
The cotters house of stone
Flys harmless by our blanket roofs
Where the winds may burst & blow
For our camps though thin are tempest proof
& buffet rain & snow

May the lot we've met our lives befall
& nothing worse attend
So heres success to gipseys all
& every gipsey friend
& while the ass that bears our camp

Can find a common free
Around old Englands heaths we'll tramp
In gipsey liberty

PEGGY BAND

O it was a lorn & a dismal night
& the storm beat loud & high
Nor a friendly light to guide me right
Was there shining in the sky
When a lonely hut my wanderings met
Lost in a foreign land
& I found the dearest friend as yet
In my lovely Peggy Band

"O father heres a soldier lad
"& weary he seems to be"
"Then welcome him in" the old man said—
& she gave her seat to me
The fire she trimmed & my cloaths she dried
With her own sweet lily hand
& oer the soldiers lot she sighed
While I blest my Peggy Band

When I told the tale of my wandering years
& the nights unknown to sleep
She made excuse to hide her tears
& she stole away to weep
A pilgrims blessing I seemed to share
As saints of the holy land
& I thought her a guardian angel there
Though he called her his Peggy Band

The night it passed & the hour to part
With the morning winged away
& I felt an anguish at my heart
That vainly bade to stay
I thanked the old man for all he did
& I took his daughters hand
But my heart was full & I could not bid
Farewell to my Peggy Band

A blessing on that friendly cot
Where the soldier found repose
& a blessing be her constant lot
Who soothed the strangers woes
I turned a last look on the door
As she held it in her hand

& my heart ached sore as I crossed the moor
To leave my Peggy Band

To the weary ways that I have gone
Full many friends befell
& Ive met with maidens many a one
To use the soldier well
But of all the maids I ever met
At home or in foreign land
Ive never seen the equal yet
Of my charming Peggy Band

BALLAD

The morning hour the sun beguiles
With glorys brightly blooming
The flower & summer meet in smiles
& so Ive met with woman
But suns must set with dewy eve
& leave the scene deserted
& flowers must with the summer leave
So I & Mary parted

O Mary I did meet thy smile
When passion was discreetest
& thou didst win my heart the while
When woman seemed the sweetest
When joys were felt that cannot speak
& memory cannot smother
When loves first beauty flushed thy cheek
More sweet then any other

Those eyes that then my passion blest
That burned in loves expression
That bosom where I then could rest
I now have no possession
These waken still in memory
Sad ceasless thoughts about thee
That say how blest Ive been with thee
& how I am without thee

SONG

Come push round the glass tis a god in disguise
For riches & joy at its bright bottom lies
What mind is more healthy then his thats at rest
& he that drinks deepest is first to be blest
Though cant may assail us we'll sit at our ease
As her preaching & practice so seldom agrees
She loves what she rails at & soaks in disguise
& sins more then we do in forging up lies

So push round the glass let us live while we may
While joys wings are wetted he can t flye away
The prude he may rail & the vile hypocrite
But a cloak both must have for to make their black white
Good wine needs no bush & day light no pall
Nor a plain honest face need not turn to the wall
So shame not the glass to abuse what we need
But drink & be merry let that be our creed

Then push round the glass & to honour the feast
If we must have a lecture let bacchus be priest
See his wig of vine leaves & his cheeks how they glow
The maxim he gives it behoves us to know
"To do unto others as we'd be done to"
Thats the soul of religion & all we need do
So let cant assail us none cares for her creed
The more she's against us the more we shall speed

BALLAD

Fair maiden when my love began
Ere thou thy beauty knew
I fearless owned my passion then
Nor met reproof from you

But now perfection wakes thy charms
& strangers turn to praise
Thy pride my faint grown heart alarms
& I scarce dare to gaze

Those lips to which mine own did grow
In loves glad infancy
With ruby ripeness now doth glow
As gems too rich for me

The full blown rose thy cheeks doth wear
Those lilys on thy brow
Forget whose kiss their buds did wear
& bloom above me now

Those eyes whose first sweet timid light
Did my young hopes inspire
Like midday suns in splendour bright
Now burn me with their fire

Nor can I weep what I bemoan
As great as are my fears
Too burning is my passion grown
To e'er be quenched by tears

BALLAD

If love be such a wilderness
So full of ills & pains & fate
Where to pass through is sure distress
As wailing doleful drones relate
Why should I to such dangers grow
While there are safer roads to go

But well I wot the pains & ills
That sighing lovers do reveal
Are fashioned most by their own wills
& as they fancy so they feel
If they must mourn 'cause one says "no"
Themselves alone do will it so

A maidens frown is not my fate
My heart for hers I ll freely give
But if for love she offers hate
I ll keep my own & rather live
Fool should I be to pain endure
Which frowns can make & smiles can cure

If I ask one that answers "no"
Am I to end my hopes therebye
She cannot make all wills think so
Then prythee tell me why should I
If she says "no" the next I wis
When met as ready may say "yes"

Let lovers fancy what they list
I ll but admire it for its joys
Nor sigh & grieve as beauty wist
Like restless childern after toys
For why should I in trouble run
Which I by heeding not may shun

That love which youth sets out to seek
As eager as the brook doth run
Is not sown on a painted cheek
Where at fools tamper & are won
But wisdom speeds till these be past
& finds it in the heart at last

BALLAD

O would I were the little bird
To love without a fear
I d up & tell my love a tale
Might win an angels ear
I d up & tell a tale of truth
A tale of trouble too
How I do love—how fain to tell
For that I dare not do

O would I were the golden cage
& she the little dove
To wear her on my breast for aye
A bosom load of love
My heart alone her pearch should be
Whereon to nest & woo
There love my fill & own it all
For that I dare not do

O would I were the little flower
The flower she favours best
I d waste my fragrance all for love
Upon her bonny breast
I'd press with joy my snowy bed
& kiss my pillow too
& love till death & say I would
But that I dare not do

O would I were but any thing
Then the poor thing I be
A bird or flower or een a flye
Less fear it owns then me
Twill try both lip & bosom where
My hopes dare never go
& sing where I must silent mourn
For what I dare not do

BALLAD

The roseys red the roseys white
The rosey blooms in sunny light
But ah it clouds the hearts delight
To muse upon its history
It tells aye many a woeful tale
Of hearts made cold of cheeks made pale
Of loves sad sigh of widows wail
In days of strife & chivalry
& freedom may it aye prevail
That strife no more may be

The roseys red the roseys white
The roseys pleasant to the sight
Now both their hues in one unite
To crown the brows of loyalty
Strife took the white rose for its crest
But concord placed it in her vest
Where it blushed red upon her breast
To join the rose of liberty
& while it blooms as freedoms guest
There let it ever be

THE HOMELESS EMIGRANTS SONG

O false love is a bitter thing
& song alone may break the spell
But silence numbs at my harp string
My woes nor song nor words may tell
Tears they will flow for many wrongs
While mine with hopeless winter freeze
& sighs & tears fill many songs
But mine must mourn for more than these

Of friends I neer must see again
That now perchance the grass grows oer
Of joys whose memorys worse then pain
To think of & to see no more
Of loves for which mine own must ach
The more to think it aches in vain
Yet more then this it takes to break
My heart for which no words remain

Tis worse then sickness worse then fears
Then palid looks & hollow eyes
Tis made of thoughts no bosom hears
That wring the sick heart till it dies
Some sigh of wounds from Cupids bow
From deeper wounds my troubles spring
Alas a heart half broken now
Hath left but little power to sing

Tis not of love I would disclose
My troubles flow from deeper streams
Tis my poor country sunk in woes
All else were vain & idle themes
No muse leads me through fancys tales
Like one to whom her powers belong
A homeless lot my heart bewails
& truths the sorrow of the song

SONG

Sweet the pleasures I do find
Lovely Jessey near thee
When every green with flowers is lined
& linnets sing to cheer thee
Then my love so fair so kind
Tis heaven while I'm near thee—Jessey
Heaven while Im near thee

Though tis not the charms of spring
Can add a charm to cheer me
When every pleasures took to wing
& left the pasture dreary
When every birds forgot to sing
Tis heaven to be near thee—Jessey
Heaven to be near thee

Left to winters frost & snow
When storms descend severly
Left with birds to pick the slow
& left with thee to cheer me
Still while lifes red tide shall flow
Heaven would be near thee—Jessey
Heaven would be near thee

Banished to some barren isle
Where famine scowled severely
Jessey blest with thee the while
Till life was left to cheer me
Still on fate & thee I'd smile
For heaven would be near thee—Jessey
Heaven would be near thee

THE SHEPHERDS LAMENT

Ah faithless love I've met thy scorning
& lain awake from night till morning
Sin' Robins ye agree'd to be
& what could be the reason Nanny
That ye should scowl & look so shanny
When e'er I mentioned love to thee

I knew ye long before another
& when ye lost your darling mother
My fretful tear was mixed with thine
& ever sin' ye left your Granny
To seek your service haughty Nanny
Have I been fooled to think ye mine

I little thought ye'd look above me
When ye were young & used to love me
& innocent as aught could be
As any lamb beside its mother
When ye would run & call me brother
& on the threshold play with me

When hand in hand in summer weather
We strolled about the fields together
O had but love a known its powers
When innoscently pleased with me
Ye held your quiltings to your knee
& crossed the brook for water flowers

But time is changed & so's my pleasure
& youth has fled & so's my treasure
& sorrow all my days must see
& times destroyed thy careful granny
& prides destroyed the heart of Nanny
She's turned her back on love & me

THE TOPERS RANT

Come come my old crones & gay fellows
That loves to drink ale in a horn
We'll sing racey songs now we're mellow
Which topers sung ere we were born
For our bottle kind fate shall be thanked
& line but our pockets with brass
We'll sooner suck ale through a blanket
Then thimbles of wine from a glass

Away with your proud thimble glasses
Of wine foreign nations supply
We topers neer drink to the lasses
Over draughts scarce enough for a flye
Club us with the hedger & ditcher
Or beggar that makes his own horn
To join us oer bottle or pitcher
Foaming oer with the essence of corn

We care not with whom we get tipsey
Or where with brown stout we regale
We'll weather the storm with a gipsey
If he be a lover of ale
We'll weather the toughest storm weary
Although we get wet to the skin
If the outside our cottage looks dreary
We're warm & right happy within

We'll sit till the bushes are dropping
Like the spout of a watering pan
For till the drams drank theres no stopping
We'll keep up the ring to a man
We'll sit till dame nature is feeling
The breath of our stingo so warm
& bushes & trees begin reeling
In our eyes like to ships in a storm

We'll sit from three hours before seven
When larks wake the morning to dance
Till nights sutty brood of eleven
When witches ride over to france
We'll sit it in spite of the weather
Till we tumble our length on the plain

When the morning shall find us together
To play the game over again

THE OFFER A BALLAD

With my hair down my back & bibbed up to my chin
Friends had made me a child all the days of my life
Had'n't love a peeped through the disguise I was in
& whispered Bob Rattle to look for a wife
He made me supprised when I heard what he said
& I felt from that hour like a bird that is free
Childish thoughts all for ever went out of my head
& I 'greed Robin Rattle should come & court me

I grew mortal sick of my mothers old fashions
Tyed a bow 'gainst her will feth & shifted a pin
& little she guessed though she fell into passions
Twas done Robin Rattle the ploughman to win
& vain had she made me consciet I d been younger
She might as well said snow in harvest would be
As tye me a child at her woolen wheel longer
When Rob offered making a woman of me

341

BALLAD

Give me lifes ease when my leafs turning yellow
Leave me no more of cares mountains to climb
Give me lifes calm when my fruits getting mellow
Let no rude winds blow to shorten my prime
Let my last pleasures be just as Ive thought 'em
Let death supprise me with no ruffian call
But soft as the leaves on the breezes of autumn
Let my bald head on its last pillow fall

Three score & ten be my last travels numbered
Three score & ten is the length I desire
Then with few pains & few struggles encumbered
Small would the blow be that death would require
Deaths labours light when by age life is wounded
& if the grave is unhaunted with pain
Long be the time ere the last trump is sounded
Long may I sleep ere I'm wakened again

THE PROMISE A BALLAD

A housed-up-mouse both night & morn
Tyed to the wheel is Nanny
Sure neer a luckless wench were born
To live as I with granny
I can't stir out a foot from home
But she bawls out for Nanny
All sweethearts they're denied to come
Mens poison unto granny

She calls me crazy wild & mad
& says I'm worse then any
If I just look upon a lad
O fye upon thee granny
Thou now art old but if I know
When ye were young as Nanny
I'll bound ye were as crazy too
& not to baulk ye granny

Last night Tom Tibbs went bye & bye
The youth was slye & shanny
But soon I read his leering eye
"Slip out an hour from granny"
So up I starts a scheme was had
"—Where are ye going Nanny"
I seek the air I'm sick & bad
Said I—& cheated granny

He led me on saying go with me
& see some pleasure Nanny
& peeped & smiled if we agree
We'll soon clear scores with granny
& honey what ye like the best
Say & I'll do't for Nanny
Well then says I to make me blest
Tom take me from my granny

& so he did & grumping gran
She said 'twou'd turn her scranny
Lud O said I if thats the plan
What made ye marry granny
Ive been now long enough at school
To know both sides a penny

343

& if in marrying Im a fool
I'm more akin to granny

& though Toms none I d chuse my sen
If I were like a many
But I'd neer met the chance agen
When once shut up with granny
With her I might have staid & staid
Till classed with wrinkled Nannys
& then gone crazed a slighted maid
—Who would be ruled by grannys

SONG

Go with your tauntings go
Neer think to hurt me so
I ll scoff at your disdain
Cold though the winter blow
When hills are free from snow
It will be spring again

So go & fare thee well
Nor think ye'll have to tell
Of wounded hearts from me
Locked up in your hearts cell
Mine still at home doth dwell
In its first liberty

Bees sip not at one flower
Spring comes not with one shower
Nor shines the sun alone
Upon one favoured hour
But with unstinted power
Makes every day his own

& for my freedoms sake
With such I'll pattern take
& rove & revel on
Your gall shall never make
Me honied paths forsake
So prythee get thee gone

& when my toil is blest
& I find a maid possest
Of truth thats not in thee
Like bird that finds its nest
I'll stop & take my rest
& love as she loves me

BALLAD

O sigh no more love sigh no more
Nor pine for earthly treasure
Who fears a shipwreck on the shore
Or meets despair with pleasure

Let not our wants our troubles prove
Although tis winter weather
Nor singly strive with what our love
Can better brave together

Thy love is proved thy worth is such
It cannot fail to bless me
If I loose thee I can't be rich
Nor poor if I possess thee

THE INCONSTANT SHEPHERD
OR SORROWS MELODIE

A maid was wooed by a haughty swain & she was fair & gay
As ever song did sing or feign in groves of arcadie
& she was won though he was proud & jealous was his heart
His temper worked her mickle woe her beauty stood no part
The eye that gazed upon her face his anger would bewray
& where was eye that met with such could care to turn away
Smiles though of gentle kind would his stormy temper bare
& ere since smiles were born what heart could frown on one so fair
Sad jealousy thy potion runs like fever through the veins
When the drained cup falls down & turns each fragment into pains
Its thoughts are worse than hellebore & poison berries are
& nought but foulest weeds themselves can thrive & harbour there
So she was wronged & pined forlorn all through such cruelty
Then on his pipe for swains can play thus sad repented he
In a bower he made for her when love first grew too young to wrong
& now morn hung the leaves with dew as if to weep the song
"O woe is me & welladay how could my reason freeze
So far on follys ice to stray to harbour jealousies
Its bitter stream takes hold of hell on sorrows frenzy bound
Nor on its shore one joy appears—all is a desert round
Dark was the thoughts I bore to her whose beauty they dislimnd
White was the bosom which they wronged & bright the eyes they
    dimmed
Fair was her face & sweet those lips where rubys did prevail
& evil was those thoughts of mine that turned them both so pale
& her fond heart so white & pure that glistened in her eye
O had I known but half its worth I had not let it die
I thought her artless ways were rude & tryed revenge to take
& wronged her heart with idle gibes till it were like to break
But as the ivy clasps the wall & woodbine twines the tree
The more I wronged the more her heart did cleave & cling to me
& all my evil ways could do & deep the wounds they made
The stubborn root would loose no hold though the branches still
    decayed
Shrinking away as shadows do decaying in decay
& wasting as the snow doth waste that weeps itself away
For beauty ever was I wis always of gentle kind
& the slightest wound inflicted there must leave a scare behind
So she faded on & loved me still & still forbore to mourn
Though I made my heart seem ice her own could not forget to burn
Till I sought new loves & then too true to bear inconstancy

It broke in deaths kind arms to rest & left its pains with me
For then I proved her all too true a double death to me"
Then he laid down his troubled lute as weary to complain
But little birds would not be still they mourned to hear the strain
& when he tried some merry tune soon went his fingers wrong
Marring the tune as if his heart would know no other song

OCEAN GLORIES—TUNE
"OLD BENBOW" A BEAUTIFUL MELODIE

Come all you seamen bold who have fought side to side
Come gallant fellows all lend an ear
Tis of an admirals fame
Brave Grenville called by name
How he fought on the main scorning fear till he died
& won a naveys fame you shall hear

The first of seven ships was his own for to meet
The Spaniards line of sail fifty five
& spite of shot & ball
He sailed amidst them all
& there his ship revenge kept at bay their whole fleet
Till scarce a gallant heart beat alive

Come gallant boys he cried I will lead—who will fight
Lives there a soul on board that would run
& out their courage burst
Each tried which should be first
Where hell had een turned tail in despair at the sight
Each rushed on glorys throne to his gun

The Spanish thunder burst on their ship all around
& courage felt a shock so severe
But like a rising sun
The gloom was oer & gone
When Grenvilles cheer was heard English tars keep your ground
I lead you on to fight not to fear

Their masters brave commands they did back all along
& the bravest nailed the flag to the mast
Brave brothers he did cry
We'll fight on till we die
To him the cannons noise was a song was a song
& thus they stood it on to the last

Bold Grenville met a shot & was brought to the ground
& courage for a while forced to bow
They dressed his wounded head
& sorrow quickly fled
When they the laurel saw springing up from the wound
& glory weaving wreaths for his brow

For still he lived & cried fight it on we will buy
A victory our foes cannot reap
Lay me in glorys bed
On the quarter deck he said
That I may face my foes & command till I die
& then in honours grave I will sleep

A tallisman to all was his sun ere it set
& glory they pursued to the grave
They fought it on & stood
Till their decks were washed in blood
& when their shot was spent they must yield & they met
A fame which battles won never gave

NELSON & THE NILE

Great Nelsons glory near the nile
Set fames bright scroll on fire
& raised a flame in englands isle
That never shall expire
His empire was the ocean-world
The heart of war his throne
Where ever Englands flag unfurled
He reigned & ruled alone
Wherever he wars vengance hurled
There victory was his own

With heart of fire that burnt the mind
& found its peace in strife
With thoughts that did outspeed the wind
& met from terror life
Upon the sea his element
In danger he grew strong
To battle as a feast he went
Its thunder loud & long
Was music & his hearts assent
Beat welcome to the song

The stubborn storms whose fury rends
Full many a gallant mast
His valour won them into friends
They worshiped as he passed
He led his fleet along the sea
The flying foe to hail
His daring filled with merry glee
The spirit of the gale
Who deemed him neptunes self to be
& spread his every sail

Yet long he sought till fortunes day
The first of august came
When Nelson bore into the bay
That deified his name
But day when dared & year when won
My pen need not defile
For victory wrote it while the sun
Did hold his light & smile

351

To see how Nelson fought & won
The battle of the Nile

The taunting foe of safety vain
Their anchors cast aground
Untill the mighty of the main
Like a tempest gathered round
& they that did the world deride
Now trembled at his name
While rocks & shores & seas defied
& danger dared his fame
To all in thunder he replied
& terror shrunk in shame

Full soon their colours & their fleet
Did ruins throne bedeck
Till weary ocean at his feet
Seemed sinking with the wreck
Their pompous ships were hurled on high
& on their wings of flame
Told to the wondering blushing sky
His glory & their shame
While mars in ecchoes made reply
& marvelled at his name

The elements supprised & won
To view so grand a fight
Drew nights black curtains from the sun
Who smiled upon the sight
The sea forgot its waves & lay
Quite still the sight to see
& neptune from his caves that day
Looked out amazedly
& threw his coral crown away
For Nelson ruled the sea

MAY QUEEN
A BALLAD

Go leave your loves unsung ye swains
For she that rivals all the rest
Hath won the wreath of may
So throw your pipes upon the plains
For nature knows the fairest maid
& chuses Sally Grey

Go wear your silks ye lady birds
In russet far above you shines
The lady of the May
Your dresses make you what you are
They cannot make you half so fair
As beautys Sally Grey

Go paint with artificial blooms
Your cheeks from natures grace removed
A rose is queen of may
& can ye think your mock perfumes
Make ye so sweet & so beloved
No—look at Sally Grey

Sweet as the dews unto the night
As sunshine to the summer morn
A lady of the may
As secresy to loves delight
Owns smiles more dearer far to one
Who doats on Sally Grey

EXPECTATION
A BALLAD

Tis saturday night & my shepherd will come
With a hollow & whistle for me
Be clear o ye skyes take your storm burtherns home
Let no rain drench our favourite tree
For I fear by the things that are hopping about
Theres a sign of a storm coming on
The Frog looks as black as the Toad that creeps out
From under its hiding stone

The cat with her tail runneth round till she reels
& the pigs race with mouthfulls of hay
I sigh at the sight—& felt sick over meals
For Im lone when my shepherds away
When dogs eat the grass it is sure to be rain
& our dogs in the orchard—een now
The swallows flye lowe & my heart is in pain
While the flyes even maddened the cow

The piegons have moped on the cote the day long
& the hens went to bed before noon
The blackbirds long still din the woods with their song
& they look upon showers as a boon
While they keep their nest dry in the wet hazel bush
& moisten their black sutty wing
Did they know but my sorrows they'd quickly be hush
Birds to make lovers happy should sing

& Ive often leaned oer the crofts mossy gate
To listen birds singing at night
When I for the surefooted Rover did wait
& rich was my bosoms delight
& sweet had it been now Im waiting anew
Till the black snail is out from the grain
But the souths ruddy clouds they have turned black & blue
& the blackbirds are singing for rain

The Thrush "wivy wit wivy wit" tother night
Sang aloud in the old sallow bush
& I called him a pert little urchin outright
To sing "heavy wet"—And the Thrush
Changed his note in a moment to "cheer up" & "cheer"

& the clouds crept away from the sun
Till my shepherd he came & when Thrushes I hear
My heart with the music is won

But the blackbird is rude & insulting & now
The more the clouds blacken the sky
The louder he sings from the green hazel bough
But he may be sad bye & bye
For the cowboy is stooping beneath the oak tree
Whose branches hang down to the ground
& beating his stick on the bushes to see
If a bird startles out from the sound

So silence is safety & bird have a care
Or your song will your dwelling betray
For yesterday morning I saw your nest there
But sung not to fright ye away
& now the boys near you—well done cunning bird
You have ceased & popt out tother side
Your nest it is safe not a leaf has he stirred
& I have my shepherd descried

LOVE OF THE FIELDS

The shepherd bends musing beneath the green thorn
& his shag dog as black as a coal
Wet with chasing the rabbits about in the corn
Lies to watch them bob out of the hole
In the bank—& to make up the picture of morn
The mare stands a knapping the foal
& when these delicious enchantments I see
O I think what a life must the glad shepherds be

Then he'll sawn by the brook where the dewberrys shoot
That for all the world look as the morn
Had breathed as it past—& the old willow root
Makes his foothold a step—& the thorn
Grows a staff—while he reaches a maiden the fruit
Whom beauty & blushes adorn
& when such delicious green pictures I see
O who can help wishing their tennant to be

Then the woodman he goes with his hatchet & bill
A singing old songs as he goes
& the wood gate it claps as twould never be still
Till echo affrightens the crows
In the oaks—& the rabbit pops off from the hill
As hid in green bushes he goes
Brushing through the green ferns by the hugh spreading tree
O I think what a joy must the forresters be

By the old spinney gate in the green narrow lane
The gipsey sits under his camp
Where the woodbines are all in full blossom again
& the ass stands the thistle to champ
On the hill—while the camp is so hid from the rain
& the grass is so free from the damp
& through the green leaves the sun gleams so divine
O I cannot help wishing his pleasures were mine

The shepherd enjoys all the riches of may
& labour grows pleasure by stealth
The woodman abides in the old forest grey
Amidst the green temple of health
In the swale—while the gipsey he builds in a day
A house without trouble or wealth

& when these delicious green pictures I see
O I wish the fields out-of-door tennant to be

To make a cot een of a hugh hollow tree
Where the badger hath burrowed a den
Or warp a rude camp on the molehilly lea
Where the sheep bleat away from the pen
On the fallows—or else in the green forest be
Where the fox seeketh safety agen
O I think though the world has grown old in its care
I should meet with the garden of paradise there

THE BOUNTY OF PROVIDENCE

I think I'm as rich as a man need to be
Though money nor land fortune ever left me
Yet Ive that which belongs as a free common right
To us all—& it giveth my bosom delight
To see the sun smile on my cottage & bring
Daily splendour as rich as he leaves with the king
—Overshadowed with care I can go to the door
& see the sun smile till the cloud passes oer

Nor land nor yet living belongs unto me
Yet I can go out in the meadows & see
The healthy green grass—& behold the shower fall
As the wealth of that being that blesses us all
& he that feels this who can say he is poor
For fortunes the birthright of joy—nothing more
& he that feels thus takes the wealth from the soil
For the mizer owns nought but the trouble & toil

My power it is nothing my riches is small
Yet my mind is as free as the richest of all
& my will to do good is as great as the best
For nature she teaches this lesson at least
As she looks upon me so to look upon all
With a joy that would no creatures blessings forestall
For the sun so exalted in glory & high
Bids the ant be as welcome to greet him as I

Having little I'll be with that little content
& take fortunes gifts in the way that she meant
To look at my lot as the best that could be
From the troubles & toil of ambition all free
With an old pocket legend wearing gold to the end
"He never is poor that keeps god for his friend"
I look on the skies & think so—for they fall
One vast hope & blessing alike over all

DECAY   A BALLAD

O poesy is on the wane
For fancys visions all unfitting
I hardly know her face again
Nature herself seems on the flitting
The fields grow old & common things
The grass the sky the winds a blowing
& spots where still a beauty clings
Are sighing "going all a going"
O poesy is on the wane
I hardly know her face again

The bank with brambles overspread
& little molehills round about it
Was more to me then laurel shades
With paths & gravel finely clouted
& streaking here & streaking there
Through shaven grass & many a border
With rutty lanes had no compare
& heaths were in a richer order
But poesy is in its wane
I hardly know her face again

I sat with love by pasture streams
Aye beautys self was sitting bye
Till fields did more then edens seem
Nor could I tell the reason why
I often drank when not a dry
To pledge her health in draughts divine
Smiles made it nectar from the sky
Love turned een water into wine
O poesy is on the wane
I cannot find her face again

The sun those mornings used to find
When clouds were other-country-mountains
& heaven looked upon the mind
With groves & rocks & mottled fountains
These heavens are gone—the mountains grey
Turned mist—the sun a homeless ranger
Pursuing on a naked way
Unnoticed like a very stranger
O poesy is on its wane
Nor love nor joy is mine again

Loves sun went down without a frown
For very joy it used to grieve us
I often think that west is gone
Ah cruel time to undecieve us
The stream it is a naked stream
Where we on sundays used to ramble
The sky hangs oer a broken dream
The brambles dwindled to a bramble
O poesy is on its wane
I cannot find her haunts again

Mere withered stalks & fading trees
& pastures spread with hills & rushes
Are all my fading vision sees
Gone gone is raptures flooding gushes
When mushrooms they were fairy bowers
Their marble pillars overswelling
& danger paused to pluck the flowers
That in their swarthy rings were dwelling
But poesys spells are on the wane
Nor joy nor fear is mine again

Aye poesy hath passed away
& fancys visions undecieve us
The night hath taen the place of day
& why should passing shadows grieve us
I thought the flowers upon the hills
Where flowers from Adams open gardens
& I have had my summer thrills
& I have had my hearts rewardings
So poesy is on its wane
I hardly know her face again

& friendship it hath burned away
Just like a very ember cooling
A make believe on april day
That sent the simple heart a fooling
Mere jesting in an earnest way
Decieving on & still decieving
& hope is but a fancy play
& joy the art of true believing
For poesy is on the wane
O could I feel her faith again

HOME HAPPINESS
BALLAD

Like a thing of the desert alone in its glee
I make a small home seem an empire to me
Like a bird in the forest whose home is its nest
My home is my all & the centre of rest
Let ambition stride over the world at a stride
Let the restless go rolling away with the tide
I look on lifes pleasures as follys at best
& like sunset feel calm when Im going to rest

I sit by the fire in the dark winters night
While the cat cleans her face with her foot in delight
& the winds all acold with rude clatter & din
Shake the windows like robbers who want to come in
Or else from the cold to be hid & away
Where the fire it burns bright & my childerns at play
Making houses of cards or a coach of a chair
While I sit enjoying their happiness there

I walk round the orchard on sweet summer eves
& rub the perfume from the black currant leaves
Which like the geranium when touched leaves a smell
That ladslove & sweet briar can hardly excell
& watch the things grow all begemed with the shower
That glitter like pearls in a sunshiny hour
& hear the pert robin just startle a tune
To cheer the lone hedger when labour is done

Joys come like the grass in the field springing there
Without the mere toil of attention or care
They come of them selves like a star in the sky
& the brighter they shine when the cloud passes bye
I wish but for little & find it all there
Where peace gives its faith to the home of the hare
Who otherwise would in her fears run away
From the shade of the flower & the breeze of the day

O the out of door blessings of leisure for me
Health riches & joy—O it owns them all three
There peace comes to me I have faith in her smile
Shes my playmate in leisure my comfort in toil
There the short pasture grass hides the lark on its nest

Though scarcely so high as the grasshoppers breast
& there its moss ball hides the wild honey bee
& there joy in plenty grows riches for me

Far away from the world its delusions & snares
Where words are but breath & its breathings but cares
Where troubles sown thick as the dews of the morn
Can scarce set a foot without meeting a thorn
There are some views the world as a light cuckaball
There are some looks on citys like stones in a wall
Nothing bigger—but these are ambition his heirs
For which I have neither the courage or cares

So I sit on my bench or enjoy in the shade
My toil as a pleasure while using the spade
While fancy is free in her pleasure to stray
Making voyages round the whole world in a day
To gather home comforts where cares never grew
Like manna the heavens rain down with the dew
Till I see the tired hedger bend wearily bye
Then like a tired bird to my corner I flye

THE MAIDENS COMPLAINT
A BALLAD

My partners jeer me all the May
& call me proud & high
& court her not the boobys say
Or bid your heart good bye
& all because a silly swain
Left home & went to sea
& wrote accross the pathless main
To throw the cause at me
He never came my heart to woo
& prythee what could Peggy do

He walked on sundays by my side
& talked of fields & flowers
I spoke again & then he sighed
& so he did for hours
He'd praise the kerchief on my breast
The ribbons on my hat
But from such ways who ever guest
That there was aught in that
He never strove my love to woo
I looked—what else could Peggy do

& then he'd turn his head away
To get at hedgrow flowers
& wade for king cups in the hay
& so he did for hours
But neer so much as gave me one
Or ask for one from me
Can love make language in a stone
Or find a speaking tree
I had not been a stone to woo
What else could cruel Peggy do

363

THE CELLAR DOOR
A BALLAD

By the old tavern door on the causway there lay
A hogshead of stingo just rolled from a dray
& there stood the blacksmith awaiting a drop
As dry as the cinders that lay in his shop
& there stood the cobler as dry as a bun
Almost crackt like a bucket when left in the sun
He'd wetted his knife upon pendil & hone
Till he'd not got a spittle to moisten the stone
So ere he could work though he'd lost the whole day
He must wait the new broach & bemoisten his clay

The cellar was empty each barrel was drained
To its dregs—& Sir John like a rebel remained
In the street—for removal too powerful & large
For two or three topers to take into charge
Odds zooks said a gipsey with bellows to mend
Had I strength I would just be for helping a friend
To walk on his legs but a child in the street
Had as much power as he to put John on his feet
Then up came the blacksmith Sir Barley said he
I should just like to storm your old tower for a spree

& my strength for your strength & bar your renown
I'd soon try your spirit by cracking your crown
& the cobler he tuckt up his apron & spit
In his hands for a burster but devil a bit
Would he move—so as yet they made nothing of land
For there lay the knight like a whale in the sand
Says the tinker if I could but drink of his veins
I should just be as strong & as stubborn again
Push along said the toper the cellars adry
Theres nothing to moistern the mouth of a flye

Says the host we shall burn out with thirst hes so big
Theres a cag of small swipes half as sour as a wig
In such like extreams why extreams will come pat
So lets e'en go & wet all our whistles with that
Says the gipsey may I never bottom a chair
If I drink of small swipes while Sir Johns lying there
& the blacksmith he threw off his apron & swore
Small swipes should bemoisten his gullet no more

364

Let it out on the floor for the dry cock-a-roach
& he held up his hammer with threatens to broach

Sir John in his castle without leave or law
& suck out his blood with a reed or a straw
Ere he'd soak at the swipes—& he turned him to start
Till the host for high treason came down a full quart
Just then passed the dandy & turned up his nose
They'd fain had him shoved but he looked at his cloaths
& nipt his nose closer & twirled his stick round
& simpered tis nuisance to lie on the ground
But bacchus he laughed from the old tavern sign
Saying go on thou shadow & let the sun shine

Then again they all tried & the tinker he swore
That the hogshead had grown twice as heavy or more
Nay nay said the toper & reeled as he spoke
We're all getting weak thats the end of the joke
The ploughman came up & cut short his old tune
Hallooed "woi" to his horses & though it was june
Said he'd help them an hour ere he'd keep them adry
"Well done" said the blacksmith with hopes running high
"He moved & by jingos success to the plough
Aye aye said the cobler we'll conquor him now

The hogshead rolled forward the toper fell back
& the host laughed aloud as his sides they would crack
To see the old tinkers toil make such a gap
In his coat as to rend it from collar to flap
But the tinker he grunted & cried "fiddle dee"
This garment hath been an old tennant with me
& a needle & thread with a little good skill
When Ive leisure will make it stand more weathers still
Then crack went his trunks from the hip to the knee
With his thrusting—no matter for nothing cared he

So long as Sir John rolled along to the door
He's a chip of our block said the blacksmith & swore
& as sure as I live to drive nails in a shoe
He shall have at my cost a full pitcher or two
& the toper he hiccuped which hindered an oath
So long as he'd credit he'd pitcher them both
But the host stopt to hint when he'd ordered the dray
Sir Barleycorns order was purchase & pay

365

& now the old knight is imprisoned & taen
To waste in the tavern mans cellar again

& now said the blacksmith let forfeits come first
For the insult swipes offered or his hoops I will burst
Here it is my old heartys—then drink your thirst full
Said the host for the stingo is worth a strong pull
Never fear for your legs if theyre broken to day
Winds only blow straws dust & feathers away
But the cask that is full like a jiant he lies
& jiants alone can his spirits capsize
If he lies in the path though a kings coming bye
John Barleycorns mighty & there will he lye

Then the toper sat down with a hiccup & felt
If he'd still an odd coin in his pocket to melt
& he made a wry face for his pocket was bare
—But he laughed & danced up "what old boy are you there"
When he felt that a stiver had got to his knee
Through a hole in his fob & right happy was he
Says the tinker Ive brawled till no breath I have got
& not met with twopence to purchase a pot
Says the toper Ive powder to charge a long gun
& a stiver Ive found when I thought I'd got none

So by helping a thirsty old friend in his need
Is my duty—take heart thou art welcome indeed
Then the smith with his tools in Sir John made a breach
& the toper he hiccuped & ended his speech
& pulled at the quart till the snob he declared
When he went to drink next that the bottom was bared
No matter for that said the toper & grinned
I had but a soak & neer rested for wind
Thats law said the smith with a look rather vexed
But the quart was a forfeit so pay for the next

Then they talked of their skill & their labour till noon
When the sober mans toil was exactly half done
& there the plough lay—people hardly could pass
& the horses let loose pinsoned up the short grass
& browsed on the bottle of flags lying there
By the gipseys old budget for mending a chair
The millers horse tyed to the old smithy door
Stood stamping his feet by the flies bitten sore

Awaiting the smith as he wanted a shoe
& he stampt till another fell off & made two

Till the miller expecting that all would get loose
Went to seek him & cursed him outright for a goose
But he dipt his dry beak in the mug once or twice
& forgot all his passion & toils in a trice
& the fly bitten horse at the old smithy post
Might stamp till his shoes & his legs they were lost
He sung his old songs & forgot his old mill
Blow winds high or low she might rest at her will
& the cobbler in spite of his bustle for pelf
Left the shop all the day to take care of itself

& the toper who carried his house on his head
No wife to be teazing no barns to be fed
Would sit out the week or the month or the year
Or a lifetime so long as he'd credit or beer
The ploughman he talked of his skill as divine
How he could plough thurrows as straight as a line
& the blacksmith he swore had he but the command
He could shoe the kings hunter the best in the land
& the cobbler declared was his skill but once seen
He should soon get an order for shoes from the queen

But the tinker he swore he could beat them all three
For gi me a pair of old bellows says he
& I'll make them roar out like the wind in a storm
& make them blow fire out of coals hardly warm
The toper said nothing but wished the quart full
& swore he could toss it all off at a pull
Ha' done said the tinker but wit was away
When the bet was to bind him he d nothing to pay
& thus in the face of lifes sun & shower weather
They drank bragged & sung & got merry together

The sun it went down—the last gleam from his brow
Flung a smile of repose on the holiday plough
The glooms they approached & the dews like a rain
Fell thick & hung pearls on the old sorrel mane
Of the horse that the miller had brought to be shod
& the morning awoke saw a sight rather odd
For a bit of the halter still hung at the door
Bit through by the horse now at feed on the moor

& the old tinkers budget lay still in the weather
While all kept on singing & drinking together

REMEMBRANCES

Summer pleasures they are gone like to visions every one
& the cloudy days of autumn & of winter cometh on
I tried to call them back but unbidden they are gone
Far away from heart & eye & for ever far away
Dear heart & can it be that such raptures meet decay
I thought them all eternal when by Langley bush I lay
I thought them joys eternal when I used to shout & play
On its bank at "clink & bandy" "chock" & "taw" & ducking stone
Where silence sitteth now on the wild heath as her own
Like a ruin of the past all alone

When I used to lie & sing by old eastwells boiling spring
When I used to tie the willow boughs together for a "swing"
& fish with crooked pins & thread & never catch a thing
With heart just like a feather—now as heavy as a stone
When beneath old lea close oak I the bottom branches broke
To make our harvest cart like so many working folk
& then to cut a straw at the brook to have a soak
O I never dreamed of parting or that trouble had a sting
Or that pleasures like a flock of birds would ever take to wing
Leaving nothing but a little naked spring

When jumping time away on old crossberry way
& eating awes like sugar plumbs ere they had lost the may
& skipping like a leveret before the peep of day
On the rolly polly up & downs of pleasant swordy well
When in round oaks narrow lane as the south got black again
We sought the hollow ash that was shelter from the rain
With our pockets full of peas we had stolen from the grain
How delicious was the dinner time on such a showry day
O words are poor receipts for what time hath stole away
The ancient pulpit trees & the play

When for school oer "little field" with its brook & wooden brig
Where I swaggered like a man though I was not half so big
While I held my little plough though twas but a willow twig
& drove my team along made of nothing but a name
"Gee hep" & "hoit" & "woi"—O I never call to mind
These pleasant names of places but I leave a sigh behind
When I see the little mouldywharps hang sweeing to the wind
On the only aged willow that in all the field remains

& nature hides her face while theyre sweeing in their chains
& in a silent murmuring complains

Here was commons for their hills where they seek for freedom still
Though every commons gone & though traps are set to kill
The little homeless miners—O it turns my bosom chill
When I think of old "sneap green" puddocks nook & hilly snow
Where bramble bushes grew & the daisy gemmed in dew
& the hills of silken grass like to cushions to the view
Where we threw the pissmire crumbs when we'd nothing else to do
All leveled like a desert by the never weary plough
All vanished like the sun where that cloud is passing now
& settled here for ever on its brow

O I never thought that joys would run away from boys
Or that boys would change their minds & forsake such summer joys
But alack I never dreamed that the world had other toys
To petrify first feelings like the fable into stone
Till I found the pleasure past & a winter come at last
Then the fields were sudden bare & the sky got overcast
& boyhoods pleasing haunts like a blossom in the blast
Was shrivelled to a withered weed & trampled down & done
Till vanished was the morning spring & set the summer sun
& winter fought her battle strife & won

By Langley bush I roam but the bush hath left its hill
On cowper green I stray tis a desert strange & chill
& spreading lea close oak ere decay had penned its will
To the axe of the spoiler & self interest fell a prey
& crossberry way & old round oaks narrow lane
With its hollow trees like pulpits I shall never see again
Inclosure like a Buonaparte let not a thing remain
It levelled every bush & tree & levelled every hill
& hung the moles for traitors—though the brook is running still
It runs a nake[d] brook cold & chill

O had I known as then joy had left the paths of men
I had watched her night & day be sure & never slept agen
& when she turned to [go] O I'd caught her mantle then
& wooed her like a lover by my lonely side to stay
Aye knelt & worshipped on as love in beautys bower
& clung upon her smiles as a bee upon a flower
& gave her heart my poesys all cropt in a sunny hour
As keepsakes & pledges all to never fade away

370

But love never heeded to treasure up the may
So it went the common road with decay

A WORLD FOR LOVE

O this world is all too rude for thee with much ado & care
O this world is but a rude world & hurts a thing so fair
Was there a nook in which the world had never been to sere
That world would prove a paradise when thou & love was near

& there to pluck the blackberry & there to reach the sloe
Now joyously & quietly would love thy partner go
Then rest when weary on a bank where not a grassy blade
Had ere been bent by troubles feet & love thy pillow made

For summer would be evergreen though sloes was in their prime
& winter smile his frowns to spring in beautys happy clime
& months would come & months would go & all in sunny moods
& every thing inspired by thee grow beautifully good

& there to seek a cot unknown to any care & pain
& there to shut the door alone on singing wind & rain
Far far away from all the world more rude then rain or wind
& who could wish a sweeter home or better place to find

Then thus to live & love with thee thou beautiful delight
Then thus to love & live with thee the summer day & night
& earth itself where thou had rest would surely smile to see
Herself grow eden once again possest of love & thee

GOD BLESS THEE

Thou lovely one thy witching face
Doth win the heedless passer bye
To marvel what a winning grace
Hath woman in her majesty
God bless thee
Hearts mutter in warm youths excess
& with fond praise caress thee
When beauty smiles can praise do less
Then wish all good to bless thee

Thou lovely one thy claim to good
Is coeternal with the sky
& heaven is of thy sisterhood
It shineth in thy timid eye
Thy love & faith an heaven hath made
God bless thee
Mens worship need not be affraid
Though as angels they caress thee
For thourt an angel ready made
They cannot help but bless thee

Praise cometh from thy tongue to me
Music & love & every thing
& in thy faith that heaven I see
That gives delight to suffering
& turns aside the thorns of care
God bless thee
In joy & hope & dark despair
My praises did caress thee
& even in death I ll love thee there
& everlasting bless thee

THE SHEPHERD

When the bloom on the black thorn shines white in the sun
& the rook begins building her nest
When the lambs round the molehillocks gambol & run
Then the shepherds glad toil is the best
From the dust of the barn where the cobwebs in ropes
Hang down from the roof & the wall
& the thresher alone oer his dull labour mopes
While the barndoor fowl cackle & squall

The shepherd while Dolly sits milking her cow
Stands telling love tales & the like
Or takes a few rounds with his partner at plough
& then he leaps over the dyke
& hies him away to his sheep in the close
Where the blackcap sings loud in his ear
& thus with his labour & pleasant discourse
He enjoys the new smiles of the year

In the morning he lets out his sheep from the pen
While the wood piegon cooes in the tree
& drives them away to the green springing glen
Where the pewet sweeps over the lea
& there he roams round till the shut of the sun
& sees the bird building its nest
& when his half play & half labour is done
He whistles away to his rest

While his dog snufts the path with a eager delight
Oft starting the rabit & hare
Who venture the new sprouting grasses to bite
As far from the wood as they dare
& first at the cottage he scrats at the door
To tell that his master is come
& there the glad shepherd drops down in his chair
& tells his day stories at home

Or takes up a book full of stories & songs
Reading such as his fancies admire
While his childern ride cock horse on poker & tongues
& his dog licks his feet at the fire
Often musing awhile oer the comforts he feels
Then to bed untill morning again

When his dog is heard barking aloud at his heels
As he whistles away to the plain

SUMMER BALLAD

Poesy now in summer stoops
Full fifty times a day
The green turns gold with buttercups
The hedges white with may
The ballad singing larks now troop
By dozens from the hay
& dozens down as soon as up
Leaves one the time to play

But sweeter ballads fill the vale
When maidens meet the morn
& the red cow stands oer the pail
Beneath the squatty thorn
Where sheep come up & rub their heads
& cows lie down to chew
Their cuds beneath the battered shade
When grass is wet with dew

The magpies nest is on the top
She cannot sing—but shows
Mays hurry while the maiden stops
& chatters till she goes
The mays field ballads much would need
If song was all its lot
& all its bustle rude indeed
If beauty owned it not

Morn sprinkles treasures in her way
Green health in every place
& I thought verses half the day
To pass so sweet a face
Dress sets not off her face so well
As it sets off her dress
Love easy knows where beauty dwells
If fancy bids it guess

She might have sweethearts half a score
& that in half a year
But she has one & wants no more
& blushes when he's near
From idle words she turns away
& frowns will fools reprove

But kindness she with kindness pays
Till almost ta'en for love

No broaches on her breast she wears
Pind down with golden pins
She gives herself no foolish airs
Nor feels the praise she wins
Though fancy many a flounce prefers
When may day comes about
Pride has but small to do with her
Thats rich enough without

She loves on sunday noons to go
Among the birds in may
Where buntings "pink" "pink" ["]pink" as though
They followed all the way
She dances round & skips the stile
Rich in her sunday dress
& meets from every face a smile
The type of happiness

& so delightful grows the walk
With loves familiar ear
Joy almost may in ballads talk
When beauty listens near
& soon as she has past the farm
& eyes are out of sight
She takes the waiting shepherds arm
& dallys with delight

She loves to spend an hour or so
With neighbours & to see
How pinks & cloves & lilys grow
Which goody shows so free
Beds edged with daisys red & white
& thrift & london pride
Appears to her so fine a sight
That nowhere owns beside

Few are the flowers her taste prefers
Yet looking up & down
She nips a leaf of lavender
To put within her gown
She loves a flower her gown to grace

377

But asks not—& recieves
A nosegay sweet—for beautys face
In welcomes favour lives

The young their silent gifts bestow
That somthing more would tell
& old folks happy are to show
They ever wish it well
She loves the garden bench at eve
& takes her sewing there
& gets by heart the last new song
A present from the fair

She has a love for many things
But will not own to one
& he who sees her home at spring
Is kept a secret on
She loves the oak upon the green
In may with apples hung
For there she sits & sings unseen
The songs her mother sung

She loves the thrush that comes to sing
Upon the hedgerow bough
& curly coated lambs of spring
That race up to the cow
The shepherd dog in shaggy suit
In e'er such haste will stand
& though the old yoe stamps her foot
Awaits the patting hand

The wouldbe sweetheart often drops
Love welcomes in her way
& she her ballad only stops
To pass the time of day
While some would compliment her health
& win esteem unseen
Beauty unconscious of its wealth
Knows not the maid they mean

She loves the green that herds the cow
& gives her labour joy
Where she plays crookhorn even now
As wild as any boy

The sweetest blessings life provides
Her village peace bestows
Though some few towns where kin resides
Is all the world she knows

& I could go when morning pays
Green welcome to her song
& I could stay when evening stays
Nor think her longest long
& lie upon the grass & think
& in the rushes make
With her sweet looks for pen & ink
Green ballads for her sake

SONNETS

SWORDY WELL

Ive loved thee Swordy well & love thee still
Long was I with thee tending sheep & cow
In boyhood ramping up each steepy hill
To play at 'roly poly' down—& now
A man I trifle oer thee cares to kill
Haunting thy mossy steeps to botanize
& hunt the orchis tribes where natures skill
Doth like my thoughts run into phantasys
Spider & Bee all mimicking at will
Displaying powers that fools the proudly wise
Showing the wonders of great natures plan
In trifles insignificant & small
Puzzling the power of that great trifle man
Who finds no reason to be proud at all

SUMMER MOODS

I love at eventide to walk alone
Down narrow lanes oerhung with dewy thorn
Where from the long grass underneath—the snail
Jet black creeps out & sprouts his timid horn
I love to muse oer meadows newly mown
Where withering grass perfumes the sultry air
Where bees search round with sad & weary drone
In vain for flowers that bloomed but newly there
While in the juicey corn the hidden quail
Cries 'wet my foot' & hid as thoughts unborn
The fairylike & seldom-seen land rail
Utters 'craik craik' like voices underground
Right glad to meet the evenings dewy veil
& see the light fade into glooms around

SUMMER EVENING

The frog half fearful jumps accross the path
& little mouse that leaves its hole at eve
Nimbles with timid dread beneath the swath
My rustling steps awhile their joys decieve
Till past—& then the cricket sings more strong
& grasshoppers in merry moods still wear
The short night weary with its fretting song
Up from behind the molehill jumps the hare
Cheat of its chosen bed—& from the bank
The yellowhammer flutters in short fears
From off its nest hid in the grasses rank
& drops again when no more noise it hears
Thus natures human link & endless thrall
Proud man still seems the enemy of all

THE VILLAGE BOY

Free from the cottage corner see how wild
The village boy along the pastures hies
With every smell & sound & sight beguiled
That round the prospect meets his wondering eyes
Now stooping eager for the cowslip peeps
As though he'd get them all—now tired of these
Accross the flaggy brook he eager leaps
For some new flower his happy rapture sees
Now tearing mid the bushes on his knees
Or woodland banks for bluebell flowers he creeps
& now while looking up among the trees
He spies a nest & down he throws his flowers
& up he climbs with new fed extacies
The happiest object in the summer hours

EVENING SCHOOLBOYS

Harken that happy shout—the schoolhouse door
Is open thrown & out the younkers teem
Some run to leapfrog on the rushy moor
& others dabble in the shallow stream
Catching young fish & turning pebbles oer
For muscle clams—Look in that mellow gleam
Where the retiring sun that rests the while
Streams through the broken hedge—How happy seem
Those schoolboy friendships leaning oer the stile
Both reading in one book—anon a dream
Rich with new joys doth their young hearts beguile
& the books pocketed most hastily
Ah happy boys well may ye turn & smile
When joys are yours that never cost a sigh

THE DEITY

Omnipotent & mighty known unknown
The world whose footstool is the heaven whose throne
Whose is it spreads this glory all around
Star studded skies & flower bewildered ground
Who is it speaks these wonders & they be
Who is it all omnipotent but thee
Thou breathed upon the sun thy powers desire
& instant kindled his eternal fire
Thou badest the unpillared skies their arch expand
Thy breath is underneath them & they stand
Thou badest the seas in tides to rise & fall
& earth to swell triumphant over all
Thy mercey coeternal with thy skill
Saw all was good & bids it flourish still

SUNDAY EVENING

Religion never more calm beauty wears
Than when each cottage joins in sunday prayers
The poor man in his ignorance of ill
His Bible reads with unpretending skill
Unused to argue strange conflicting creeds
He puts plain comments to the page he reads
Though venturing not in warm enthusiasts ways
To offer his own ignorance for praise
He in his Prayer books beautious homilies
His simple reverence to his God reveals
& while his listening childern clasp his knees
A parents blessing from his bosom steals
Prayers are the wings on which the soul doth fly
To gather blessings from a bounteous sky

ON A SKULL

Lifes monitor & fear inspiring friend
Picture of our frail origin & end
Is thine deaths quiet sleep—tis horrible
With worms & dust & coffined bones to dwell
Dost lie in fear of waking wrapt around
In deaths dark sealed impenetrable cloud
Dost ever dream & speak without a sound
Twould make deaths self to shudder in his shroud
Thy shadows hangeth like a gloomy pall
With more or less of terror over all
Life looking on this glass of time doth freeze
With fear at its own image which its sees
To think the living head with thoughts so full
Is but the flattered portrait of a skull

SEDGE BIRDS NEST

Fixed in a white thorn bush its summer guest
So low een grass oertopt its tallest twig
A sedge bird built its little benty nest
Close by the meadow pool & wooden brig
Where schoolboys every morn & eve did pass
In robbing birds & cunning deeply skilled
Searching each bush & taller clump of grass
Where ere was liklihood of bird to build
Yet did she hide her habitation long
& keep her little brood from dangers eye
Hidden as secret as a crickets song
Till they well fledged oer widest pools could flye
Proving that providence is often bye
To guard the simplest of her charge from wrong

THE SHEPHERDS TREE

Hugh Elm thy rifted trunk all notched & scarred
Like to a warriors destiny I love
To stretch me often on such shadowd sward
& hear the laugh of summer leaves above
Or on thy buttressed roots to sit & lean
In carless attitude—& there reflect
On times & deeds & darings that have been
Old cast aways now swallowed in neglect
While thou art towering in thy strength of heart
Stirring the soul to vain imaginings
In which lifes sordid being hath no part
The wind of that eternal ditty sings
Humming of future things that burns the mind
To leave some fragment of itself behind

AN IDLE HOUR

Sauntering at ease I often love to lean
Oer old bridge walls & mark the flood below
Whose ripples through the weeds of oily green
Like happy travellers mutter as they go
& mark the sunshine dancing on the arch
Time keeping to the merry waves beneath
& on the banks see drooping blossoms parch
Thirsting for water in the days hot breath
Right glad of mud drops plashed upon their leaves
By cattle plunging from the steepy brink
While water flowers more than their share recieve
& revel to their very cups in drink
Just like the world some strive & fare but ill
While others riot & have plenty still

THE SHEPHERD BOY

Pleased in his lonliness he often lies
Telling glad stories to his dog—& een
His very shadow that the loss supplies
Of living company. Full oft he ll lean
By pebbled brooks & dream with happy eyes
Upon the fairey pictures spread below
Thinking the shadowed prospect real skies
& happy heavens where his kindred go
Oft we may track his haunts where he hath been
To spend the leisure which his toils bestow
By 'nine peg morris' nicked upon the green
Or flower stuck gardens never meant to grow
Or figures cut on trees his skill to show
Where he a prisoner from a shower hath been

LORD BYRON

A splendid sun hath set when shall our eyes
Behold a morn so beautiful arise
As that which gave his mighty genius birth
& all eclipsed the lesser lights on earth
His first young burst of twilight did declare
Beyond that haze a sun was rising there
As when the morn to usher in the day
Speeds from the east in sober garb of grey
At first till warming into wild delight
She casts her mantle off & shines in light
The labours of small minds an age may dream
& be but shadows on times running stream
While genius in an hour makes what shall be
The next a portion of eternity

ON SEEING THE BUST OF THE PRINCESS VICTORIA BY BEHNES

Sweet opening vision of a royal line
How many hopes & anxious thoughts arise
That time must in her mysterys define
How many pleasing fancies fill our eyes
While musing thus & gazing upon thine
That open look the artist sweetly caught
Turned upward as to view the beaming sky
In all that rich young vacancy of thought
That makes man envy early infancy
Sweetly concieved & exquisitly wrought
The statue even childhoods joy imparts
& sculptures genius makes a proud display
Life almost from the chilly marble starts
& beauty breaths reality in clay

EVENING PASTIME

Musing beside the crackling fire at night
While singing kettle merrily prepares
Womans solacing beverage I delight
To read a pleasant volume where the cares
Of life are sweetened by the muses voice—
Thomson or Cowper or the Bard that bears
Lifes humblest name though natures favoured choice
Her pastoral Bloomfield—& as evening wears
Weary with reading list the little tales
Of laughing childern who edge up their chairs
To tell the past days sport which never fails
To cheer the spirits—while my fancy shares
Their artless talk mans sturdy reason fails
& memorys joy grows young again with theirs

NATURE

How many pages of sweet natures book
Hath poesy doubled down as favoured things
Such as the wood leaves in disorder shook
By startled stockdoves hasty clapping wings
Or green woodpecker that soft tapping clings
To grey oak trunks till scared by passing clowns
It bounces forth in airy ups & downs
To seek fresh solitudes the circling rings
The idle puddock makes around the towns
Watching young chickens by each cottage pen
& such are each days party coloured skies
& such the landscapes charms oer field & fen
That meet the poets never weary eyes
& are too many to be told agen

THE WREN

Why is the cuckoos melody preferred
& nightingales rich song so fondly praised
In poets ryhmes Is there no other bird
Of natures minstrelsy that oft hath raised
Ones heart to extacy & mirth as well
I judge not how anothers taste is caught
With mine theres other birds that bear the bell
Whose song hath crowds of happy memories brought
Such the wood Robin singing in the dell
& little Wren that many a time hath sought
Shelter from showers in huts where I did dwell
In early spring the tennant of the plain
Tenting my sheep & still they come to tell
The happy stories of the past again

A SPRING MORNING

Spring cometh in with all her hues & smells
In freshness breathing over hills & dells
Oer woods where May her gorgeous drapery flings
& meads washed fragrant with their laughing springs
Fresh as new opened flowers untouched & free
From the bold rifling of the amorous bee
Tha happy time of singing birds is come
& loves lone pilgrimage now finds a home
Among the mossy oaks now coos the dove
& the hoarse crow finds softer notes for love
The foxes play around their dens & bark
In joys excess mid woodland shadows dark
& flowers join lips below & leaves above
& every sound that meets the ear is love

TO A FRIEND—IN ILLNESS

In friendships gentle name that claims akin
With poesys warmth its feelings to explain
Lady my feeble pen would fainly win
The welcome praises from thy lips again
Although the Muse shrinks from my hand the while
That with weak hold would yet her stay detain
Mingling sad tears with every withering smile
Dreaming of pleasures past & present pain—
Telling my sick heart that its hopes are vain
Wishing for health it neer may know again
Well I can better bear my sinking lot
Knowing that when my life shall cease to be
My very faults though known shall be forgot
& my poor memory find a friend in thee

SPRING

Now that the spring the quickening earth espouses
& natures feathered folk keep holiday
Each with sweet song in bush & tree carouses
Who would not from dull citys flee away
From smoke enveloped streets & gloomy houses
To fields where forth healths merry maidens fare
To milk their red cows & when that be done
To spend in sport the time they have to spare
Pressing the gold locks of the enarmoured sun
On pleasant banks with young love toying there
& whoso wisheth for a blest estate
That in the golden mean would fear no fall
Need neither wish to be or rich or great
While a poor milk maid lives enjoying all

AUTUMN

Me it delights in mellow autumn tide
To mark the pleasaunce that mine eye surrounds
The forest trees like coloured posies pied
The uplands mealy grey & russet grounds
Seeking for joy where joyance most abounds
Not found I ween in courts & halls of pride
Where folly feeds on flatterys sights & sounds
& with sick heart but seemeth to be merry
True pleasaunce is with humble food supplied
Like shepherd swain who plucks the bramble berry
With savoury appetite from hedgerow briars
Then drops content by molehills sunny side
Proving therebye low joys & small desires
Are easiest fed & soonest satisfied

TO A YOUNG LADY

Maiden the blooms of happiness surround thee
The worlds bright side like thy young visions fair
Gay & unclouded smile in raptures round thee
With joys unconscious of encroaching care
The poesy of life hath sweetly found thee
Ah would thy sunshine had no clouds to share
& the young flowers with which her joys have crowned thee
Would they were dreams as lasting as theyre fair
But nature maiden hath its winter—care
Or more or less in ambush waits to wound thee
Then cheat thy gentle heart with no frail token
From witching hope—far better joys pursue
I know her closest bonds are easy broken
& feel the picture I have drawn too true

CROWLAND ABBEY

In sooth it seems right awful & sublime
To gaze by moonlight on the shattered pile
Of this old abbey struggling still with time
The grey owl hooting from its rents the while
& tottering stones as wakened by the sound
Crumbling from arch & battlement around—
Urging dread echoes from the gloomy aisle
To sink more silent still—The very ground
In desolations garment doth appear—
The lapse of age & mystery profound—
We gaze on wrecks of ornamented stones
On tombs whose sculptures half erased appear
& rank weeds battening over human bones
Till even ones very shadow seems to feel a fear

A PLEASANT PLACE

Now summer cometh I with staff in hand
Will hie me to the sabbath of her joys—
To heathy spots & the unbroken land
Of woodland heritage unknown to noise
& toil—save many a playful band
Of dancing insects that well understand
The sweets of life & with attuned voice
Sing in sweet concert to the pleasant may
There by a little bush I ll listening rest
To hear the nightingale a lovers lay
Chaunt by his mate who builds her carless nest
Of oaken leaves on thorn stumps mossed & grey
Feeling with them I too am truly blest
By making sabbaths of each common day

VANITY OF FAME

What boots the toil to follow common fame
With youths wild visions of anxiety
& waste a life to win a feeble claim
Upon her page which she so soon turns bye
To make new votaries room who share the same
Rewards—& with her faded memories lie
Neighbours to shadows—tis a sorry game
To play in earnest with—to think ones name
Buoyant with visions of eternity
& as familiar now in the worlds ear
As flowers & sunshine to the summers eye
Shall be forgot with other things that were
& like old words grown out of use thrown by
In the confused lap of still obscurity

MEMORY

I would not that my being all should die
& pass away with every common lot
I would not that my humble dust should lie
In quite a strange & unfrequented spot
By all unheeded & by all forgot
With nothing save the heedless winds to sigh
& nothing but the dewy morn to weep
About my grave far hid from the worlds eye
I feign would have some friend to wander nigh
& find a path to where my ashes sleep
Not the cold heart that merely passes bye
To read who lieth there but such that keep
Past memories warm with deeds of other years
& pay to friendship some few friendly tears

DEATH OF BEAUTY

Now thou art gone the fairey rose is fled
That erst gay fancys garden did adorn
Thou wert the dew on which their folly fed
The sun by which they glittered in the morn
Now thou art gone their pride is withered
The dress of common weeds their youth bewray
Now vanity neglects them in her play
Thou wert the very index of their praise
Their borrowed bloom all kindled from thy rays
Like dancing insects that the sun alures
They little heeded it was gained from thee
Vain joys what are they now their suns away
What but poor shadows that blank night obscures
As the grave hideth & dishonours thee

FAME

Whats future fame a melody loud playing
In crowds where one is wanting whose esteeming
Would love to hear it best—a sun displaying
A solitary glory whose bright beaming
Smiles upon withered flowers & lone delaying
Lingers behind its world—a crown vain gleaming
Around a shade whose substance death hath banished
A living dream oer which hope once was dreaming
A busy echoe on each lip delaying
When he that woke it into life is vanished
A picture that from all eyes praise is stealing
A statue towering over glorys game
That cannot feel while he that was all feeling
Is past & gone & nothing but a name

TO THE MEMORY OF BLOOMFIELD

Some feed on living fame with consious pride
& in that gay ship popularity
They stem with painted oars the hollow tide
Proud of the buzz which flatterys aids supply
Joined with to days sun gilded butterfly
The breed of fashion haughtily they ride
As though her breath were immortality
Which is but bladder puffs of common air
Or water bubbles that are blown to die
Let not their fancys think tis muses fare
While feeding on the publics gross supply
Times wave rolls on—mortality must share
A mortals fate & many a fame shall lie
A dead wreck on the shore of dark posterity

Sweet unassuming minstrel not to thee
The dazzling fashions of the day belong
Natures wild pictures field & cloud & tree
& quiet brooks far distant from the throng
In murmurs tender as the toiling bee
Make the sweet music of thy gentle song
Well nature owns thee let the crowd pass by
The tide of fashion is a stream too strong
For pastoral brooks that gently flow & sing
But nature is their source & earth & sky
Their annual offerings to her current bring
Thy gentle muse & memory need no sigh
For thine shall murmur on to many a spring
When their proud streams are summer burnt & dry

The shepherd musing oer his summer dreams
The mayday wild flowers in the meadow grass
The sunshine sparkling in the valley streams
The singing ploughman & hay making lass—
These live the summer of thy rural themes
Thy green memorials these & they surpass
The cobweb praise of fashion—every may
Shall find a native "Giles" beside his plough
Joining the skylarks song at early day
& summer rustling in the ripening corn
Shall meet thy rustic loves as sweet as now
Offering to Marys lips the "brimming horn"
& seasons round thy humble grave shall be
Fond lingering pilgrims to remember thee

BEAUTY

Daughters of england where has nature given
Creatures like you so delicately formed
Ye earthly types of beauty in its heaven
With tender thoughts & blushes ever warmed
Where is the heart with apathy so blessed
That womans beauty failed to lead astray
Where is the eye can for a moment rest
On beautys face & calmly turn away
O lovely woman muse of many themes
The sweet reality of fancys dreams
Where is the soul that never lost its rest
Nor felt the thrilling aching & the strife
From stolen glances on a heaving breast
As white as marble statues warmed with life

THE MARCH NIGHTINGALE

Now sallow catkins once all downy white
Turn like the sunshine into golden light
The rocking clown leans oer the spinny rail
In admiration at the sunny sight
The while the Blackcap doth his ears assail
With such a rich & such an early song
He stops his own & thinks the nightingale
Hath of her monthly reckoning counted wrong
"Sweet jug jug jug" comes loud upon his ear
Those sounds that unto may by right belong
Yet on the awthorn scarce a leaf appears
How can it be—spell struck the wondering boy
Listens again—again the sound he hears
& mocks it in his song for very joy

THE THRUSHES NEST

Within a thick & spreading awthorn bush
That overhung a molehill large & round
I heard from morn to morn a merry thrush
Sing hymns to sunrise while I drank the sound
With joy & often an intruding guest
I watched her secret toils from day to day
How true she warped the moss to form her nest
& modelled it within with wood & clay
& bye & bye like heathbells gilt with dew
There lay her shining eggs as bright as flowers
Ink spotted over shells of greeny blue
& there I witnessed in the sunny hours
A brood of natures minstrels chirp & flye
Glad as that sunshine & the laughing sky

THE SYCAMORE

In massy foliage & a sunny green
The splendid sycamore adorns the spring
Adding rich beauty to the varied scene
That natures breathing arts alone can bring
Hark how the insects hum around & sing
Like happy ariels hid from heedless view
& merry bees that feed with eager wing
On the broad leaves glazed oer with honey dew
The fairey sunshine gently flickers through
Upon the grass & buttercups below
& in its foliage winds their sport renew
Waving romantic shadows too & fro
That oer the mind in sweet disorder flings
A flitting dream of beauties fading things

THE CRABTREE

Spring comes anew & brings each little pledge
That still as wont my childish heart decieves
I stoop again for violets in the hedge
Among the Ivy & old withered leaves
& often mark amid the clumps of sedge
The pooty shells I gathered when a boy
But cares have claimed me many an evil day
& chilled the relish which I had for joy
Yet when crab blossoms blush among the may
As wont in years gone bye I scramble now
Up mid the brambles for my old esteems
Filling my hands with many a blooming bough
Till the heart stirring past as present seems
Save the bright sunshine of those fairey dreams

WINTER

Old January clad in crispy rime
Comes trampling on & often makes a stand
The hasty snowstorm neer disturbs his time
He mends no pace but beats his dithering hand
& Febuery like a timid maid
Smiling & sorrowing follows in his train
Huddled in cloak of mirey roads affraid
She hastens on to greet her home again
Then march the prophetess by storms inspired
Gazes in rapture on the troubled sky
& then in headlong fury madly fired
She bids the hail storm boil & hurry bye
Yet neath the blackest cloud a sunbeam flings
Its cheering promise of returning springs

THE BEANS IN BLOSSOM

The southwest wind how pleasant in the face
It breaths while sauntering in a musing pace
I roam these new ploughd fields & by the side
Of this old wood where happy birds abide
& the rich blackbird through his golden bill
Utters wild music when the rest are still
Now luscious comes the scent of blossomed beans
That oer the path in rich disorder leans
Mid which the bees in busy songs & toils
Load home luxuriantly their yellow spoils
The herd cows toss the mole hills in their play
& often stand the strangers steps at bay
Mid clover blossoms red & tawney white
Strong scented with the summers warm delight

BOYS AT PLAY

The shepherd boys play by the shaded stile
While sunshine gleams with warm & idle smile
Or hide neath hedges where the linnets sing
& leaves spread curtains round the bubbling spring
While winds with idle dalliance wave the woods
& toy with nature in her youthful moods
Fanning the feathers on the linnets breast
& happy maid in lightsome garments drest
Sweeping her gown in many an armorous shade
As if enarmoured of the form displayed
Upon the southwest wind the boiling showers
Bring sweet arivance of all sorts of flowers
Enjoying like the laughing boys at play
Sabbaths of sunshines outdoor holiday

THE SHEPHERDS FIRE

On the rude heath yclad in furze & ling
& oddling thorn that thick & prickly grows
Shielding the shepherd when the rude wind blows
& boys that sit right merry in a ring
Round fires upon a molehill toasting sloes
& crabs that froth & frizzle on the coals
Loud is the gabble & the laughter loud
The rabbits scarce dare peep from out their holes
Unwont to mix with such a noisey crowd
Some run to eke the fire—while many a cloud
Of smoke curls up some on their haunches squat
With mouth for bellows puffing till it flares
Or if that fail one fans his napless hat
& when the feast is done they squabble for their shares

NOVEMBER

Sybil of months & worshipper of winds
I love thee rude & boisterous as thou art
& scraps of joy my wandering ever finds
Mid thy uproarious madness—when the start
Of sudden tempests stir the forrest leaves
Into hoarse fury till the shower set free
Still the hugh swells & ebb the mighty heaves
That swing the forrest like a troubled sea
I love the wizard noise & rave in turn
Half vacant thoughts & self imagined rhymes
Then hide me from the shower a short sojourn
Neath ivied oak & mutter to the winds
Wishing their melody belonged to me
That I might breath a living song to thee

OLD POESY

Sweet is the poesy of the olden time
In the unsullied infancy of rhyme
When nature reigned omnipotent to teach
& truth & feeling owned the powers of speech
Rich is the music of each early theme
& sweet as sunshine in a summer dream
Giving to stocks & stones in raptures strife
A soul of utterance & a tongue of life
Sweet wild flower images in disarray
Which art & fashion fling as weeds away
To sport with shadows of inferior kind
Mere magic lanthorns of the shifting mind
Automatons of wonder working powers
Shadows for life & artificial flowers

To turn from music of this modern art
To fames old pages that real life impart
We seem as startled from unnatural dreams
To hear the summer voice of woods & streams
& feel the sunny air right green & young
Breath music round as though a syren sung
& greet as arts vain painted scenes are bye
The soul stirred impulse of a living sky
As in long draughts of summers parched hours
Falls the refreshment of great rains & showers
The birds resume their song the leaves their green
& brooks as long dry as the land hath been
Brimful of the skys bounty gladly go
Seeming to sing & wonder why they flow

TO DEWINT

Dewint I would not flatter nor would I
Pretend to critic skill in this thine art
Yet in thy landscapes I can well descry
Thy breathing hues as natures counterpart
No painted freaks—no wild romantic sky
No rocks nor mountains as the rich sublime
Hath made thee famous but the sunny truth
Of nature that doth mark thee for all time
Found on our level pastures spots forsooth
Where common skill sees nothing deemed divine
Yet here a worshipper was found in thee
Where thy young pencil worked such rich surprise
That rushy flats befringed with willow tree
Rival'd the beauties of italian skies

A LIVING PICTURE

Her hair was swarthy brown & soft of hue
As the sweet gloom that falls with evens dew
That on her fine white forhead did divide
In the triumphant negligence of pride
Her eyes were dark but they wore lights to shine
That love adores & poets call divine
& her cheeks summer blooms wore hues the while
Of loves soft innosence without its guile
& on the pouting of her amorous lip
Where love delicious nectar longed to sip
Beauty sat throned in that bewitching spell
That love adores & language cannot tell
Where charms triumphant made each gazer pay
Heartaches for looking—ere he turned away

POESY A MAYING

Now comes the bonny May dancing & skipping
Across the stepping stones of meadow streams
Bearing no kin to april showers a weeping
But constant sunshine as her servant seems
Her heart is up—her sweetness all a maying
Streams in her face like gems on beautys breast
The swains are sighing all & well adaying
Love sick & gazing on their lovely guest
The sunday paths to pleasant places leading
Are graced by couples linking arm in arm
Sweet smiles enjoying or some book areading
Where love & beauty are the constant charm
For while the bonny May is dancing bye
Beauty delights the ear & beauty fills the eye

The birds they sing & build & nature scorns
On Mays young festival to keep a widow
There childern too have pleasures all their own
A plucking ladysmocks along the meadow
The little brook sings loud among the pebbles
So very loud that waterflowers which lie
Where many a silver curdle boils & dribbles
Dance too with joy as it goes singing bye
Among the pasture molehills maidens stoop
To pluck the luscious majoram for their bosoms
The greenswards smothered oer with buttercups
& white thorns they are breaking down with blossoms
Tis natures livery for the bonny May
Who keeps her court & all have holiday

Princess of months—so natures choice ordains
& lady of the summer still she reigns
In spite of aprils youth who charms in tears
& rosey June who wins with blushing face
July sweet shepherdess who wreaths the shears
Of shepherds with her flowers of winning grace
& suntanned august with her swarthy charms
The beautiful & rich—& pastoral gay
September with her pomp of fields & farms
& wild novembers sybilline array
In spite of beautys calender the year
Garlands with beautys prize the bonny May
Where'er she goes fair nature hath no peer
& months do loose their queen when shes away

Up like a princess starts the merry morning
In draperies of many coloured cloud
& skylarks minstrels of the early dawning
Pipe forth their hearty anthems long & loud
The bright enarmoured sunshine goes a maying
& every flower his laughing eye beguiles
& on the milkmaids rosey face a playing
Pays court to beauty in his softest smiles
For mays divinity of joy begun
Adds life & lustre to the golden sun
& all of life beneath its glory straying
Is by mays beauty into worship won
Till golden eve ennobles all the west
& day goes blushing like a bride to rest

TO CHARLES LAMB

Friend Lamb thou chusest well to love the lore
Of our old bygone bards whose racey page
Rich mellowing Time made sweeter then before
The blossom left for the long garnered store
Of fruitage now right luscious in its age
Although to fashions taste—what more
Can be expected from the popular rage
For tinsels gauds that are to gold preferred
Me much it grieved as I did erst presage
Vain fashions foils had every heart deterred
From the warm homely phrase of other days
Untill thy muses auncient voice I heard
& now right fain yet fearing honest bard
I pause to greet thee with so poor a praise

BOSTON CHURCH

Majestic pile thy rich & splendid tower
Oerlooks the ocean with aspiring pride
Dareing the insults rude of wind & shower
& greeting time with presence dignified
Firm as a rock yet seems thy massy power
Though thou hast seen prides mightiest thrust aside
& ages crumble at thy feet in dust
& the proud sea claim as her rightful dower
Wrecks of its thousand ships to hold in trust
As dark oblivions harvests of the storm
Yet waves may lash & the loud hurricane
Threaten thy cloud crowned dwelling—& deform
The sky in glooms around thee—all is vain
Empires may pass away but thoult remain

Smiling in sunshine as the storm frowns bye
Whose dreadful rage seemed to thy quiet thrall
As small birds twitterings that beneath thee flye
Winds call aloud & they may louder call
For deaf to dangers voice sublime & grand
Thou towerest in thy old majesty oer all
Tempests that break the tall mast like a wand
Howl their rage weary round thee & no more
Impression makes than summer winds that bow
The little trembling weeds upon thy wall
Lightenings have seared their centurys round thy brow
& left no footmarks—so in shadows hoar
Time decks & spares thee till that doom is hurled
That sears the ocean dry & wrecks the world

ISAAC WALTON

Some blame thee honest Isaac—aye & deem
Thy pastime cruel by the silent stream
Of the unwooded Lea—but he that warms
In eloquence of grief oer suffering worms
Throws by his mourning quill & hunts the hare
Whole hours to death yet feels no sorrow there
Yet this mock sentimental man of moods
On every pastime but his own intrudes
Not so with thee thou man of angel mind
That like thy master gentle was & kind
Fit emblem of the prime apostles days
& worthy even of the scripture praise
& men of Gods own heart must surely be
Such honest soul that most resemble thee

NUTTING

The sun had stooped his westward clouds to win
Like weary traveller seeking for an Inn
When from the hazelly wood we glad descried
The ivied gateway by the pasture side
Long had we sought for nutts amid the shade
Where silence fled the rustle that we made
When torn by briars & brushed by sedges rank
We left the wood & on the velvet bank
Of short sward pasture ground we sat us down
To shell our nutts before we reached the town
The near hand stubble field with mellow glower
Showed the dimmed blaze of poppys still in flower
& sweet the molehills smelt we sat upon
& now the thymes in bloom but where is pleasure gone

THE WOODMAN

Now evening comes & from the new laid hedge
The woodman rustles in his leathern guise
Hiding in dyke ylined with brustling sedge
His bill & mittins from thefts meddling eyes
& in his wallets storeing many a pledge
Of flowers & boughs from early sprouting trees
& painted pootys from the ivied hedge
About its mossy roots—his boys to please
Who wait with merry joy his coming home
Anticipating presents such as these
Gained far afield where they nor night nor morn
Find no school leisure long enough to go
Where flowers but rarely from their stalks are torn
& birds scarce loose a nest the season through

SHADOWS

The fairest summer hath its sudden showers
The clearest sky is never without clouds
& in the painted meadows host of flowers
Some lurking weed in poisonous death enshrouds
Sweet days that upon golden sunshine springs
A gloomy night in mourning waits to stain
The honey bees are girt with sharpest stings
& sweetest joys oft breed severest pains
While like to autumns storms sudden & brief
Mirths parted lips oft close in silent grief
Amid this checkered lifes dissasterous state
Where hope lives green amid the desolate
As nature in her happy livery waves
Oer ancient ruins pallaces & graves

MORNING PLEASURES

The dewy virtues of the early morn
Breaths rich of health & leads the mind to joy
While like a thrilling pleasure newly born
Each little hamlet wakes its shouting boy
Right earlily to wander out afield
& brush the dewdrops from the bending corn
To see what nests the hedgerow thorns may shield
Or gather cuckoos from the neighbouring lawn
Where mid the dark Dog mercury that abounds
Round each mossed stump the woodlark hides her nest
& delicate bluebell that her home surrounds
Bows its soft fragrance oer her spotted breast
Till from the boys rude steps she startled flies
Who turns the weeds away & vainly seeks the prize

HONESTY

There is a valued though a stubborn weed
That blooms but seldom & thats found but rare
In sunless places where it cannot seed
Would earth for truths sake had more room to spare
Cant hates it—hypocrites condemn it—& the herd
Seeking self interest frown & pass it bye
Tis trampled on—tis bantered—& deterred
Tis scoffed—& mocked at—yet it doth not die
But like a diamond for a century lost
Buried in darkness & obscurity
When found again it looses not in cost
But keeps its value & its purity
By time unsullied—still the prince of gems
& first of jewels in all diadems

411

The rich man claims it—but he often buys
Its substitute that is not what it seems
While poverty enobled in disguise
Its simple bloom oft worships & esteems
Knaves boast possesion—but they forge its name
Mobs laud & praise it—but with them tis noise
Or the mere passport for some hidden game
Beneath whose garb self interest lurks & lies
Tis by the good man only deemed a prize
Too valued to be scoffed at or opprest
Tis ever more respected by the wise
Though thousands treat it as a common jest
& that thou mayest not slight so grand a dower
Tis honesty go thou & wear the flower

HAYMAKING

Tis haytime & the red complexioned sun
Was scarcely up ere blackbirds had begun
Along the meadow hedges here & there
To sing loud songs to the sweet smelling air
Where breath of flowers & grass & happy cow
Fling oer ones senses streams of fragrance now
While in some pleasant nook the swain & maid
Lean oer their rakes & loiter in the shade
Or bend a minute oer the bridge & throw
Crumbs in their leisure to the fish below
—Hark at that happy shout—& song between
Tis pleasures birthday in her meadow scene
What joy seems half so rich from pleasure won
As the loud laugh of maidens in the sun

412

SLANDER

There is a viper that doth hide its head
In the recesses of the human heart
There is a serpent that doth make its bed
On manhoods prime & Gods own counterpart
It feeds upon the honours of the great
It mars the reputation of the just
It eats its being into worths estate
& levels all distinctions in the dust
Goodness is smitten by its bitter gibes
Greatness is wounded by the slime it breeds
It lives the worst of all its evil tribes
For poisonous actions & for damning deeds
Nay slanders keener then a serpents breath
It poisons deeper & it brings not death

It feeds on falshood & on clamour lives
& truth like sunshine waters in its eyes
It cannot bear the searching light she gives
But in her splendour—struggles—wreaths—& lies
A crushed & wounded worm that vainly turns
All ways for rest & ease & findeth none
Of its own venom breath it wastes & burns
Away—like putrid waters to the sun
—Its stains as footmarks in a frosty morn
Left on the bruising grass by early swain
Truths Spring soon comes & laughs them all to scorn
Stains dissapear & grass is green again
So hearts that feed the falshood slander frames
Are all that wear at last the venom of its fames

STEPPING STONES

The stepping stones that stride the meadow streams
Look picturesque amid springs golden gleams
Where steps the traveller with a warey pace
& boy with laughing leisure in his face
Sits on the midmost stone in very whim
To catch the struttles that beneath him swim
While those accross the hollow lakes are bare
& winter floods no more rave dangers there
But mid the scum left where it roared & fell
The schoolboy hunts to find the pooty shell
Yet there the boisterous geese with golden broods
Hiss fierce & daring in their summer moods
The boys pull off their hats while passing bye
In vain to fright—themselves being forced to fly

THE GARDEN BENCH

I sit to see the landscape fade away
In musing shadows with departing day
Leaving the shepherds storys half untold
While weary flocks go bleating to the fold
& midges dancing in the evening sun
Bids labour welcome that its toil is done
A wonted quiet oer the bosom steals
Which calm seclusive quiet ever feels
Glad as the hope that meets a lovers smile
Or sweet as labour resting from its toil
& sweet it is some pleasant tale to weave
Neath the swart twilight of a summers eve
Of some sweet being that in thought doth move
An angels beauty with a womans love

PLEASANT PLACES

Old stone pits with veined ivy overhung
Wild crooked brooks oer which was rudely flung
A rail & plank that bends beneath the tread
Old narrow lanes where trees meet overhead
Path stiles on which a steeple we espy
Peeping & stretching in the distant sky
& heaths oerspread with furze blooms sunny shine
Where wonder pauses to exclaim "divine"
Old ponds dim shadowed with a broken tree
These are the picturesque of taste to me
While painting winds to make compleat the scene
In rich confusion mingles every green
Waving the sketchy pencil in their hands
Shading the living scenes to fairey lands

THE HAIL STORM IN JUNE 1831

Darkness came oer like chaos—& the sun
As startled with the terror seemed to run
With quickened dread behind the beetling cloud
The old wood sung like nature in her shroud
& each old rifted oak trees mossy arm
Seemed shrinking from the presence of the storm
& as it nearer came they shook beyond
Their former fears—as if to burst the bond
Of earth that bound them to that ancient place
Where danger seemed to threaten all their race
Who had withstood all tempests since their birth
Yet now seemed bowing to the very earth
Like reeds they bent like drunken men they reeled
Till man from shelter ran & sought the open field

ETERNITY OF TIME

Eternal grand eternity of time
Where things of greatest standing grow sublime
Less from long fames & universal praise
Then wearing as the "ancients of old days"
The word once speaking seems but half the way
To reach that night leap of eternal day
The Milton centurys each a mighty boast
The shakspear eras—worlds without their host
Engraved up[on] the adamant of fame
By pens of steal in characters of flame
To whom the forrest oaks eternal stay
Are but as points & commas in their way
These less then nothings are to ruins doom
When suns grow dark & earth a vast & lonely tomb

THE POESY OF FLOWERS

What would the rosey be but as the rose
A merely sweet undignifying flower
But cloathed by womans dignifying grace
It looks upon us with a living power
Then quickly every blush from beauty glows
As mirrors—there reflecting beautys face
Her lips & luscious cheeks shine in its leaves
& in the lily—there her bosom heaves
Flowers thus personify the hearts delight
& beauty gives us rapture in their sight
Flowers merely flowers—would seem but cold esteems
With heart-associations & love-dreams
But mixed like life with mind—where ere we roam
They link like houshold feelings with our home

THE FAIREY RINGS

Here in the greensward & the old molehills
Where ploughshares never come to hurt the things
Antiquity hath charge of—fear instills
Her footsteps—& the ancient fairey rings
Shine black & fresh & round—the gipseys fire
Left yesternight scarce leaves more proof behind
Of midnight sports when they from day retire
As in these rings my fancy seems to find
Of fairey revels—& I stoop to see
Their little footmarks in each circling stain
& think I hear them in their summer glee
Wishing for night that they may dance again
Till shepherds tales told neath the leaning tree
While shunning showers seem bible truths to me

Aye almost scripture truths my poorer mind
Grows into worship of these mysterys
While fancys doth her ancient scrolls unbind
That time hath hid in countless centurys
& when the mornings mist doth leave behind
The fuzball round & mushroom white as snow
They strike me—in romantic moods enshrined
As shadows of things modeled long ago
Halls palaces & marble columned domes
& modern shades of faireys ancient homes
Erected in these rings & pastures still
For midnight balls & revelry—& then
Left like the ruins of all ancient skill
To wake the wonder of more common men

THE MORNING WIND

Theres more then music in this early wind
Awaking like a bird refreshed from sleep
& joy what Adam might in eden find
When he with angels did communion keep
It breaths all balm & insence from the sky
Blessing the husbandman with freshening flowers
Joys manna from its wings doth fall & lie
Harvests for early wakers with the flowers
The very grass with joys devotion moves
Cowslaps in adoration & delight
This way & that bow to the breath they love
Of the young winds that with their dewpearls play
Till smoaking chimneys sicken the young light
& feelings fairey visions fade away

HARES AT PLAY

The birds are gone to bed the cows are still
& sheep lie panting on each old molehill
& underneath the willows grey-green bough
Like toil a resting—lies the fallow plough
The timid hares throw daylight fears away
On the lane road to dust & dance & play
Then dabble in the grain by nought deterred
To lick the dew fall from the barleys beard
Then out they sturt again & round the hill
Like happy thoughts—dance—squat—& loiter still
Till milking maidens in the early morn
Gingle their yokes & sturt them in the corn
Through well known beaten paths each nimbling hare
Sturts quick as fear—& seeks its hidden lair

THE FLOOD

On Lolham Brigs in wild & lonely mood
Ive seen the winter floods their gambols play
Through each old arch that trembled while I stood
Bent oer its wall to watch the dashing spray
As their old stations would be washed away
Crash came the ice against the jambs & then
A shudder jarred the arches—yet once more
It breasted raving waves & stood agen
To wait the shock as stubborn as before
—White foam brown crested with the russet soil
As washed from new ploughed lands—would dart beneath
Then round & round a thousand eddies boil
On tother side—then pause as if for breath
One minute—& ingulphed—like life in death

Whose wrecky stains dart on the floods away
More swift then shadows in a stormy day
Things trail & turn & steady—all in vain
The engulphing arches shoot them quickly through
The feather dances flutters & again
Darts through the deepest dangers still afloat
Seeming as faireys whisked it from the view
& danced it oer the waves as pleasures boat
Light hearted as a merry thought in may—
Trays—uptorn bushes—fence demolished rails
Loaded with weeds in sluggish motion stray
Like water monsters lost each winds & trails
Till near the arches—then as in affright
It plunges—reels—& shudders out of sight

Waves trough—rebound—& fury boil again
Like plunging monsters rising underneath
Who at the top curl up a shaggy main
A moment catching at a surer breath
Then plunging headlong down & down—& on
Each following boil the shadow of the last
& other monsters rise when those are gone
Crest their fringed waves—plunge onward & are past
—The chill air comes around me ocean blea
From bank to bank the water strife is spread
Strange birds like snow spots oer the huzzing sea
Hang where the wild duck hurried past & fled
—On roars the flood—all restless to be free
Like trouble wandering to eternity

HEDGE SPARROW

The tame hedge sparrow in its russet dress
Is half a robin for its gentle ways
& the bird loving dame can do no less
Then throw it out a crumble on cold days
In early march it into gardens strays
& in the snug clipt box tree green & round
It makes a nest of moss & hair & lays
When een the snow is lurking on the ground
Its eggs in number five of greenish blue
Bright beautiful & glossy shining shells
Much like the firetails but of brighter hue
Yet in her garden home much danger dwells
Where skulking cat with mischief in its breast
Catches their young before they leave the nest

SHEPHERDS HUT

The Shepherds hut propt by the double ash
Hugh in its bulk & old in mossy age
Shadowing the dammed-up brook—where plash & plash
The little mills did younkers ears engage
Delightful hut rude as romances old
Where hugh old stones made each an easy chair
& brakes & ferns for luxurys manifold
& flint & steel the all want needed there
—The light was struck & then the happy ring
Crouched round the blaze—O there were happy times
Some telling tales & others urged to sing
Themes of old things in rude yet feeling ryhmes
That raised the laugh or stirred the stifled sigh
Till pity listened in each vacant eye

Those rude old tales—mans memory augurs ill
Thus to forget the fragments of old days
Those long old songs—their sweetness haunts me still
Nor did they perish for my lack of praise
But old desciples of the pasture sward
Rude chroniclers of ancient minstrelsy
The shepherds vanished all & disregard
Left their old music like a vagrant bee
For summers breeze to murmur oer & die
& in these ancient spots—mind ear & eye
Turn listeners—till the very wind prolongs
The theme as wishing in its depths of joy
To reccolect the music of old songs
& meet the hut that blessed me when a boy

WOOD PICTURES IN WINTER

The woodland swamps with mosses varified
& bullrush forrests bowing by the side
Of shagroot sallows that snug shelter make
For the coy more hen in her bushy lake
Into whose tide a little runnel weaves
Such charms for silence through the choaking leaves
& whimpling melodies that but intrude
As lullabys to ancient solitude
—The wood-grass plats which last year left behind
Weaving their feathery lightness to the wind
Look now as picturesque amid the scene
As when the summer glossed their stems in green
While tasty hare brunts through the creepy gap
Seeks their soft beds & squats in safetys lap

WOOD PICTURES IN SUMMER

The one delicious green that now prevades
The woods & fields in endless lights & shades
& that deep softness of delicious hues
That over head—blends—softens & subdues
The eye to extacy & fills the mind
With views & visions of enchanting kind
While on the velvet down beneath the swail
I sit on mossy stump & broken rail
Or lean oer crippled gate by hugh old tree
Broken by boys disporting there at swee
While sunshine spread from an exaustless sky
Gives all things extacy as well as I
& all wood-swaily places even they
Are joys own tennants keeping holiday

WOOD PICTURES IN SPRING

The rich brown-umber hue the oaks unfold
When springs young sunshine bathes their trunks in gold
So rich so beautiful so past the power
Of words to paint—my heart aches for the dower
The pencil gives to soften & infuse
This brown luxuriance of unfolding hues
This living luscious tinting woodlands give
Into a landscape that might breath & live
& this old gate that claps against the tree
The entrance of springs paradise should be
Yet paint itself with living nature fails
—The sunshine threading through these broken rails
In mellow shades—no pencil eer conveys
& mind alone feels fancies & pourtrays

A WOODLAND SEAT

Within this pleasant wood biside the lane
Lets sit & rest us from the burning sun
& hide us in the leaves & entertain
An hour away—to watch the wood brook run
Through heaps of leaves drop dribbling after drop
Pining for freedom till it climbs along
In eddying fury oer the foamy top
& then loud laughing sings its whimpling song
Kissing the misty dewberry by its side
With eager salutations & in joy
Making the flag leaves dance in graceful pride
Giving & finding joy—here we employ
An hour right profitable thus to see
Life may meet joys where few intrusions be

& mark the flowers around us how they live
Not only for themselves as we may feel
But the delight which they to others give
For nature never will her gifts consceal
From those who love to seek them—here amid
These trees how many doth disclose their pride
From the unthinking rustic only hid
Who never turns him from the road aside
To look for beautys which he heedeth not
—It gives us greater zest to feel the joys
We meet in this sweet solemn suited spot
& with high extacys ones mind employs
To bear the worst that fickle life prepares
Finding her sweets as common as her cares

In every trifle somthing lives to please
Or to instruct us—every weed or flower
Heirs beauty as a birthright by degrees
Of more or less though taste alone hath power
To see & value what the herd pass bye
—This common Dandelion mark how fine
Its hue—the shadow of the days proud eye
Glows not more rich of gold—that nettle there
Trod down by careless rustics every hour
Search but its slighted blooms—kings cannot wear
Robes prankt with half the splendour of a flower
Pencilled with hues of workmanship divine
Bestowed to simple things—denied to power
& sent to gladden hearts so mean as mine

TO MYSTERY

Mystery thou subtle essence—ages gain
New light from darkness—still thy blanks remain
& reason trys [to] chase old night from thee
When chaos fled thy parent took the key
Blank darkness—& the things age left behind
Are lockt for aye in thy unspeaking mind
Towers temples ruins on & under ground
So old—so dark—so mystic—so profound
Old time himself so old is like a child
& cant remember when their blocks were piled
Or caverns scooped & with a wondering eye
He seems to pause like other standers bye
Half thinking that the wonders left unknown
Was born in ages older than his own

THE DINNER IN THE FIELDS

How pleasant when athirst in burning days
To kneel adown where clear the fountain strays
Over its bed of pebbles—oer the brink
& just where bubbles blubber up to drink
How cooling by the parched lips it runs
While some thick willow shadows out the sun
& how delicious is the taste—een wine
Can[t] relish better where the wealthy dine
Then sweet spring water to the thirsty swain
Who sits & eats his dinner on the plain
& visits with a relish dear to toil
The shaded spring where clear the waters boil
An ancient luxury where the humble dwell
Which Jacob craved from rachel at the well

THE MILKING SHED

Good God & can it be that such a nook
As this can raise such sudden rapture up
—Two dotterel trees an oak & ash that stoop
Their aged bodys oer a little brook
& raise their sheltering heads above & oer
A little hovel raised on four old props
Old as themselves to look on & what more
Nought but an awthorn hedge & yet one stops
In admiration & in joy to gaze
Upon these objects feeling as I stand
That nought in all this wide worlds thorny ways
Can match this bit of feelings fairy land
How can it be—time owns the potent spell
Ive known it from a boy & love it well

THE SALLOW

Pendant oer rude old ponds or leaning oer
The woodlands mossy rails—the sallows now
Put on their golden liveries & restore
The spring to splendid memories ere a bough
Of white thorn shows a leaf to say tis come
& through the leafless underwood rich stains
Of sunny gold show where the sallows bloom
Like sunshine in dark places & gold veins
Mapping the russet landscape into smiles
At springs approach nor hath the sallow palms
A peer for richness—ploughmen in their toils
Will crop a branch—smit with its golden charms
While at its root the primrose' brunny eye
Smiles in his face & blooms deliciously

THE HAPPY BIRD

The happy whitethroat on the sweeing bough
Swayed by the impulse of the gadding wind
That ushers in the showers of april—now
Singeth right joyously & now reclined
Croucheth & clingeth to her moving seat
To keep her hold—& till the wind for rest
Pauses—she mutters inward melodies
That seem her hearts rich thinkings to repeat
& when the branch is still—her little breast
Swells out in raptures gushing symphonies
& then against her brown wing softly prest
The wind comes playing an enraptured guest
This way & that she swees—till gusts arise
More boisterous in their play—& off she flies

THE BREATH OF MORNING

How beautiful & fresh the pastoral smell
Of tedded hay breaths in this early morn
Health in these meadows must in summer dwell
& take her walks among these fields of corn
I cannot see her—yet her voice is born
On every breeze that fans my hair about
& though the sun is scarcely out of bed
Leaning on ground like half awakened sleep
The boy hath left his mossy thatched shed
& bawling lustily to cows & sheep
& taken at the woodbines overhead
Climbs up to pluck them from the thorny bower
Half drowned by dropples pattering on his head
From leaves bemoistened by nights secret shower

DECAY

Amidst the happiest joy a shade of grief
Will come—to mark in summers prime a leaf
Tinged with the autumns visible decay
As pining to forgetfulness away
Aye blank forgetfulness that coldest lot
To be—& to have been—& then be not
Een beautys self loves essence heavens prime
Mate for eternity in joys sublime
Earths most divinest is a mortal thing
& nurses times sick autumn from its spring
& fades & fades till wonder knows it not
& admiration hath all praise forgot
Coldly forsaking an unheeding past
To fade & fall & die like common things at last

GLINTON SPIRE

Glinton thy taper spire predominates
Over the level landscape—& the mind
Musing—the pleasing picture contemplates
Like elegance of beauty much refined
By taste—that almost deifys & elevates
Ones admiration making common things
Around it glow with beautys not their own
Thus all around the earth superior springs
Those straggling trees though lonely seem not lone
But in thy presence wear superior power
& een each mossed & melancholly stone
Gleaning cold memories round oblivions bower
Seem types of fair eternity—& hire
A lease from fame by thy enchanting spire

THE MEADOW HAY

I often roam a minute from the path
Just to luxuriate on the new mown swath
& stretch me at my idle length along
Hum louder oer some melody or song
While passing stranger slackens in his pace
& turns to wonder what can haunt the place
Unthinking that an idle ryhmster lies
Buried in the sweet grass & feeding phantasys
This happy spirit of the joyous day
Stirs every pulse of life into the play
Of buoyant joy & extacy—I walk
& hear the very weeds to sing & talk
Of their delights as the delighted wind
Toys with them like playfellows ever kind

BURTHORP OAK

Old noted oak I saw thee in a mood
Of vague indifference—& yet with me
Thy memory like thy fate hath lingering stood
Like an old hermit in the lonely sea
Of grass that waves around thee—Solitude
Paints not a lonlier picture to the view
Burthorp then thy one solitary tree
Age rent & shattered to a stump—Yet new
Leaves come upon each rift & broken limb
With every spring—& poesys visions swim
Around it of old days & chivalry
& desolate fancys bid the eyes grow dim
With feelings that earths grandeur should decay
& all its olden memories pass away

MIDSUMMER

Midsummers breath gives ripeness to the year
Of beautiful & picturesque & grand
Tinting the mountain with the hues of fear
Bare climbing dizziness—where bushes stand
Their breakneck emminence with danger near
Like lives in peril—though they wear a smile
Tis sickly green as in a homeless dream
Of terror at their fate—while underhand
Smiles with home hues as rich as health to toil
In mellow greens & darker lights that cheer
The ploughman turning up the healthy soil
& health & pleasure glistens every where
—So high ambitions dwell as dangers guests
& quiet minds as small birds in their nests

OBSCURITY

Old tree oblivion doth thy life condemn
Blank & recordless as that summer wind
That fanned the first few leaves on thy young stem
When thou wert one years shoot—& who can find
Their homes of rest or paths of wandering now
So seems thy history to a thinking mind
As now I gaze upon thy sheltering bough
Thou grew unnoticed up to flourish now
& leave thy past as nothing all behind
Where many years & doubtless centurys lie
That ewe beneath thy shadow—nay that flie
Just settled on a leaf—can know with time
Almost as much of thy blank past as I
Thus blank oblivion reigns as earths sublime

PLEASURES OF FANCY

A Path old tree goes bye thee crooking on
& through this little gate that claps & bangs
Against thy rifted trunk what steps hath gone
Though but a lonely way—yet mystery hangs
Oer crowds of pastoral scenes recordless here
The boy might climb the nest in thy young boughs
Thats slept half an eternity—in fear
The herdsman may have left his startled cows
For shelter when heavens thunder voice was near
Here too the woodman on his wallet laid
For pillow may have slept an hour away
& poet pastoral lover of the shade
Here sat & mused half some long summers day
While some old shepherd listened to the lay

THE TRUTH OF TIME

Go vile hypocrisy with subtle tongue
& smooth spruce visage that can hide a lie
In fairest speech & meditate a wrong
Under prayers masking—put that covering bye
That hid thy speckled snakes thy whole life long
Here truth reigns absolute—nay pass not bye
That mask must off—& thy deformity
In nakedness of deeds must stand & show
The hypocrite that seemed a saint below
That like a gamester shuffled so the cards
To win by cheating honestys awards
Poor honesty that like a carrion crow
Was made by thee—aye quake from foot to brow
Eternitys thy judge & deaths thy partner now

THE FOUNTAIN OF HOPE

Truth old as heaven is & God is truth
& hope is never old but still a youth
& when I ope the volume which began
Its essence & its mystery with man
I see that divine shadow mystery
& all the attributes of majesty
The high consception—power unspeakable
Where deity as three—almighty dwell
I rise above myself oer reasons shrine
& feel my origin as love divine
Older then earth 'bove worlds however high
An essence to be crushed but never die
That like a light hereafter shall arise
A star or comet in those mighty skies
Where God the sun smiles on it like a flower
& bids it live in light neath his almighty power

EVENING PRIMROSE

When once the sun sinks in the west
& dewdrops pearl the evenings breast
All most as pale as moonbeams are
Or its companionable star
The evening primrose opes anew
Its delicate blossoms to the dew
& shunning-hermit of the light
Wastes its fair bloom upon the night
Who blindfold to its fond caresses
Knows not the beauty it posseses
Thus it blooms on till night is bye
& day looks out with open eye
Bashed at the gaze it cannot shun
It faints & withers & is done

HOME PICTURES IN MAY

The sunshine bathes in clouds of many hues
& mornings feet are gemed with early dews
Warm daffodils about the garden beds
Peep through their pale slim leaves their golden heads
Sweet earthly suns of spring—the gossling broods
In coats of sunny green about the road
Waddle in extacy—& in rich moods
The old hen leads her flickering chicks abroad
Oft scuttling neath her wings to see the kite
Hang wavering oer them in the springs blue light
The sparrows round their new nests chirp with glee
& sweet the robin springs young luxury shares
Tutting its song in feathery gooseberry tree
While watching worms the gardeners spade unbears

SUDDEN SHOWER

Black grows the southern sky betokening rain
& humming hive bees homeward hurry bye
They feel the change—so let us shun the grain
& take the broad road while our feet are dry
Aye there some dropples moistened in my face
& pattered on my hat—tis coming nigh
Lets about & find a sheltering place
The little things around like you & I
Are hurrying through the grass to shun the shower
Here stoops an ash tree—hark the wind gets high
But never mind this Ivy for an hour
Rain as it may will keep us dryly here
That little wren knows well his sheltering bower
Nor leaves his dry house though we come so near

CARLESS RAMBLES

I love to wander at my idle will
In summers luscious prime about the fields
& kneel when thirsty at the little rill
To sip the draught its pebbly bottom yields
& where the maple bush its fountain shields
To lie & rest a swaily hour away
& crop the swelling peascod from the land
Or mid the upland woodland walks to stray
Where oaks for aye oer their old shadows stand
Neath whose dark foliage with a welcome hand
I pluck the luscious strawberry ripe & red
As beautys lips—& in my fancys dreams
As mid the velvet moss I musing tread
Feel life as lovely as her picture seems

LOVE IN YOUTH

Words paint not womans beauty springs young hour
Grow flowers to paint her she herselfs a flower
Fairer then aught but blossoms & they bear
But faint remembrance to a thing so fair
The red rose in her cheeks doth blushing lie
Lit up like sunshine by her laughing eye
& the white lilys on her beating breast
Spread warm & nuzzling like two doves at rest
Her lips are two twin roseys which the morn
Kisses & leaves its dewy pearls thereon
Smiles hang about them as if loath to give
Room to those frowns that bade hope cease to live
& joy in all youths motions seem to say
Beauty & youth here make their holiday

Thou page of [living] beauty can the eye
Find aught so rich as natures works supply
With some the person—some the mind adds grace
Though rosey cheeks ill suits an harlots face
—Thine is the beauty such as all esteems
With heart as innocent as infants dreams
Pure as the virgin flower untouched & free
From the bold freedom of the amorous bee
Thy voice was rich as fame thy praise een now
Comes like the glory round an angels brow
For fame is nothing worth the muses care
Unless to grace it womans love be there
& praise is but a shadow cloathed in bays
Without the honey dew of beautys praise

THE OLD WILLOW

The juicey wheat now spindles into ear
& trailing pea blooms ope their velvet eyes
& weeds & flowers by crowds far off & near
In all their sunny liveries appear
For summers lustre boasts unnumbered dyes
How pleasant neath this willow by the brook
Thats kept its ancient place for many a year
To sit & oer these crowded fields to look
& the soft dropping of the shower to hear
Ourselves so sheltered een a pleasant book
Might lie uninjured from the fragrant rain
For not a drop gets through the bowering leaves
But dry as housed in my old hut again
I sit & troubleous care of half its claim decieve

AMBITION

Ambition what a pomp creating word
Tis libelous of comfort though tis heard
As comforts aid & counsellor—O fie
That hearts should smile at what should make them sigh
The swelling thought that gives the heart relief
The ever craving wish that will not sleep
Till comes the sudden gush of care & grief
& anxious hope that gives it small relief
Soothing the rude extremeties of fate
Till every hope hath left it desolate
Like grandeur that with fading pride doth dwell
Oer ancient walls till every stone hath fell
It falls & leaves—the song of every wind
A broken shadow of its hopes behind

THE WRYNECKS NEST

That summer bird its oft repeated note
Chirps from the dotterel ash & in the hole
The green woodpecker made in years remote
It makes its nest—where peeping idlers strole
In anxious plundering moods—& bye & bye
The wrynecks curious eggs as white as snow
While squinting in the hollow tree they spy
The sitting bird looks up with jetty eye
& waves her head in terror too & fro
Speckled & veined in various shades of brown
& then a hissing noise assails the clown
& quick with hasty terror in his breast
From the trees knotty trunk he sluthers down
& thinks the strange bird guards a serpents nest

PROVIDENCE

Folks talk of providence with heedless tongue
That leads to riches & not happiness
Which is but a new tune for fortunes song
& one contentment cares not to possess
It knows her seldom & it shuns her long
& that kind providence least understood
Hath been my friend that helps me bear with wrong
& learns me out of evil to find good
To hearten up against the heartless deeds
Of faithless friends who led me blindly on
To make my poor faith wither mid the weeds
Of their deceptions—yet when all were gone
A voice within told me of one true friend
& this is providence right worthy to commend

It hides the future & leaves room for hope
To smile—& promise joys that may not come
& cares from which our fortunes cant elope
Are robbed of half their terrors being dumb
& all unable to foretell their speed
This blessed ignorance is half the sum
Of providence—thus all are blest indeed
The weak & strong the timid & the bold
Thus will the hare feel safe in its retreat
Where lay the murdering wolf an hour before
& upon boughs warm with the eagles feet
The wren will perch & dream of harm no more
Kind providence amid contending strife
Bids weakness feel the liberty of life

THE WHEAT RIPENING

What time the wheat field tinges rusty brown
& barley bleaches in its mellow grey
Tis sweet some smooth mown baulk to wander down
Or cross the fields on footpaths narrow way
Just in the mealy light of waking day
As glittering dewdrops moise the maidens gown
& sparkling bounces from her nimble feet
Journeying to milking from the neighbouring town
Making life light with song—& it is sweet
To mark the grazing herds & list the clown
Urge on his ploughing team with cheering calls
& merry shepherds whistling toils begun
& hoarse tongued birdboy whose unceasing calls
Join the larks ditty to the rising sun

THE HAPPINESS OF IGNORANCE

Ere I had known the world & understood
How many follies wisdom names its own
Distinguishing things evil from things good
The dread of sin & death—ere I had known
Knowledge the root of evil—had I been
Left in some lone place where the world is wild
& trace of troubling man was never seen
Brought up by nature as her favourite child
As born for nought but joy where all rejoice
Emparadised in ignorance of sin
Where nature tries with never chiding voice
Like tender nurse nought but our smiles to win
The future dreamless beautiful would be
The present—foretaste of eternity

TO CHARLES LAMB
ON HIS ESSAYS

Elia thy reveries & visioned themes
To cares lorn heart a luscious pleasure proves
Wild as the mystery of delightful dreams
Soft as the anguish of remembered love
Like records of past days their memory dances
Mid the cool feelings manhoods reason brings
As the unearthly visions of romances
Peopled with sweet & uncreated things
& yet thy themes thy gentle worth enhances
Then wake again thy wild harps tenderest strings
Sing on sweet bard let fairy loves again
Smile in thy dreams with angel extacies
Bright oer our soul will break the heavenly strain
Through the dull gloom of earths realities

FORREST FLOWERS

Ye simple weeds that make the desert gay
Disdained by all een by the youngsters eye
Who lifts his stick a weapon in his play
& lops your blossoms as he saunters bye
In mockery of merriment—yet I
Hail you as favourites of my early days
& every year as mid your haunts I lie
Some added pleasure claims my lonely gaze
Starpointed thistle with its ruddy flowers
Wind waving rush left to bewildered ways
Shunning the scene which cultures toil devours
Ye thrive in silence where I glad recline
Sharing with finer blooms springs gentle showers
That shows ye're prized by better taste then mine

THE ASS

Poor patient creature how I grieve to see
Thy wants so ill supplied—to see thee strain
& stretch thy tether for the grass in vain
Which heavens rain waters for all else but thee
The fair green field the fullnes of the plain
Add to thy hunger colt & heifer pass
& roll as though they mocked thee on the grass
Which would be luxury to the bare brown lane
Where thourt imprisoned humble patient ass
Cropping foul weeds & scorning to complain
Mercey at first "sent out the wild ass free"
A ranger "of the mountains" & what crimes
Did thy progenitors that thou shouldst be
The slave & mockery of latter times

SUNRISE

Morning awakes sublime—glad earth & sky
Smile in the splendour of the day begun
Oer the broad easts illumined canopy
Shade of its makers majesty the sun
Gleams in its living light—from cloud to cloud
Streaks of all colours beautifully run
As if before heavens gate there hung a shroud
To hide its grand magnificence—O heaven
Where entrance een to thought is disallowed
To view the glory that this scene is giving
What may blind reason not expect to see
When in immortal worlds the soul is living
Eternal as its maker & as free
To taste the unknowns of eternity

SUNSET

Welcome sweet eve thy gently sloping sky
& softly whispering wind that breaths of rest
& clouds unlike what daylight galloped bye
Now stopt as weary huddling in the west
Each by the farewell of days closing eye
Left with the smiles of heaven on its breast
Meek nurse of weariness how sweet to meet
Thy soothing tenderness to none denied
To hear thy whispering voice—ah heavenly sweet
Musing & listening by thy gentle side
Lost to lifes cares thy coloured skies to view
Picturing of pleasant worlds unknown to care
& when our bark the rough sea flounders through
Warming in hopes its end shall harbour there

NOTHINGNESS OF LIFE

I never pass a venerable tree
Pining away to nothingness & dust
Ruins vain shades of power I never see
Once dedicated to times cheating trust
But warm reflection makes the saddest thought
& views lifes vanity in cheerless light
& sees earths bubbles youth so eager sought
Burst into emptiness of lost delight
& all the pictures of lifes early day
Like evenings striding shadows haste away
Yet theres a glimmering of pleasure springs
From such reflections of earths vanity
That pines & sickens oer lifes mortal things
& leaves a relish for eternity

THE INSTINCT OF HOPE

Is there another world for this frail dust
To warm with life & be itself again
Somthing about me daily speaks there must
& why should instinct nourish hopes in vain
Tis natures prophecy that such will be
& every thing seems struggling to explain
The close sealed volume of its mystery
Time wandering onward keeps its usual pace
As seeming anxious of eternity
To meet that calm & find a resting place
Een the small violet feels a future power
& waits each year renewing blooms to bring
& surely man is no inferior flower
To die unworthy of a second spring

ROUND OAK SPRING

Sweet brook Ive met thee many a summers day
& ventured fearless in thy shallow flood
& rambled oft thy sweet unwearied way
Neath willows cool that on thy margin stood
With crowds of partners in my artless play
Grasshopper beetle bee & butterflye
That frisked about as though in merry mood
To see their old companion sporting bye
Sweet brook lifes glories once were thine & mine
Shades cloathed thy spring that now doth naked lie
On thy white boiling sand the sweet woodbine
Darkened & dipt its flowers—I mark & sigh
& muse oer troubles since we met the last
Like two fond friends whose happiness is past

THE MAJIC OF BEAUTY

An imperfection as perfections guest
Is greatest beauty—charms immaculate
& tawny moles upon a womans breast
Grow very jewels in their fair estate
So is it where the hearts consceptions wait
On beauty as her lacquey—up we climb
& from the very sun oer heavens own gate
Snatch a rich jewel—gracing common time
Making earth heaven—in our fancys dreams
& woman as an idol in esteem
Fairest companion of fair thoughts—& kin
To graces perfectness in heavens own grace
To worship such therefore can be no sin
If heavens own copy lives in beautys face

THE HEDGE ROSE

The wild rose swells its prickly buds anew
& soon shall wear the summers witching hue
Those hues which nature as its dowery heirs
& beauty like a blossom wins & wears
On her soft cheeks when shepherds in the grove
Reach down the blushing flowers & talk of love
The very bees that such intrusions scare
Frit from the blossom that he culls her there
Flye round mistaken as they leave the bower
& take the maids sweet blushes for a flower
Thus wild dog roseys hung in every hedge
Wakens at joys hearts core its sweetest pledge
Shedding to summer lanes their rich perfume
& whispering memorys raptures while they bloom

THE FEAR OF FLOWERS

The nodding oxeye bends before the wind
The woodbine quakes lest boys their flowers should find
& prickly dog rose spite of its array
Can t dare the blossom seeking hand away
While thistles wear their heavy knobs of bloom
Proud as the war horse wears its haughty plume
& by the road side dangers self defies
On commons where pined sheep & oxen lie
In ruddy pomp & ever thronging mood
It stands & spreads like danger in a wood
& in the village street where meanest weeds
Can t stand untouched to fill their husks with seed
The haughty thistle oer all danger towers
In every place the very whasp of flowers

THE HEAT OF NOON

There lies a sultry lusciousness around
The far stretched pomp of summer which the eye
Views with a dazzled gaze—& gladly bounds
Its prospects to some pastoral spots that lie
Nestling among the hedge confining grounds
Where in some nook the haystacks newly made
Scents the smooth level meadow land around
While underneath the woodlands hazley hedge
The crowding oxen make their swaily beds
& in the dry dyke thronged with rush & sedge
The restless sheep rush in to hide their heads
From the unlost & ever haunting flie
& under every trees projecting shade
Places as battered as the road is made

EMMONSAILS HEATH IN WINTER

I love to see the old heaths withered brake
Mingle its crimpled leaves with furze & ling
While the old Heron from the lonely lake
Starts slow & flaps his melancholly wing
& oddling crow in idle motions swing
On the half rotten ash trees topmost twig
Beside whose trunk the gipsey makes his bed
Up flies the bouncing woodcock from the brig
Where a black quagmire quakes beneath the tread
The fieldfare chatters in the whistling thorn
& for the awe round fields & closen rove
& coy bumbarrels twenty in a drove
Flit down the hedgrows in the frozen plain
& hang on little twigs & start again

THE FIRETAILS NEST

Tweet pipes the Robin as the cat creeps bye
Her nestling young that in the elderns lie
& then the Bluecap tootles in its glee
Picking the flies from orchard apple tree
& Pink the Chaffinch cries its well known strain
Urging its kind to utter pink again
While in a quiet mood hedge sparrows trie
An inward stir of shadowed melody
—Around the rotten tree the firetail mourns
As the old hedger to his toil returns
Chopping the grain to stop the gap close bye
The hole where her blue eggs in safety lie
Of every thing that stirs she dreameth wrong
& pipes her "tweet tut" fears the whole day long

MONARCHY OF NATURE

Ive often thought me that a king should be
The head of every empire when Ive seen
The little toilings of the honey bee
Who forms a colony & owns a queen
& hurds his stores for winter in his hive
While wild & straggling tribes in bank & wall
Bore little holes—nor further store contrive
Then what themselves may want—& may be all
May be consumed ere winters storms are past
& then with famines tribes they pine & die
While tempest proof against the rudest blast
The hive bees monarchy doth live & thrive
Like populous citys & when winters bye
Crowds upon crowds again their busy labours ply

BLAKE

Blake though insulted by a kings decree
Thy fame stirs onward like the mighty sea
That throws its painted gems upon the shore
To deck crowns heirs with glitter little more
While all thats truly noble & sublime
Is rolling onward to the throne of time
Time the insulted arbiter of fame
Merits reward & tyrants lasting shame
That rusts crowns into baubles—kings to dust
Then Blake thy glory kindled in its trust
& like the sea thy hearts own element
Shining in light & earths amaze it went
Pursuing on a worth ennobled way
Heroe-inspiring theme of glorys dauntless day

THE WRYNECKS NEST

Yon summer bird its oft repeated note
Chirps from that dotterel ash & in the hole
The green woodpecker made in years remote
It makes its nest where idle birdboys stroll
In anxious robbing moods—& bye & bye
The wrynecks curious eggs all white as snow
While peeping in the hollow tree they spy
The sitting bird looks up with jetty eye
& waves her head in terror too & fro
Snake-speckled in the varied shades of brown
& then a hissing noise the startled clown
Heereth & bursting terror throbs his breast
Quick from the knotty trunk he sluthers down
Thinking the strange bird guards a serpents nest

MERIT

Hard words to vague pretention seres like death
& kills its feeble efforts with a breath
But insults thrown on merits struggling way
Are help-mates to her journey—not decay
As fires lies smouldering till the wind sweeps past
Then bursts to flame & kindles with the blast
So from the throws of envy hate & strife
Genius bursts forth & breaths eternal life
In vain the taunt would blight the scoff would sere
Like cobweb network falls the gibe & sneer
& genius like a sunburst from the cloud
Throws forth her light her mind is heard aloud
The nights of malice into lights decay
& aids her exaltations into day

ASHTON LAWN

I had a joy & keep it still alive
Of hoarding in the memorys treasured book
Old favourite spots that with affections thrive
& to my inward fancys shine & look
Like well-done pictures in some winning page
Such was old Langley bush by time forsook
With its old sheltered thorn tree mossed with age
& such the roman bank by swordy well
Where idless would a leisure hour engage
To hunt where ditchers toild the pooty shell
Among the sand & grit existing still
Though buried with its sixteen hundred years
Thus man in myriads dies—while time reveres
The simplest things above his mightiest skill

In Ashton lawn condemned to slow decay
Close to the south-east nook a ruined hill
Lies choaked in thorns & briars—yet to this day
Reality may trace the castle still
A fragment of the moat still forms a pond
Beset with hoof tracked paths of horse & cow
That often go to drink & all beyond
Greensward with little molehills on its brow
& fairy-rings in its old mysterys dark
Still wear its ancient name & shepherds call
The closen all around it still "old parks"
Still traced by buried fragments of a wall
The castles self will soon be nothings heir
Pickt up to mend old roads—old garden walls repair

GREENSWARD

Rich healthiness bedyes the summer grass
Of each old close—& everywhere instills
Gladness to travellers while they pause & pass
The narrow pathway through the old molehills
Of glad neglected pastures—& Ive thought
While sitting down upon their quiet laps
That no delights that rich men ever bought
Could equal mine—where quiet came unsought
While the cow mused beside the broken gaps
At the rich hay close sweeping to the wind
& as to pleasure natures gifts not few
Comes to the heart as unto grass the dew
For e'en her meanest gifts where e'er we find
Are worth a praise as music to the mind

THE MOLE

Rude architect rich instincts natural taste
Is thine by heritage—thy little mound
Bedecking furze clad heath & rushy waste
Betraced with sheeptracks shine like pleasure ground
No rude inellegance thy work confounds
But scenes of picturesque & beautiful
Lye mid thy little hills of cushioned thyme
On which the cowboy when his hands are full
Of wild flowers leans upon his arm at rest
As though his seat were feathers—when I climb
Thy little fragrant mounds I feel thy guest
& hail neglect thy patron who contrives
Waste spots for the[e] on natures quiet breast
& taste loves best where thy still labour thrives

FIRST SIGHT OF SPRING

The hazel blooms in threads of crimson hue
Peep through the swelling buds & look for spring
Ere yet a white thorn leaf appears in view
Or march finds throstles pleased enough to sing
To the old touchwood tree woodpeckers cling
A moment & their harsh toned notes renew
In happier mood the stockdove claps his wing
The squirrel sputters up the powdered oak
With tail cocked oer his head & ears errect
Startled to hear the woodmans understroke
& with the courage that his fears collect
He hisses fierce half malice & half glee
Leaping from branch to branch about the tree
In winters foliage moss & lickens drest

COTTAGE FEARS

The evening gathers from the gloomy woods
& darkling creeps oer silent vale & hill
While the snug village in nights happy moods
Is resting calm & beautifully still
The windows gleam with light the yelping curs
That guards the henroost from the thieving fox
Barks now & then as somthing passing stirs
& distant dogs the noises often mocks
While foxes from the woods send dismal cries
Like somthing in distress the cottager
Hears the dread noise & thinks of danger nigh
& locks up door in haste—nor cares to stir
From the snug safety of his humble shed
Then tells strange tales till time to go to bed

450

COLOURS OF AUTUMN

Now that the year is drawing to a close
Such mellow tints on trees & bushes lie
So like to sunshine that it brighter glows
As one looks more intently—on the sky
I turn astonished that no sun is there
The ribboned strips of orange blue & red
Streaks through the western sky a georgeous bed
Painting days end most beautifully fair
So mild so quiet breaths the balmy air
Scenting the perfume of decaying leaves
Such fragrance & such lovliness they wear
Trees hedgrows bushes that the heart recieves
Joys for which language owneth words too few
To paint that glowing richness which I view

THE HOLLOW TREE

How oft a summer shower hath started me
To seek for shelter in an hollow tree
Old hugh ash dotterel wasted to a shell
Whose vigorous head still grew & flourished well
Where ten might sit upon the battered floor
& still look round discovering room for more
& he who chose a hermit life to share
Might have a door & make a cabin there
They seemed so like a house that our desires
Would call them so & make our gipsey fires
& eat field dinners of the juicey peas
Till we were wet & drabbled to the knees
But in our old tree house rain as it might
Not one drop fell although it rained till night

451

PLEASANT SPOTS

There is a wild & beautiful neglect
About the fields that so delights & cheers
Where nature her own feelings to effect
Is left at her own silent work for years
The simplest thing thrown in our way delights
From the wild careless feature that it wears
The very road that wanders out of sight
Crooked & free is pleasant to behold
& such the very weeds left free to flower
Corn poppys red & carlock gleaming gold
That makes the cornfields shine in summers hour
Like painted skys—& fancys distant eye
May well imagine armys marching bye
In all the grand array of pomp & power

THE FERN OWLS NEST

The weary woodman rocking home beneath
His tightly banded faggot wonders oft
While crossing over the furze crowded heath
To hear the fern owls cry that whews aloft
In circling whirls & often by his head
Wizzes as quick as thought & ill at rest
As through the rustling ling with heavy tread
He goes nor heeds he tramples near its nest
That underneath the furze or squatting thorn
Lies hidden on the ground & teazing round
That lonely spot she wakes her jarring noise
To the unheeding waste till mottled morn
Fills the red east with daylights coming sounds
& the heaths echoes mocks the herding boys

HAPPY THOUGHTS

As pleasant as unlooked for summer showers
Where woods & fields lay gaping day by day
As a sweet reccompence of sunny hours
When oppressed sky imprisoned lay
In one thick cloud for days—in these sweet moods
I feel within me bidding once again
My spirits stir at liberty & play
With happy thoughts that ramble far away
Along the waggon rifted lanes & woods
That give bold outline to the level plain
Where old embowering oaks lift overhead
An arch of branching grains—& then to lye
On the brown heath where sheep are scantly fed
& view the smiles of an unbounded sky

Aye theres a wholsome feeling out of doors
That nourishes the heart with happy themes
The very cattle on the flaggy moors
To the minds eye a pleasant picture seems
& occupations of home husbandry
Some with the plough some singing by the side
Of the slow waggon—& when these I see
They give such blameless pictures void of strife
Such sweet employments neath a smiling sky
I even feel that better lot of life
That in such spots calm providence is bye
& sweet domestic peace whose quiet eye
Feels most delight in its own humble home
& checks the restless mood that often longs to roam

MEADOW PATHS

The meadow with its sweep of level green
Goes winding onward from admiring eyes
Strangers can't say there winter floods have been
So vivid & so beautiful it lies
Its rich grass fanning to the young soft winds
While clumps of early daisys ope their eyes
& please the passenger that often winds
The little paths that cross it here & there
Winding to market village feast or fair
& more then happy doth the schoolboy go
With little basket swinging at his side
Tracing their verdant carpets too & fro
Morning & night with leisure gratified
While earth with Gods rich blessings overflow

STRAY WALKS

How pleasant are the fields to roam & think
Whole sabbaths through unnoticed & alone
Beside the little molehill skirted brink
Of the small brook that skips oer many a stone
Of green woodside where many a squatting oak
Far oer grass screeds their white stained branches hing
Forming in pleasant close a happy seat
To nestle in while small birds chirp & sing
& the loud blackbird will its mate provoke
More louder yet its chorus to repeat
How pleasant is it thus to think & roam
The many paths scarce knowing which to chuse
All full of pleasant scenes—then wander home
& oer the beautys we have met to muse

Tis sunday & the little paths that wind
Through closen green by hedges & wood sides
& like a brook corn crowded slope divides
Of pleasant fields—their frequent passers find
From early morn to mellow close of day
On different errands climbing many stiles
Oer hung with awthorn tempting haste to stay
& cool some moments of the road away
When hot & high the uncheckt summer smiles
Some journeying to the little hamlet hid
In dark surrounding trees to see their friends
While some sweet leisures aimless road pursue
Wherever fancys musing pleasure wends
To woods or lakes or church thats never out of view

PASTORAL LIBERTY

O for the unshackled mood as free as air
& pleasure wild as birds upon the wing
The unwronged impulse won from seasons fair
Like birds perrenial travels with the spring
Come peace & joy the unworn path to trace
Crossing ling-heaths & hazel crowded glen
Where health salutes me with its ruddy face
& joy breaths freely from the strife of men
O lead me any where but in the crowd
On some lone island rather would I be
Than in the world worn knowledge noising loud
Wealth gathering up & loosing—leave with me
Calm joy & humble hope for quiet won
To live in peace unhurt & hurting none

EARLY IMAGES

Come early morning with thy mealy grey
Moist grass & fitful gales that winnow soft
& frequent—I ll be up with early day
& roam the social way where passing oft
The milking maid who greets the pleasant morn
& shepherd with his hook in folded arm
Rocking along accross the bending corn
& hear the many sounds from distant farm
Of cackling hens & turkeys gobbling loud
& teams just plodding on their way to plough
Down russet tracks that strip the closen green
& hear the mellow low of distant cow
& see the mist upcreeping like a cloud
From hollow places in the early scene

& mark the jerking swallow jerk & fling
Its flight oer new mown meadows happily
& cuckoo quivering upon narrow wing
Take sudden flitting from the neighbouring tree
& heron stalking solitary thing
Mount up into high travel far away
& that mild indecision hanging round
Skys holding bland communion with the ground
In gentlest pictures of the infant day
Now picturing rain—while many a pleasing sound
Grows mellower distant in the mealy grey
Of dewy pastures & full many a sight
Seems sweeter in its indistinct array
Than when it glows in mornings stronger light

THE MILKMAIDS SONG

Hark to that beautiful melody it is
The milkmaid singing love songs to her cow
With a voice like nightingales—list who would miss
Such music for a little lack of sleep
By rising an hour or two before
The common day gets marred by vulgar sounds
The air is pleasant too & giveth store
Of health that early risers purchase cheap
This singing milkmaid seeks this happy place
Early & late her morn & evening rounds
The passer bye neer meets a sweeter face
With ready smiles to greet the pleasant day
How doth such greetings happy thoughts surround
Cheating a pleasant walk of half the way

THE CLUMP OF FERN

Pleasures lie scattered all about our ways
Harvest for thought & joy to look & glean
Much of the beautiful to win our praise
Lie where we never heeded aught had been
By this wood stile half buried in the shade
Of rude disorder—bramble woodbine all
So thickly wove that nutters scarcely made
An entrance through—& now the acorns fall
The gatherers seeking entrance pause awhile
Ere they mount up the bank to climb the stile
Half wishing that a better road was nigh
Yet here mid leaf strewn mornings autumn mild
While pleasing sounds & pleasing sights are bye
Things beautiful delight my heart to smile

Here underneath the stiles moss covered post
A little bunch of fern doth thrive & spring
Hid from the noisey wind & coming frost
Like late reared young neath the wood piegons wing
Ive seen beneath the furze bush clumps of ling
So beautiful in pinky knotts of bloom
That made the inmost hearts emotions breath
A favourite love for the unsocial heath
That gives man no inviting hopes to come
To fix his dwelling & disturb the scene
So in my lonliness of mood this green
Large clump of crimpled fern leaves doth bequeath
Like feelings—& wherever wanderers roam
Some little scraps of happiness is seen

A AUTUMN MORNING

The autumn morning waked by many a gun
Throws oer the fields her many coloured light
Wood wildly touched close tanned & stubbles dun
A motley paradise for earths delight
Clouds ripple as the darkness breaks to light
& clover fields are hid with silver mist
One shower of cobwebs oer the surface spread
& threads of silk in strange disorder twist
Round every leaf & blossoms bottly head
Hares in the drowning herbage scarcely steal
But on the battered pathway squats abed
& by the cart rut nips her morning meal
Look where we may the scene is strange & new
& every object wears a changing hue

FORREST TREES

The woods how lovely with their crowds of trees
Each towering over each like hills oer hills
The oaks excess for darkest covert made
The mind with a sublime of pleasure fills
Then winged ash more sparingly displayed
A lightness oer the pensive eye distills
& elms in hanging branches mass oer mass
Determined still the woods to overlook
& willows feigning fondness for the grass
That leans oer pastoral pond & little brook
Like gipseys smoak beside the wood displays
Its lonely patch of green inclining greys
While the white poplar in the hedge so tall
Like leafy steeples overtops them all

A AWTHORN NOOK

The smooth & velvet sward my fancy suits
In pleasant places where the awthorns look
As left for arbours & the old tree roots
Lie crampt & netted oer the guggling brook
& shepherd on his elbow lolls to read
His slips of ballads bought at neighbouring fair
Seeming unconsious of the beautys there
The stilly quiet of the grassy screed
Skirting the busy brook—the happy fare
Of little birds that in the bushes breed
Are all unnoticed save that carless way
That sees & feels not—there I love to pass
The green hours leisure of a summers day
Stretching at length upon the couching grass

459

SAND MARTIN

Thou hermit haunter of the lonely glen
& common wild & heath—the desolate face
Of rude waste landscapes far away from men
Where frequent quarrys give thee dwelling place
With strangest taste & labour undeterred
Drilling small holes along the quarrys side
More like the haunts of vermin than a bird
& seldom by the nesting boy descried
Ive seen thee far away from all thy tribe
Flirting about the unfrequented sky
& felt a feeling that I can t describe
Of lone seclusion & a hermit joy
To see thee circle round nor go beyond
That lone heath & its melancholly pond

TWILIGHT IN SUMMER

Such splendid pomp the summers richness brings
That sunset far beyond her journey flings
Illuminating streaks of golden stain
& where the dial looks for smiles in vain
Oer the cold bosom of the gloomy north
Streaks of her smiling bounty issue forth
So bright as if the sun made longer stay
& sought for heaven by that lonely way
As if to leave no part of earth or sky
Without his smile to glad the gazing eye
So providence in every place appears
To chace the gloom that struggles into fears
& leaves a smile from summer every where
The lone to cherish & the sad to cheer

FIELD THOUGHTS

Field thoughts to me are happiness & joy
Where I can lye upon the pleasant grass
Or track some little path & so employ
My mind in trifles pausing as I pass
The little wild flower clumps by nothing nurst
But dews & sunshine & impartial rain
& welcomly to quench my summer thirst
I bend me by the flaggy dyke to gain
Dewberrys so delicious to the taste
& then I wind the flag fringed meadow lake
& mark the pike plunge with unusual haste
Through water weeds & many a circle make
While bursts of happiness from heaven fall
There all have hopes here fields are free for all

A WALK

Being refreshed with thoughts of wandering moods
I took my staff & wandered far away
Through swampy fenland void of heaths & woods
To see if summers luxury could display
In such drear places aught of beautiful
& sooth it gives me much delight to say
That painters would feel exquisite to cull
Rich bits of landscape I have seen to day
Down by the meadow side our journey lay
Along a sloping bank profusely spread
With yarrow ragwort fleabane all in flower
As showy almost as a garden bed
But thistles like unbidden guests would come
& throw a dreary prospect in the way

461

Then oer some arches intersecting walls
We clambered & pursued the dreary fen
Upon whose dreary edge old Waldron hall
Stood like a lone place far removed from men
Hid under willows tall as forrest trees
Yet there we met with places rich to please
Green closen osier clumps & black topt reeds
In little forrests shooting crowds on crowds
So thickly set no opening scarce alowed
The bird a passage in their shade to breed
& now a fishers hut—I could but look
In lone seclusion in my journey lay
Placed on a knoll of that wild reedy nook
As if some Crusoe had been cast away

In that rude desolate flat when winter floods
Rave seas of danger round its little bay
So thought I in supprises startled moods
To meet that little picture in my way
Then swept the brown bank in a rounding way
& flag-clumps vivid green & little woods
Of osiers made the wilderness be gay
& some green closen so intensly green
I could have wasted half a summers day
To gaze upon their beauty so serene
As if calm peace had made its dwelling there
For in such places she hath often been
An unhoused dweller in the open air
An hermit giving blessings to the scene

Now came the river sweeping round the nooks
By thirsty summers pilgrimage subdued
Dark & yet clear the glassy water looks
As slow & easy in majestic mood
It sweeps along by osier crowded glen
Untill it winds an almost naked flood
Along the flats of the unwooded fen
Yet even there prolific summer dwells
& garnishes its sides in vivid green
Of flags & reeds the otters pathless den
—Now lanes without a guide post plainly tells
Their homward paths—while from a stile is seen
The open church tower & its little bells
& chimneys low where peaceful quiet dwells

My journey feels refreshed with green delight
Though woods nor heaths nor molehill pastures led
A pleasant varied way—yet richly spread
Corn crowded grounds in awthorn hedges dight
That shelter gave to many a little bird
Where yellowhammers "peeped" in saddened plight
At peeping cowboy that its pleasure marred
Who carried in his hat its stubbly nest
& sung in rapture oer his stolen prize
The eggs in his rude mind where strangely guest
As written on by some strange phantasys
Strange prodigys that happy summer brings
To minds as happy & my journey tells
My mind that joy in poor seclusion dwells

SUMMER HAPPINESS

The sun looks down in such a mellow light
I cannot help but ponder in delight
To see the meadows so divinely lye
Beneath the quiet of the evening sky
The flags & rush in lights & shades of green
Look far more rich than I have ever seen
& bunches of white clover bloom again
& plats of lambtoe still in flower remain
In the brown grass that summer scythes have shorn
In every meadow level as a lawn
While peace & quiet in that silent mood
Cheers my lone heart & doth my spirits good
The level grass the sun the mottled sky
Seems waiting round to welcome passers bye

Summer is prodigal of joy the grass
Swarms with delighted insects as I pass
& crowds of grasshoppers at every stride
Jump out all ways with happiness their guide
& from my brushing feet moths flirt away
In safer places to pursue their play
In crowds they start I marvel well I may
To see such worlds of insects in the way
& more to see each thing however small
Sharing joys bounty that belongs to all
& here I gather by the world forgot
Harvests of comfort from their happy mood
Feeling Gods blessing dwells in every spot
& nothing lives but ows him gratitude

THE WELLAND

Theres somthing quite refreshing to behold
A broad & winding river wirl away
Here waterlilys studding nooks with gold
There yielding rushes bowing gentle sway
& trailing weeds whose easy curves delay
The waters for a moment—till they pass
& in a stiller motion sweep & bend
A broad & liquid mirror smooth as glass
In whose clear bosom are distinctly penned
Trees flowers & weeds in a delightful mass
Like happy thoughts in quiets easy mood
Oer which the fisher prows his boat along
& welland on thy reedy banks I find
Calm musings too I'm fain to cherish long

MOWERS DINNER HOUR

Upon the shady sward in meadow nook
Where spreads a tree to keep the waters cool
As sweet as pictures in a pleasant book
The mowers sit at dinner by the pool
Healthy & stubborn as their hard employ
Oercanopied in boughs & pleasant shade
Theirs is the envied seat of real joy
& luxury never sweeter dinner made
Than they of humbler means on the rich grass
With home brewed ale held up to merry lass
Who laughing comes to turn the bleaching hay
Ah did they know how happily they pass
Their time in toil they'd never wish for wealth
But keep their low estate & so ensure their health

COTTAGE COMFORT

The moon looks through the window late at eve
& throws the patterns of the diamond panes
Upon the cottage floor—while fancys leave
Illustrious calmness round—such as were vain
To look or search for in a higher state
Where calm contentment seldom wait on gain
Who far too throng to sit & contemplate
Her quiet lonliness—drives after wealth
With all the worlds anxiety & bent
Not taking heed for happiness or health
For they by humbler paths their journey went
Well be the hermits wish my nourishment
Some quiet nook that leaves the crowd by stealth
Peace from the world a cottage & content

FOOTPATHS

Theres somthing rich & joyful to the mind
To view through close & field those crooked shreds
Of footpaths that most picturesqly wind
From town to town or some tree hidden sheds
Where lonely cottager lifes peace enjoys
Far far from strife & all its troubled noise
The pent up artizan by pleasure led
Along their winding ways right glad employs
His sabbath leisure in the freshening air
The grass the trees the sunny sloping sky
From his weeks prison gives delicious fare
But still he passes almost vacant bye
The many charms that poesy finds to please
Along the little footpaths such as these

466

Now tracking fields where passenger appears
As wading to his waist in crowding grain
Where ever as we pass the bending ears
Pat at our sides & gain their place again
Then crooked stile with little steps that aids
The climbing meets us—& the pleasant grass
& hedgrows old with arbours ready made
For weariness to rest in pleasant shades
Surround us & with extacy we pass
Wild flowers & insect tribes that ever mate
With joy & dance from every step we take
In numberless confusion—all employ
Their little aims for peace & pleasures sake
& every summers footpath leads to joy

Now sudden as a pleasure unawares
A wooden plank strides oer a little brook
That unto thirst the sweetest boon prepares
Paved oer with pebbles to the very brink
& so invitingly its waters look
Though not a thirst it urges us to drink
Then comes a sloping hill & whats beyond
We stray to look & find a little pond
Where dotterel trees bend as if falling in
& sallow bushes of their station fond
Stretch from each side & welcome [surety] win
Where snug the hermit morehen loves to lie
Who from the passing footstep plunges in
& from his old haunt seldom dares to fly

Now almost hid in trees a little gate
Cheats us into the darkness of the wood
We almost think the day is wearing late
So dreamy is the light that dwells around
& so refreshing is its sombre mood
We feel at once shut out from sun & sky
All the deliciousness of solitude
While sauntering noisless oer the leafy ground
The air we breath seems loosing every trace
Of earth & all its trouble & the mind
Yearns for a dwelling in so sweet a place
From troubles noise such stillness seemeth bye
Yet soon the side brings some unwelcome spire
To bid the charm of solitude retire

Yet still the little path winds on & on
Down hedgrow sides & many a pastoral charm
We soon forget the charm of poesy gone
In the still woodland with its silent balm
& find some other joy to dream upon
A distant notice of some nestling farm
Crowded with russet stacks that peep between
Hugh homestead elms or orchards squatting trees
Where apples shine sun tanned & mellow green
Home comforts for dull winters reveries
When the dull evening claimeth news & friends
Calm pleasure thus home nearing fancy sees
That maketh vanished fancy full amends
As the crooked footpath at the village ends

MEADOW BUTTERFLYES

Brown butterflies in happy quiet rest
Upon the blooming ragworts golden breast
Giving unto the mind a sweet employ
That everything in nature meets with joy
Ah sweet indeed for trifles such as these
Full often give my aching bosom ease
When I in little walks my mind employ
Aright—& feel those happy reveries
That nature in her varied lessons tend
To bring our thinkings to a happy end
& in her varied moods for ever tries
To make us that great blessing comprehend
That spreads around us in a fond caress
Emblems & moods of future happiness

THE REED BIRD

A little slender bird of reddish brown
With frequent haste pops in & out the reeds
& on the river frequent flutters down
As if for food & so securely feeds
Her little young that in their ambush needs
Her frequent journeys hid in thickest shade
Where danger never finds a path to show
A fear on comforts nest securely made
In woods of reeds round which the waters flow
Save by a jelted stone that boys will throw
Or passing rustle of the fishers boat
It is the reed bird prized for pleasant note
Ah happy songster man can seldom share
A spot so hidden from the haunts of care

THE WOODLARKS NEST

The woodlark rises from the coppice tree
Time after time untired she upward springs
Silent while up then coming down she sings
A pleasant song of varied melody
Repeated often till some sudden check
The sweet toned impulse of her rapture stops
Then stays her trembling wings & down she drops
Like to a stone amid the crowding kecks
Where underneath some hazels mossy root
Is hid her little low & humble nest
Upon the ground larks love such places best
& here doth well her quiet station suit
As safe as secresy her six eggs lie
Mottled with dusky spots unseen by passers bye

Yet chance will somtimes prove a faithless guest
Leading some wanderer by her haunts to roam
& startled by the rustle from her rest
She flutters out & so betrays her home
Yet this is seldom accident can meet
With her weed hidden & surrounded nest
Ive often wondered when agen my feet
She fluttered up & fanned the anemonie
That blossomed round in crowds—how birds could be
So wise to find such hidden homes again
& this in sooth oft puzzled me—they go
Far off & then return—but natures plain
She giveth what sufficeth them to know
That they of comfort may their share retain

FIELD CRICKET

Sweet little minstrel of the sunny summer
Housed in the pleasant swells that front the sun
Neighbour to many a happy yearly comer
For joys glad tidings when the winters done
How doth thy music through the silk grass run
That cloaths the pleasant banks with herbage new
A chittering sound of healthy happiness
That bids the passer bye be happy too
Who hearing thee feels full of pleasant moods
Picturing the cheerfulness that summers dress
Brings to the eye with all her leaves & grass
In freshness beautified & summers sounds
Brings to the ear in one continued flood
The luxury of joy that knows no bounds

I often pause to seek thee when I pass
Thy cottage in the sweet refreshing hue
Of sunny flowers & rich luxuriant grass
But thou wert ever hidden from the view
Brooding & piping oer thy rural song
In all the happiness of solitude
Busy intruders do thy music wrong
& scare thy gladness dumb where they intrude
Ive seen thy dwelling by the scythe laid bare
& thee in russet garb from bent to bent
Moping without a song in silence there
Till grass should bring anew thy home content
& leave thee to thyself to sing & wear
The summer through without another care

471

THE YARROW

Dweller in pastoral spots life gladly learns
That nature never mars her aim to please
Thy dark leaves like to clumps of little ferns
Imbues my walks with feelings such as these
Oertopt with swarms of flowers that charms the sight
Some blushing into pink & others white
On meadow banks roadsides & on the leas
Of rough neglected pastures—I delight
More even then in gardens thus to stray
Amid such scenes & mark thy hardy blooms
Peering unto the autumns mellowing day
The mowers scythe swept summer blooms away
Where thou defying dreariness wilt come
Bidding the lonliest russet paths be gay

THE RAGWORT

Ragwort thou humble flower with tattered leaves
I love to see thee come & litter gold
What time the summer binds her russet sheaves
Decking rude spots in beautys manifold
That without thee were dreary to behold
Sunburnt & bare—the meadow bank the baulk
That leads a waggonway through mellow fields
Rich with the tints that harvests plenty yields
Browns of all hues—& everywhere I walk
Thy waste of shining blossoms richly shields
The sun tanned sward in splendid hues that burn
So bright & glaring that the very light
Of the rich sunshine doth to paleness turn
& seems but very shadows in thy sight

A SEAT IN THE MEADOWS

I love to stroll the meadow when its mown
& all the crowd of luscious scented hay
Is cleared away & left the sward alone
Beneath the quiet of a lovely day
& there I love green leisure to delay
Beside some lake to find a pleasant seat
To sit luxuriantly in dangers way
& almost let the water touch my feet
A somthing so refreshing bland & cool
From the calm surface of the water steals
What time the noontide spangles oer the pool
Bringing back bits of joy past time consceals
& youths past visions flit accross the brain
What books nor pictures never meet again

UNIVERSAL GOODNESS

I look on nature less with critics eyes
Than with that feeling every scene supplies
Feelings of reverence that warms & clings
Around the heart while viewing pleasing things
& heath & pastures hedgrow stunted tree
Are more than alps with all its hills to me
The bramble for a bower the old molehill
For seat delights me wander where I will
I feel a presence of delight—& fear
Of love & majesty far off & near
Go where I will its absence cannot be
& solitude & God are one to me
A presence that ones gloomiest cares caress
& fills up every place to guard & bless

THE LANE

The cartway leading over every green
A russet strip then winding half unseen
Up narrow lanes & smothered oer in shade
By oak & ash in meeting branches made
That touch & twine & shut out all the sky
& teams will snatch to crop them driving bye
Then over fields deep printed freely strays
Yet crooked & rambling half uncertain ways
While far away fields stretch on either side
& skys above head spread a circle wide
Letting low hedges trees snug close & fields of grain
An unknown world to shepherds when descried
& then the timid road retreats again
A leaf hid luxury in a narrow lane

PARTRIDGE COVEYS

Among the stubbles when the fields grow grey
& mellow harvest gathers to a close
The painful gleaner twenty times a day
Start up the partridge broods that glad repose
Upon the grassy slip or sunny land
Yet ever it would seem in dangers way
Where snufting dogs their rustling haunts betray
& tracking gunners ever seem at hand
Oft frighted up they startle to the shade
Of neighbouring wood & through the yellow leaves
Drop wearied where the brakes & ferns hath made
A solitary covert—that decieves
For there the fox prowls its unnoticed round
& danger dares them upon every ground

ON SEEING TWO SWALLOWS LATE IN OCTOBER

Lone occupiers of a naked sky
When desolate november hovers nigh
& all your fellow tribes in many crowds
Have left the village with the autumn clouds
Carless of old affections for the scene
That made them happy when the fields were green
& left them undisturbed to build their nests
In each old chimney like to welcome guests
Forsaking all like untamed winds they roam
& make with summers an unsettled home
Following her favours to the farthest lands
Oer untraced oceans & untrodden sands
Like happy images they haste away
& leave us lonely till another may

But little lingerers old esteem detains
Ye haply thus to brave the chilly air
When skys grow dull with winters heavy rains
& all the orchard trees are nearly bare
Yet the old chimneys still are peeping there
Above the russet thatch where summers tide
Of sunny joys gave you such social fare
As makes you haply wishing to abide
In your old dwellings through the changing year
I wish ye well to find a dwelling here
For in the unsocial weather ye would fling
Gleanings of comfort through the winter wide
Twitting as wont above the old fireside
& cheat the surly winter into spring

THE BRAMBLE

Spontaneous flourisher in thickets lone
Curving a most impenetrable way
To all save nutters when a tree has shown
Ripe clusters to the autumns mellow day
& long the brustle of the rude affray
Clings to thy branches—scraps of garments torn
Of many hues red purple green & grey
From scrambling maid who tugs the branches down
& inly smiles at the strange garb she wears
While rough in hasty speech the brushing clown
Leg hoppled as in tethers turns & swears
& cuts the bramble strings with oath & frown
Yet scorn wronged bush taste marks thee worthy praise
Green mid the underwood of winter days

THE SURRY TREE

Tree of the tawny berry rich though wild
When mellowed to a pulp yet little known
Though shepherds by its dainty taste beguiled
Swarm with clasped leg the smooth trunk timber grown
& pulls the very topmost branches down
Tis beautiful when all the woods tan brown
To see thee thronged with berrys ripe & fine
For daintier palates fitting then the clown
Where hermits of a day may rove & dine
Luxuriantly amid thy crimson leaves
When different shades in different garbs appear
& furze spread heath a deeper green recieves
& fancy every sort of feeling weaves
& autumn comes & mellows all the year

THE SPINDLE TREE

Tis pleasant in our walks to meet with things
Simple yet new—paths frequent traced diserns
Such the spurge laurel that obscurely springs
Among the underwood & different ferns
That hid themselves in leaves the summer through
Now shining rich & resolutely green
When leaves save weeds are else but scant & few
Yet one gay bush is beautifully seen
As full of berries as its twigs can be
Glittering & pink as blossoms washed in dew
Gleams the gay burthen of the spindle tree
The old mans beard the saplings grains pursues
Like feathers hung with rime—but autumns showers
Makes their rich berries shine like summer flowers

LABOURS LEISURE

O for the feelings & the carless health
That found me toiling in the fields—the joy
I felt at eve with not a wish for wealth
When labour done & in the hedge put by
My delving spade—I homeward used to hie
With thoughts of books I often read by stealth
Beneath the black thorn clumps at dinners hour
It urged my weary feet with eager speed
To hasten home where winter fires did shower
Scant light now felt as beautiful indeed
Where bending oer my knees I used to read
With earnest heed all books that had the power
To give me joy in most delicious ways
& rest my spirits after weary days

Aye when long summer showers lets labour win
Sweet leisure—how I used to mark with joy
The south grow black & blacker to the eye
Till the rain came & pepsed me to the skin
No matter anxious happiness was bye
With her refreshing pictures through the rain
Carless of bowring bush & sheltering tree
I homeward hied to feed on books again
For they were then a very feast to me
The simplest things were sweetest melody
& nothing met my eager taste in vain
& thus to read I often wished for rain
Such leisure fancys fed my lowly lot
Possessing nothing & still wanting not

It is an happiness that simplest hearts
Find their own joy in what they undertake
That nature like the seasons so imparts
That every mind its own home comfort makes
That be our dwelling in the fields or woods
No matter custom so endears the scenes
We feel in lonliness sweet company
& many a varied pleasure intervenes
Which the wide world unnoting passes bye
Pursuing what delights it varied joy
Thus happiness is with us joys succeed
Spontaneous every where like summer weeds
The cheerful commoners of every spot
Blessing the highest & the lowliest lot

HEAVY DEW

The night hath hung the morning smiles in showers
The kingcups burnished all so rich within
Hang down their slender branches on the grass
The bumble bees on the hugh thistle flowers
Clings as half sleeping yet & motion lacks
Not even stirring as I closely pass
Save that they lift their legs above their backs
In trembling dread when touched—yet still they lie
Fearful of danger without power to flye
The shepherd makes a mort of crooked tracks
His dog half drowned & dripping to the skin
Stops oft & shakes his shaggy hide in vain
Wading through grass like rivers to the chin
Then snorts & barks & brushes on again

APRIL SHOWERS

Delightful weather for all sorts of moods
& most for him—grey morn & swarthy eve
Found rambling up the little narrow lane
Where primrose banks amid the hazly woods
Peep most delightfully on passers bye
While aprils little clouds about the sky
Mottle & freak & unto fancy lie
Idling & ending travel for the day
Till darker clouds sail up with cumberous heave
South oer the woods & scares them all away
Then comes the rain pelting with pearly drops
The primrose crowds until they stoop & lie
All fragrance to his mind that musing stops
Beneath the awthorn till the shower is bye

NUTTERS

The rural occupations of the year
Are each a fitting theme for pastoral song
& pleasing in our autumn paths appear
The groups of nutters as they chat along
The woodland rides in strangest dissabille
Maids jacketed grotesque in garments ill
Hiding their elegance of shape—her ways
Her voice of music makes her woman still
Aught else the error of a carless gaze
Might fancy uncooth rustics noising bye
With laugh & chat & scraps of morning news
Till met the hazel shades & in they hie
Garbed suiting to the toil—the morning dews
Among the underwood are hardly dry

Yet down with crack & rustle branches come
& springing up like bow unloosed when free
Of their ripe clustering bunches brown—while some
Are split & broken under many a tree
Up springs the blundering pheasant with the noise
Loud brawls the maiden to her friends scared sore
& loud with mimic voice mischevous boys
Ape stranger voices to affright her more
Eccho long silent answers many a call
Straggling about the wildwoods guessing way
Till by the wood side waiting one & all
They gather homward at the close of day
While maids with hastier step from sheperds brawl
Speed on half shamed of their strange dissaray

MIST IN THE MEADOWS

The evening oer the meadow seems to stoop
More distant lessens the diminished spire
Mist in the hollows reeks & curdles up
Like fallen clouds that spread—& things retire
Less seen & less—the shepherd passes near
& little distant most grotesquely shades
As walking without legs—lost to his knees
As through the rawky creeping smoke he wades
Now half way up the arches dissappear
& small the bits of sky that glimmer through
Then trees loose all but tops—I meet the fields
& now the indistinctness passes bye
The shepherd all his length is seen again
& further on the village meets the eye

SIGNS OF WINTER

Tis winter plain the images around
Protentious tell us of the closing year
Short grows the stupid day the moping fowl
Go roost at noon—upon the mossy barn
The thatcher hangs & lays the frequent yaum
Nudged close to stop the rain that drizzling falls
With scarce one interval of sunny sky
For weeks still leeking on that sulky gloom
Muggy & close a doubt twixt night & day
The sparrow rarely chirps the thresher pale
Twanks with sharp measured raps the weary frail
Thump after thump right tiresome to the ear
The hedger lonesome brustles at his toil
& shepherds trudge the fields without a song

The cat runs races with her tail—the dog
Leaps oer the orchard hedge & knarls the grass
The swine run round & grunt & play with straw
Snatching out hasty mouthfuls from the stack
Sudden upon the elm tree tops the crow
Uncerimonious visit pays & croaks
Then swops away—from mossy barn the owl
Bobs hasty out—wheels round & scared as soon
As hastily retires—the ducks grow wild
& from the muddy pond fly up & wheel
A circle round the village & soon tired
Plunge in the pond again—the maids in haste
Snatch from the orchard hedge the mizled cloaths
& laughing hurry in to keep them dry

ANGLING

Angling has pleasures that are much enjoyed
By tasteful minds of nature never cloyed
In pleasant solitudes where winding floods
Pass level meadows & oerhanging woods
Verged with tall reeds that rustle in the wind
A soothing music in the anglers mind
& rush right complasant that ever bows
Obesceience to the stream that laughs below
He feels delighted into quiet praise
& sweet the pictures that the mind essays
While gentle whispers on the southern wind
Brings health & quiet to the anglers mind
Smooth as the gentle river whirls along
& sweet as memory of some happy song

The morn is still & balmy all that moves
The trees are south gales which the angler loves
That stirs the waveing grass in idle whirls
& flush the cheeks & fan the jetty curls
Of milking maidens at their morns employ
Who sing & wake the dewy fields to joy
The sun just rising large & round & dim
Keeps creeping up oer the flat meadows brim
As rising from the ground to run its race
Till up it mounts & shows a ruddy face
Now is the time the angler leaves his dreams
In anxious movements for the silent streams
Frighting the heron from its morning toil
First at the river watching after coil

Now with the rivers brink he winds his way
For a choice place to spend the quiet day
Marking its banks how varied things appear
Now cloathed in trees & bushes & now clear
While steep the bank climbs from the waters edge
Then almost choaked with rushes flags & sedge
Then flat & level to the very brink
Tracked deep by cattle running there to drink
At length he finds a spot half shade half sun
That scarcely curves to show the waters run
Still clear & smooth quick he his line unlaps
While fish leap up & loud the water claps
Which fills his mind with pleasures of supprise
That in the deep hole some old monster lies

Right cautious now his strongest line to take
Lest some hugh monster should his tackle break
Then half impatient with a cautious throw
He swings his line into the depths below
The water rat hid in the shivering reeds
That feeds upon the slime & water weeds
Nibbling their grassy leaves with crizzling sound
Plunges below & makes his fancys bound
With expectations joy—down goes the book
In which glad leisure might for pleasure look
& up he grasps the angle in his hand
In readiness the expected prize to land
While tip toe hope gives expectations dream
Sweet as the sunshine sleeping on the stream

None but true anglers feel that gush of joy
That flushes in the patient minds employ
While expectation upon tiptoe sees
The float just wave it cannot be a breeze
For not a waver oer the waters pass
Warm with the joyous day & smooth as glass
Now stronger moved it dances round then stops
Then bobs again & in a moment drops
Beneath the water—he with joys elate
Pulls & his rod bends double with the weight
True was his skill in hopes expecting dream
& up he draws a flat & curving bream
That scarcely landed from the tackle drops
& on the bank half thronged in sedges stops

Now sport the waterflyes with tiny wings
A dancing crowd imprinting little rings
& the rich light the suns young splendours throw
Is by the very pebbles caught below
Behind the leaning tree he stoops to lean
& soon the stirring float again is seen
A larger yet from out its ambush shoots
Hid underneath the old trees cranking roots
The float now shakes & quickens his delight
Then bobs a moment & is out of sight
Which scarce secured—down goes the cork again
& still a finer pants upon the plain
& bounds & flounces mid the newmown hay
& luck but ceases with the closing day

WINTER FIELDS

O for a pleasant book to cheat the sway
Of winter—where rich mirth with hearty laugh
Listens & rubs his legs on corner seat
For fields are mire & sludge—& badly off
Are those who on their pudgy paths delay
There striding shepherd seeking driest way
Fearing nights wetshod feet & hacking cough
That keeps him waken till the peep of day
Goes shouldering onward & with ready hook
Progs off to ford the sloughs that nearly meet
Across the lands—croodling & thin to view
His loath dog follows—stops & quakes & looks
For better roads—till whistled to pursue
Then on with frequent jumps he hirkles through

BIRDS & SPRING

The happy birds in their delight bring home
To our own doors the news that spring is come
Eave haunting sparrow that no song employs
Pull off the apple blooms for very joys
& that delightful neighbour ever merry
The Robin with a bosom like a cherry
Comes to the threshold welcome pert & bold
Where crumbs lay littered when the day was cold
& whistles out so loud the folks within
Jump with supprise & wonder at the din
& when they run to see supprise will smile
Scarcely believing Robins sung so loud
But spring is come & he is overproud
To see young leaves that nothing comes to spoil

WINTER EVENING

The crib stocks fothered—horses suppered up
& cows in sheds all littered down in straw
The threshers gone the owls are left to whoop
The ducks go waddling with distended craw
Through little hole made in the henroost door
& geese with idle gabble never oer
Bate careless hog untill he tumbles down
Insult provoking spite to noise the more
While fowl high perched blink with contemptous frown
On all the noise & bother heard below
Over the stable ridge in crowds the crow
With jackdaws intermixed known by their noise
To the warm woods behind the village go
& whistling home for bed go weary boys

SNOW STORM

Winter is come in earnest & the snow
In dazzling splendour—crumping underfoot
Spreads a white world all calm & where we go
By hedge or wood trees shine from top to root
In feathered foliage flashing light & shade
Of strangest contrast—fancys pliant eye
Delighted sees a vast romance displayed
& fairy halls descended from the sky
The smallest twig its snowy burthen bears
& woods oer head the dullest eyes engage
To shape strange things—where arch & pillar bears
A roof of grains fantastic arched & high
A little shed beside the spinney wears
The grotesque zemblance of an hermitage

One almost sees the hermit from the wood
Come bending with his sticks beneath his arm
& then the smoke curl up its dusky flood
From the white little roof his peace to warm
One shapes his books his quiet & his joys
& in romances world forgetting mood
The scene so strange so fancys mind employs
It seems heart aching for his solitude
Domestic spots near home & trod so oft
Seem daily—known for years—by the strange wand
Of winters humour changed—the little croft
Left green at night when morns loth look obtrudes
Trees bushes grass to one wild garb subdued
Are gone & left us in another land

A THAW

The snows are gone or nearly chance may show
Beside the dripping hedge some little hills
Fast drop the eves till pudges plash below
& every rut & hollow quickly fills
In huzzing crowds cote-piegons too & fro
Traverse the villages & at the stack
Hang flapping—in an instant up they go
From slaughtering gun its momentary crack
While barn & dove cote sound the echo back
They circle round & round & settle soon—
The homstead cows their old accustomed track
Keep to the foddering place throughout the day
Untill the boys hoarse brawl at hazy noon
Comes with his fork & litters heaps of hay

THE BLACKCAP

Under the twigs the blackcap hangs in vain
With snowwhite patch streaked over either eye
This way & that he turns & peeps again
As wont where silk-cased insects used to lie
But summer leaves are gone the day is bye
For happy holidays & now he fares
But cloudy like the weather yet to view
He flirsts a happy wing & inly wears
Content in gleaning what the orchard spares
& like his little couzin capped in blue
Domesticates the lonely winter through
In homestead plots & gardens where he wears
Familiar pertness—yet but seldom comes
With the tame robin to the door for crumbs

NIGHT WIND

Darkness like midnight from the sobbing woods
Clamours with dismal tidings of the rain
Roaring as rivers breaking loose in floods
To spread & foam & deluge all the plain
The cotter listens at his door again
Half doubting wether it be floods or wind
& through the thickening darkness looks affraid
Thinking of roads that travel has to find
Through nights black depths in dangers garb arrayed
& the loud glabber round the flaze soon stops
When hushed to silence by the lifted hand
Of fearing dame who hears the noise in dread
& thinks a deluge comes to drown the land
Nor dares she go to bed untill the tempest drops

BIRDS NESTS

How fresh the air the birds how busy now
In every walk if I but peep I find
Nests newly made or finished all & lined
With hair & thistle down & in the bough
Of little awthorn huddled up in green
The leaves still thickening as the spring gets age
The Pinks quite round & snug & closely laid
& linnets of materials loose & rough
& still hedge sparrow moping in the shade
Near the hedge bottom weaves of homely stuff
Dead grass & mosses green an hermitage
For secresy & shelter rightly made
& beautiful it is to walk beside
The lanes & hedges where their homes abide

489

WOOD RIDES

Who hath not felt the influence that so calms
The weary mind in summers sultry hours
When wandering thickest woods beneath the arms
Of ancient oaks & brushing nameless flowers
That verge the little ride who hath not made
A minutes waste of time & sat him down
Upon a pleasant swell to gaze awhile
On crowding ferns bluebells & hazel leaves
& showers of ladysmocks so called by toil
When boys sprote gathering sit on stulps & weave
Garlands while barkmen pill the fallen tree
—Then mid the green variety to start
Who hath [not] met that mood from turmoil free
& felt a placid joy refreshed at heart

THE HEDGE WOODBINE

The common woodbine in the hedgerow showers
A multitude of blossoms & from thence
The tinctured air all fragrance on the sense
Flings richest sweets that almost overpowers
& faintness pauls the taste which goes away
When some old ballad beautifully sung
Comes through the hedge with crowded fragrance hung
From merry maidens tossing up the hay
To list the sunny mirth we inly feel
That none but beautys self could sing so well
& pastoral visions on our fancys dwell
Our joys excess joys inmost thoughts consceal
The woodbine hedge—the maids half toil half play
—Words like to clouds obscure & wear away

EARLY MORNING

Morn with her sober shadows tall & thin
Stalks forth afield with slow & solemn stride
Like thinking poet some new joy to win
& in its little clump of trees espied
The mossy cottage hidden like a nest
Smokes from its plastered chimney while the lark
Sings oer her nestlings in the neighbouring corn
There toil made stirring by the restless cock
His early breakfast hastily prepares
& stooping hies afield its earliest guest
& happiest—for he sings from light to dark
Tracking the grassy pathways night & morn
He ask[s] of passing stranger whats o'clock
& heeds but little save his own affairs

HAPPINESS OF EVENING

The winter wind with strange & fearful gust
Stirs the dark wood & in the lengthy night
Howls in the chimney top while fears mistrust
Listens the noise by the small glimmering light
Of cottage hearth where warm a circle sits
Of happy dwellers telling morts of tales
Where some long memory wakens up by fits
Laughter & fear & over all prevails
Wonder predominant—they sit & hear
The very hours to minutes & the song
Or story be the subject what it may
Is ever found too short & never long
While the uprising tempest loudly roars
& boldest hearts fear stirring out of doors

Fears ignorance their fancy only harms
Doors safely locked fear only entrance wins
While round the fire in every corner warms
Till nearest hitch away & rub their shins
& now the tempest in its plight begins
The shutters jar the woodbine on the wall
Rustles agen the panes & over all
The noisey storm to troublous fancy dins
& pity stirs the stoutest heart to call
"Who's there" as slow the door latch seemly stirred
But nothing answered so the sounds they heard
Was no benighted traveller—& they fall
To telling pleasant tales to conquor fear
& sing a merry song till bedtime creepeth near

GLOSSARY

Note: old plural forms like "eldern", "childern", "folken" are not separately listed, nor are those words which are fairly obvious variant spellings of familiar words like "lare" (=lair) and "feet" (=feat). Since Clare was consulted by Anne Elizabeth Baker for her *Glossary of Northamptonshire Words and Phrases* (2 vols, London and Northampton, 1854), we give where relevant her definition, distinguished by inverted commas.

awes	Haws, the fruit of the hawthorn tree.
bashed	Abashed.
bate or *bait*	Harass.
bauk or *baulk*	"Narrow slip of grass land dividing two ploughed or arable lands in open or common fields."
beaver	A hat, originally of beaver fur.
beavering hour	Time for refreshment.
beeflye	*Bombylius major*, emerges from rat-tailed maggot in early spring and hums like a bee.
bee-spell	Perhaps connected with *be-spelt*, which Baker defines as "Bewitched, mischievous, but not vicious," though the context implies a type of spotted patterning.
bents	"Long, coarse, rushy stems of rye and other grasses running to seed, called grass Bents and hay Bents according to the season."
blackcap	Clare's March Nightingale, one of our earliest warbler migrants, *Sylvia atricapilla*; but his sonnet "The Blackcap" concerns the Great Tit.
blackthorn	Sloe, *Prunus spinosa*, Clare's black thorn; he uses *thorn* or *white thorn* for hawthorn and whitethorn, too.
blea	Bleak, chill, sunless, cold.
bloodwall	"The dark, double Wall-flower." Also the wild wallflower found on old walls.
bluecap	(a) Blue Cornflower, "The corn blue-bottle. *Centaurea Cyanus.*" (b) The Blue Tit.
bogbean	Buckbean, *Menyanthes trifoliata*.

493

bottle of flags	Bundle of reeds.
brake	Bracken or fern.
brig	Bridge.
brun-coloured ⎱ *brunny* ⎰	Nut-brown or freckled with brown.
brunt	To burst, push.
brustle	To make a rustling noise.
budget	Pack.
bumbarrel	The Long-tailed Tit.
burdock	One of the various burdocks, *Arctium lappa, A. pubens,* or *A. minus,* or the bur from them.
burr	"A haziness or mist, covering or encircling the moon."
cag	Keg.
carlock	Charlock, *Sinapis arvensis.*
cat gallows (sticks)	"Two sticks stuck vertically in the ground and a third placed horizontally upon them. It is a favourite boyish pastime to jump over them."
Ceres	*Cereus,* one of the cactus species, here torch thistle.
chock and taw	A marble game: "CHOCK or CHUCK. An under-handed throw with a jerk, as boys throw stones into the water to make ducks and drakes. CHOCK or CHOCK-HOLE. A game of marbles played by *chocking* or pitching marbles into a hole made for the purpose, instead of shooting at a ring."
chockholes	See above.
clamm	Mechanical device for holding something fast.
cleavers	Goosegrass, *Galium aparine.*
clink and bandy	A boys' game probably like "knurr and spell" or "buck and stick". Played with a small pointed piece of wood and a stick. The small piece of wood was put on the ground, struck on its pointed end to make it rise in the air, and then hit away with the stick as far as possible. Baker gives for "clink" or "click" "A smart blow," and "BANDY. A knobbed stick used to strike the ball at the game of hockey."
closen	"Small enclosures, or fields; a retention of the old Saxon plural."
clouted	Studded, clothed, patched.

cockleflower	Corn cockle, *Agrostemma githago*, though sometimes applied to other corn weeds.
coil	Stir, bustle, movement; but perhaps a variant of *cull* suggesting collection, gathering, prey.
cowslap peeps	cowslip eyes.
coy	To coax, entice.
crab	Crab apple.
crane, act the crane	Clare explains in the Introduction to *The Village Minstrel* (London, 1821): "A man holds in his hand a long stick, with another tied at the top in the form of an L reversed, which represents the long neck and beak of the crane. This, with himself, is entirely covered with a large sheet. He mostly makes excellent sport, as he puts the whole company to the rout, picking out the young girls, and pecking at the bald heads of the old men."
crank	To turn, twist.
crankle	To bend, wind in and out.
croodle	"CROODLING. Shrinking, and contracting the body from cold."
crookthorn	A boys' game.
cross plumb skittles	A game played by knocking down skittles with a weighted string hanging from a cross.
cross row	The alphabet.
cuck	To chuck, throw underhand.
cuckaball	Cuckoo-ball, an ancient country game, or the ball it is played with, made of rags and/or flowers.
cuckoos	Clare uses this word for Cuckoo-pint, Lords-and-ladies, Wild Arum. He also uses *cuckoos* for Cuckoo-flowers, Lady's Smock, *Cardamine pratensis.*
culverkey	Cowslip.
dewberry	A less common kind of blackberry, with a grape-like bloom.
dotterel	Clare explains: "*Dotterel*-trees, old stumping trees in hedge rows, that are headed or lopped every ten or twelve years for fire-wood."
drabbled	"Dirtied or splashed with walking in the mud."
ducking stone	"DUCKS. A boyish pastime, played with three stones, surmounted by a fourth, which is attempted to be struck off, by casting another stone at it from a short distance."

earthern tongue	A fern, *Ophioglossum*, now rare.
edding	Grass at the head of a field.
elting	"ELTING-MOULDS. The soft ridges of fresh-ploughed land." Doughy.
emelous	Emulous.
E–O	A gambling game, rather like roulette, where the falling of a ball into niches marked E and O (presumably Even and Odd) on the turning centre of the table determines the winner of the stakes.
eyebright	One of the *Euphrasia officinalis* (agg.).
feth	(An interjection) faith!
finweed	Restharrow, *Ononis repens*.
firetail	The Redstart.
flags	Reeds for thatching, though Clare also uses the word for Yellow Iris and Bulrush.
flaze	"To blaze; to flare as a candle does, when a current of air causes it to burn unsteadily, and melt away fast."
flitting	"FLIT. To remove from one house or lodging to another."
flusker	"To fly with sudden and disordered motion."
fother	To feed (farm animals).
foulroyce	Red Dogwood, *Cornus sanguinea*.
frail	Flail.
frit	Frightened, terrified.
fuzball	The Puff-ball fungus.
glabber	To chatter.
glib	Smooth, slippery, voluble.
goss	Common Gorse, furze.
grain	"GRAINS. The main branches of trees, rising from the trunk; which are measurable for timber."
guess	(In compounds like "another guess thing" where it is a corruption of "gates" = way) sort of.
gulled	Hollowed.
haloo	Halo.
hants	Haunts.
hartsomely	With good heart or cheer, blithely.
haynish	Wretched, awkward.
heathbell	The flower of the Heath; the Bluebell.
hirkle	To cower, crouch, shrink so as to keep warm.
hirple	To limp, walk lame, stumble.

hopple	"To tie the legs together."
horse blob	The Marsh Marigold, *Caltha palustris*.
hovel	Animal shed in field; with no derogatory sense.
hugh	Huge.
hurd	Hoard.
huzzing	Making a buzzing and spluttering noise
idless	Idleness.
ignis fatus	*Ignis fatuus*, will o' the wisp, phosphoric light over the Fen, delusive hope.
jeer	To scoff at (used transitively).
jelt	"JILT. To throw, to fling."
keck	"The dried stalk of the hemlock, cow's parsley, or any other umbelliferous plant; sometimes the plants themselves are so called."
kingcup	"Marsh marigold. *Caltha palustris*. The same name is sometimes given to the butter-cup."
knap	Bite, to nibble.
knopple	Small knob.
ladslove	Southernwood, *Artemisia abrotanum*.
ladycow	Ladybird.
ladysmocks	See *cuckoos*. Baker also gives "The great bindweed. *Convolvulus sepium*."
lambtoe	"Probably another name for the *Lotus corniculatus*," Bird's Foot Trefoil.
landrail	Corncrake.
lawn	"An open space in the midst of a chace or forest," a small pasture.
leam	To shell (nuts).
ling	Heath, heather, *Calluna vulgaris*. Beesom *ling* was used to make besoms.
lodge	"The house situate on a farm."
long legged shepherd	Cranefly.
lown	Man of low birth or condition.
mizled	"MIZZLE. To rain in small drops, little more than a falling mist." Damp.
moise	To moisten.
mort	"A quantity, a great number." Most often used in the plural.

motely	Motley.
mouldywharp	Mole.
mozzly	Perhaps related to "muzzled"=speckled with white or grey, speckled, mingled.
muscle clams	Freshwater Mussels.
nap	To bite, nibble.
nappy	Ale.
netherd	Neatherd, cowherd.
nine peg morris	Nine men's morris, peg morris, or merels, an ancient game played between two players each with nine pegs, pebbles, counters, or pins. The playing area can be marked out on a board or merely by making holes in the ground.
oddling	"One differing from the rest of a family, brood, or litter."
paul	To cloy, weaken, dull.
peg morris	See *nine peg morris*.
pencil	Paintbrush.
pendil	Sharpening stone.
pepsed	"PEPSE. To throw at. ... Synonymous with *pelt.*"
pettichap	Chiffchaff.
pie	Magpie.
pilewort	Lesser Celandine, *Ranunculus ficaria.*
pingle	"A clump of trees, or underwood, not large enough for a SPINNEY."
pink	The Chaffinch; occasionally Clare may mean the Yellowhammer.
pinson	To snip, pincer.
pismire	Ant.
plat	Flat stretch (of ground).
pleachy	"Mellow, powdery," dried, bleached.
pluft	"PLUFFED. Swollen, bloated, puffy."
poesy	Clare's spelling for "posy", but he more often means "poetry".
pooty	"The girdled snail shell," *Cepaea nemoralis.*
pound	Pen for stray animals.
prog	"To prick; to poke into holes and corners."
puddock	"This name is applied indiscriminately to the fan-tail kite or buzzard ... and the fork'd-tail kite." Its "shrill peelew" suggests Clare means the buzzard.

pudge	Puddle.
pudgy	Muddy, full of puddles.
pursy	Short-winded, fat.
quailed	Quelled.
rack	"A thin cloud."
ramp	To grow luxuriantly. "It is used most to [describe] wild, luxuriant vegetable growth."
rawky	"Misty, foggy; and Clare adds, wet under foot."
redcap	Goldfinch.
restharrow	A field shrub with tough roots, Ononis repens.
riddle	Red dye for marking sheep.
rout	Route.
sawn	To saunter, loiter.
sawney	A silly, half-witted person.
scranny	Wild, distracted, crazy.
screed	Patch of land.
scurvy grass	A cruciferous plant, *Cochlearia officinalis*.
sedge bird	Sedge Warbler.
self heal	The plant Brunella used to be used as a cure for quinsy. Probably here *Prunella vulgaris*.
sen	Self.
shanny	"Shame-faced," shy.
shepherd's purse	A common cruciferous weed, *Capsella bursa-pastoris*.
shoaf	Sheaf.
shocks	Sheaves of corn; earthy roots.
shoy	Shy.
slive (past tense *slove*)	"To sneak, to skulk, to creep about, or do anything slyly."
sluther	To slide.
snib	Snub, cut.
snub, snubby	Cut short, stumpy.
soodle	"To go slowly and unwillingly along."
sprote	"SPRAWTS. ... Small twigs." Firewood.
statute	Michaelmas annual fair.
stingo	Strong ale.
stiver	Small coin.
stoven	"A stump, either growing or put into the ground as a post."
stowk	A stook.
streak	To stretch.

strinkle	To sprinkle.
struttle	Stickleback.
stubbing scythe	Sickle for hacking stubble or roots up.
surry tree	Wild Service Tree, *Sorbus torminalis.*
suthering	"Heavy sighing or whistling of the wind."
swail, swale	Shade, a shady place.
swaily, swaly	Shady, cool.
swath, swathy	Perhaps = swarthy.
swee	Swing.
swipes	Small beer.
swoof	Sough or deep sigh.
swop	To swoop.
take your own trundle	Go your own way.
tasty	Attractive.
taws	Marbles.
teazel	Teasel, *Dipsacus fullonum,* a bur once used by fullers for raising the nap of cloth.
tent	"To watch, to attend."
throng	Busy.
throstle	Clare's Mavis or Song-thrush, as distinct from the Missel Thrush or Storm-cock.
tittle	To tickle.
tongues	Tongs.
totter grass	Quaking grass, *Briza media.*
tormentil	An abundant low-growing herb, *Potentilla erecta.*
town	Used by Clare for village.
unbrunt	Unhindered by.
urgin	Urchin.
watchet	Light blue.
water blob	Marsh Marigold, *Caltha palustris.*
whew	The cry of a bird; to make the noise.
whimble	Gimlet, auger.
woodchat	Wood-wren or Wood-warbler.
woodlark	Tree-pipit.
wormwood	A bitter plant, *Artemisia absinthium.*
yarrow	Milfoil, *Achillea millefolium.*
yaum	Length of dampened straw for thatching.
yoe	Ewe.

INDEX OF TITLES AND FIRST LINES

INDEX OF TITLES AND FIRST LINES

Definite or indefinite articles are included at the beginning of first lines but not of titles. Each of the sonnets of a sonnet group is indexed separately.

506

507

508

511

514